C+H
7⁵⁰

HARVARD HISTORICAL STUDIES

PUBLISHED UNDER THE DIRECTION OF
THE DEPARTMENT OF HISTORY

FROM THE INCOME OF

THE HENRY WARREN TORREY FUND

VOLUME LVIII

GENESIS
and GEOLOGY

A STUDY IN THE RELATIONS OF SCIENTIFIC
THOUGHT, NATURAL THEOLOGY, AND
SOCIAL OPINION IN GREAT BRITAIN, 1790–1850

CHARLES COULSTON GILLISPIE

Cambridge
HARVARD UNIVERSITY PRESS

DISTRIBUTED IN GREAT BRITAIN BY

OXFORD UNIVERSITY PRESS

LONDON

SBN 674-34480-4

PRINTED IN THE UNITED STATES OF AMERICA

TO

V. L. C. G.

AND

R. L. G.

PREFACE

THIS STUDY ORIGINATED in the idea that issues arising out of the growth and dissemination of science may be approached by the historian as problems in intellectual history and that the writing of such studies is desirable for the understanding both of science and of history. My interest is in the nineteenth century, which was a period when the relation of science to religious belief was generally regarded as a matter of acute concern. This was particularly true in England, and in England the Darwinian controversy was the most widely discussed and certainly the most dramatic issue affecting science, an issue, moreover, on which scientists themselves were at first sharply divided. Much of the heat of the debate, even among scientists, was generated out of opposing views regarding the implications of Darwin's theory for religion and for morality; but so much has already been written upon this subject that, although it is not exhausted, I thought it might be more profitable to undertake research in the period before the publication of *On the Origin of Species*. Accordingly, I proposed to give an account of the immediate background of the pattern of scientific disagreement which culminated in disputes about Darwin's book and to attempt to analyze the causes of that disagreement. In doing so, I have been led into an investigation of the development of geology rather than of biology.

For the most part, this book deals with the opinions of people who were scientists or naturalists themselves, and I have chosen to approach the subject in this way for several reasons. In the first place, although it is coming to be a commonplace, it should nevertheless be pointed out that no science has ever been entirely composed of some neat collection of truths in which scientists, a body of men set apart by their knowledge, all concur. Scientists have never been isolated from their times. Scientific thought does, however, seem to possess the possibility of definitely if gradually disposing of error, though not necessarily of arriving at final fact. When the scientist is thinking as a scientist, his attitude includes an honest respect for ascertained facts about nature and a particular way of handling those facts as the irreducible raw material of thought. This is not to say that the ideal respect for facts is lived up to on every occasion or that scientific method prevents disagreement about their interpretation. And here the historical treatment, even in the hands of the layman, may be a useful tool for charting the manner in which science has developed. It may isolate some of the preconceptions which have influenced the scientist's interpretation, acceptance, or rejection of facts, and it may discover how far the origin of those preconceptions is to be found in the social, intellectual, and theological climate of his times.

In the subject treated in this book, the theological climate was obviously of particular importance. This suggests a further reason for writing about the opinion of scientists themselves. Contemporary scientific literature of the years before 1850 or thereabouts makes it immediately apparent that neither the conflict between religion and science, as later held by John W. Draper,[1] nor even that between theology and science, as set out in the classic account by Andrew D. White,[2] was the simple, universal, black-and-white affair that it seemed in the optimistic perspective of late nineteenth-century positivist rationalism.[3] W. E. H. Lecky's discussion of the theological characteristics of the eighteenth century confirms this point.

Few of the grounds upon which the more serious scepticism of the nineteenth century is based then existed. One of the most remarkable differences between eighteenth century Deism and modern freethinking is the almost entire absence in the former of arguments derived from the discoveries of physical science. These discoveries had unquestionably a real though indirect influence in discrediting many forms of superstition, but the direct antagonism between science and theology which appeared in Catholicism at the time of the discoveries of Copernicus and Galileo was not seriously felt in Protestantism till geologists began to impugn the Mosaic account of the creation.[4]

As will appear throughout this study, though I agree with Lecky's statement, I do not agree with him — or with the most common interpretation among later historians of ideas — in

regarding tenderness towards the Bible as the basis of the difficulty between science and Protestant Christianity. Indeed, during the seven decades between the birth of modern geology and
the publication of *On the Origin of Species*, the difficulty as
reflected in scientific literature appears to be one of religion (in
a crude sense) *in* science rather than one of religion *versus*
science. The most embarrassing obstacles faced by the new
sciences were cast up by the curious providential materialism of
the scientists themselves and of those who relied upon them to
show that the materials of a material universe exhibit the sort
of necessity which results from control instead of the sort which
springs from self-sufficiency. The work of the scientists supported a providentialist view which managed to be at the same ·
time mundane and supernatural — mundane as to appearances
and supernatural as to inferences.

Whether the last century, as distinct from the whole of history, witnessed something like an inevitable and definitive warfare between science and religion, I do not know. The scope of
this study is not nearly so ambitious as that, however. Indeed,
its limitations are rather narrow, even for a monograph, but to
extend them would destroy whatever unity my treatment has
and would also, at the moment, exceed the boundaries of my
research. I have hoped that within its limits what follows will
be of some interest, and I had, therefore, better make clear what
those limits are.

In the first place, although the first chapter takes a running
start from the attitude of natural philosophers to the larger
meanings of their work in the relatively unspecialized atmosphere of the seventeenth and eighteenth centuries, my detailed
treatment of the subject begins with the closing decades of the
eighteenth century. To find the ultimate origins of the attitudes
I discuss would, of course, take me back to the beginnings of
western thought, but it was near the turn of the nineteenth
century that geology put on distinctively modern dress, the first
of the descriptive sciences to do so. Old issues regarding the
order of nature together with newer issues regarding the history
of nature were then caught up in the development of geology.
This, it seems to me, forms the most significant aspect of the

immediate background of the debate over evolution. Using the growth of geology as the directing thread, I have carried the story down to the Darwinian controversy, but have stopped short of it (except for some general concluding remarks). Secondly, having decided that the issues discussed arose from a quasi-theological frame of mind within science, I have written from that point of view and have excluded the purely clerical opponents of science as a whole. Thirdly, I have not fretted about epistemology. The nature and validity of the reality revealed by scientific investigations were not matters about which any of the people who figure in this book made any difficulty. I have also dispensed with any treatment of the atheistic and primarily rationalist tradition, never very strong in Victorian England. The sources of rationalistic atheism were not the same as the sources of scientific agnosticism.[5]

Lastly, and perhaps most seriously, I have dealt only with British opinion. This, to be sure, reflects the work of European scientists, but even so it was no more than a special case of the reception of theories and discoveries which are not supposed to have taken any account of national boundaries. Scientific thought, though it may not be quite so independent of its environment as is sometimes said, is certainly far less apt to be shaped by class or national influences than, say, the concepts of political economy or the interpretation of history. Opinion about science, however, is undoubtedly a social phenomenon and can be expected to reflect interpretative attitudes characteristic of the time and place, and this is true both of the opinion of scientists and of other people.

For the period covered by this study, it would undoubtedly be desirable to compare continental opinions with British and Roman Catholic reactions with Protestant ones, and these are projects which might well repay further research. Since the subject involves geology primarily, however, there are certain reasons for beginning with Great Britain. Although it is not necessary to go the whole way with Dr. Singer in being "struck by the overwhelming share of British investigators in the early development of geology as a science," [6] it is true that the work of British geologists was very productive and that geology was a popular science in Britain, partly, perhaps, because it was an outdoor science and in its early days a peculiarly individualistic one.[7] The first of the now numerous national geological societies was founded in London in 1807. In England itself the Geological Society of London was the earliest of many specialized scientific societies. Moreover, in contrast to the backwardness of the British government in most scientific matters, England was also the first country to establish a geological survey (1835). Finally, popular science enjoyed a great vogue in England in the early nineteenth century, more so than on the Continent. It is clear from the literature that the meaning of science for society was important to scientists as well as to other leaders of opinion in England.

In the period here under discussion, from 1790 or so to 1850, this meaning, so far as it was controversial, appears to have grown out of the development of the descriptive sciences and particularly of geology. If this study seems to give undue prominence to the work of geologists, it is only following the example of the contemporary public.[8] There were a number of reasons for this interest. In the first place, the descriptive sciences — just then emerging from the chrysalis of "natural history" — were continually revolutionizing their basic conceptions in a notably dramatic fashion, while the physical sciences were expanding by fitting technical and — to the layman — less interesting details into a framework unaffected philosophically by its own growth. This difference was appreciated at the time. Everyone spoke of geology as a newborn science, one which had begun only with James Hutton or with Abraham Gottlob Werner. Its disputes were described as the inevitable squalls and squabbles of childhood.[9] This very inconvenience, however, made the subject particularly well suited to popularization because, as a contemporary scientist remarked, it dealt with "a lower order of facts," comprehensible to almost anyone.[10] In the positivist succession, geology logically follows chemistry and precedes biology. Whether this succession is necessary or not, the layman is apt to regard one particular science as the exemplar of basic scientific concepts in any given period. The prevailing preoccupation with geology need not, therefore, be thought surprising.

The reader may be interested in knowing how I have selected the people whose opinions I discuss. Having decided to write about the opinions of scientists, I have not brought in anyone who was not a serious and productive naturalist, recognized as such at the time, and I have tried not to overlook any important British geologist whose work was relevant to the subject and who participated in the discussions I treat. It is obvious, however, that some were much better scientists than others. In *The Great Chain of Being*, Professor Lovejoy quotes G. H. Palmer to the effect that one may often learn more about the mind of an age from its inferior writers than from its greatest ones, who transcend their time.[11] Second- and third-rate scientists may, it seems to me, have a similar interest for the history of scientific opinion. All the people in Chapters II through VI have a just claim to be considered productive scientists, but the attention they receive is proportional to the importance of their contributions to the controversies in geology, which is my subject, rather than to the importance of their contributions to science. Nevertheless, the only important figure whose real contributions to scientific knowledge I would have difficulty in demonstrating is Robert Chambers: though he was something of an amateur naturalist and published a few minor memoirs, the interests of symmetry are what really require his inclusion because his *Vestiges of Creation* provoked some very heated rejoinders by people who unquestionably were scientists. These remarks, finally, do not apply to Chapter I, which is introductory, or to Chapter VII, which discusses popular science and natural theology in general terms. In writing these chapters, I have simply chosen characteristic expressions of what seem to have been widely held points of view, and my choice was necessarily somewhat arbitrary. There is one matter of definition that I ought to make clear here. By "Providence" and "providential," I mean the idea that God created the universe with a purpose and that He supervises its operation with an eye to fulfilling that purpose.

I should like to express my gratitude to those who have assisted me in the preparation and revision of this study and who, of course, are not responsible for the faults which remain. I may first of all take this opportunity to acknowledge my deep and general indebtedness to Professor H. C. F. Bell of Wesleyan University, who introduced me to the study of history, and to Professor David E. Owen of Harvard University, who guided my graduate work and advised me in the research for the dissertation, of which this study is an outgrowth. Professor I. Bernard Cohen of Harvard has given me the benefit of his expert criticism of the manuscript, and his knowledge of the history of science has saved me a number of deplorable mistakes in a field where I am not an expert. Professor Robert R. Palmer and Dr. Walter L. Woodfill, two of my colleagues at Princeton University, were very generous with their time in reading the manuscript. Their comments on matters of organization, expression, and interpretation were of great value to me. The officials of the various libraries at Harvard University were very helpful, and the Master and the Senior Common Room of Kirkland House were most hospitable to a former member of their staff and provided me with accommodations in which to work during the final revision. Publication was made possible by the liberality of the custodians of the Research Fund at Princeton University. And finally, my wife has been of the greatest help with the manuscript and has worked over it as no wife with a house to run should have to work.

CHARLES COULSTON GILLISPIE

Princeton, New Jersey
January 1951

GENESIS AND GEOLOGY

CONTENTS

I

THROUGH NATURE UP TO NATURE'S GOD

If it were seasonable, *Lindamor*, to entertain ourselves but with those attributes of God, which are Legible or Conspicuous in the Creation; We might there discern the admirable Traces of such immense Power, such unsearchable Wisdom, and such exuberant Goodness, as may justly ravish us to an Amazement at them, rather than a bare admiration of them. And I must needs acknowledge, *Lindamor*, that when with bold Telescopes I survey the Old and Newly discover'd Stars and Planets that adorn the upper Region of the World; and when with excellent Microscopes I discern in otherwise Invisible Objects, the unimitable Subtilty of Nature's curious Workmanship; and when, in a word, by the help of Anatomical Knives, and the light of Chymical Furnaces, I study the Book of Nature . . . I find my self oftentimes reduc'd to exclame with the Psalmist, *How manifold are thy works, O Lord? in wisdom hast thou made them all!*

— *The Honourable Robert Boyle* [1]

Extinguished theologians lie about the cradle of every science as the strangled snakes beside that of Hercules.

— *Thomas Henry Huxley* [2]

I

Two centuries separated Huxley's devoted hatred of theologians from Robert Boyle's perfect confidence that science lifted the mind towards the worship of God. If there existed during most of this period a warfare between science and theology, scientists concerned would have been among the first to know of it. In England, however, they were not aware of being embattled until well into the nineteenth century. But the mutual tolerance of scientist and theologian did not reflect indifference to one another's calling. Neither had ever regarded the other's truths as irrelevancies. On the contrary, ever since the time of Bacon, scientists had been congratulating themselves upon unfolding a divinely ordained system of nature, through "the opening and laying out of a road for the human understanding direct from the sense, by a course of experiment orderly conducted and well built up."[3]

In seventeenth-century England, natural philosophers surrounded their labors with a notably devotional atmosphere. Boyle and Newton, for example, did not make the sharp modern distinction between science and theology, and they were highly serious about both their theological and their scientific studies. They would have been deeply shocked at the condescension with which some later critics have described their religious writings as aberrations unworthy of genius. If an absorption in the divine plan was an aberration, it was an aberration of the times and not of the man. Lesser scientists, men like John Ray, John Wilkins, Nehemiah Grew, and many others untouched by genius, also turned their talents to expressing the majesty and wonder of God's revelation to mankind, a message which could be read not only in the inspired writings but also in His book of nature.[4]

Writings of the scientists fell into the Puritan posture of awed confidence in the face of a universe unfolding into comprehensibility at the touch of the "new philosophy." It was a sobering prospect, certainly, because God was in it and through it, but it was a prospect to be contemplated steadfastly. Those who were investigating and admiring the Lord's work were necessarily participating in the Lord's work. Puritan devotionalism and Puritan utilitarianism positively encouraged and facilitated the prosecution of scientific researches, and both Puritan and scientist looked forward to an improvement of man's estate as the reward of their respective labors. The prevailing view of religion and the Baconian view of philosophy together produced a positive, restless impatience with scholastic thinking. Both emphasized an individual interpretation of different sorts of experience, and the Puritan's opinion of scholastic methods in theology was cut from the same cloth as his attitude towards received authority in natural science.[5] One critic of the universities, in attacking the school theology, asked,

What is it else, but a confused *Chaos*, of needless, frivolous, fruitless, triviall, vain, curious, impertinent, knotty, ungodly, irreligious, thorny, and hel-hatc'ht disputes, altercations, doubts, questions, and endless janglings, multiplied and spawned forth even to monstrosity and nauseousness? [6]

— a question that appears to demand an answer similar to his opinion of Aristotelian science, which he described as

meerly verbal, speculative, abstractive, formal and notional, fit to fill the brains with monstrous and airy *Chymaeras*, speculative and fruitless conceits, but not to replenish the intellect with sound knowledge, and demonstrative verity, nor to lead men practically to dive into the internal center of natures abstruse and occult operations: But is onely conversant about the shell, and husk, handling the accidental, external and recollacious qualities of things, confusedly, and continually tumbling over obscure, general and equivocal terms, which are onely fit to captivate young *Sciolists*, and raw wits, but not to satisfy a discreet and wary understanding, that expects *Apodictical*, and experimental manuductions into the more interiour clossets of nature . . .

And whereas names should truely express notions, and they be congruous to things themselves, the *Aristotelian Philosophy* leads us into an endless Labyrinth, having nothing in manner but *Syllogisms*, or rather *Paralogisms* to statuminate and uphold the Fabrick thereof: For they have altogether laid aside Induction as too mechanical and painful, which onely can be serviceable to Physical Science, and have invented words, terms, definitions, distinctions, and limitations consonant enough amongst themselves, but no way consorting or sympathizing with nature it self.[7]

The author of a recent study devoted to a detailed discussion of a great many similar expressions of opinion graphically remarks that "our modern scientific utilitarianism is the offspring of Bacon begot upon Puritanism." [8]

If the Protestant ethic, as Max Weber described it, did indeed resolve itself in social values emphasizing anti-traditionalism, utilitarianism, a worldly asceticism, methodical diligence in an approved vocation, the individual interpretation of experience, the desirability of free speculation, and the rationalization of appearances, this same collection of qualities, divorced from theological implications, could serve equally well to describe a climate of opinion conducive to the cultivation of experimental scientific inquiry. These virtues were not, however, divorced from theological implications. There was no reason that they should have been. Natural philosophers were particularly well situated for carrying into practical effect the glorification of God, because they were in direct contact with His works. Natural philosophy and religion were not the same realm, of course, but science and theology paralleled each other in being concerned with manifestations of divinity in a universe which was assumed to be permanently divine, increasingly intelligible, and so designed that man could better his lot by improving his understanding of physical phenomena. Materialism was, it is true, beginning to distress orthodox theologians by the end of the century, but they do not seem to have charged science with responsibility for its progress. John Harris, for example, author of the *Lexicon Technicum*,[9] attacked the Hobbesian school in his Boyle lectures for 1698. He regarded immorality and pride as the cause of atheism [10] and nowhere even hinted that science was to blame. Indeed, Hobbes had himself been an opponent of the new philosophy.

So long as the Puritan approach to religion remained vital, and even for some time afterwards, the theistic tendencies of the order of nature did not become an impersonal and mechanistic abstraction. There was a wealth of wonder in the well-known passage which expresses Newton's view of Nature's God:

Whereas the main Business of Natural Philosophy is to argue from Phaenomena without feigning Hypotheses, and to deduce Causes from Effects, till we come to the very first Cause, which certainly is not mechanical . . . Whence is it that Nature doth nothing in vain, and whence arises all that Order and Beauty which we see in the World? . . . And these things being rightly dispatched, does it not appear from Phaenomena that there is a Being incorporeal, living, intelligent, omnipresent, who in infinite Space, as it were in his Sensory, sees the things themselves intimately, and throughly perceives them, and comprehends them wholly by their immediate presence to himself? [11]

Newton's feeling about the Deity retained a strong sense of the divine. He expressed it, however, in conceptions which long outlasted his own appreciation of the insufficiency of mechanistic interpretations. Already the existence of a divinity appears "from Phaenomena," and already this is a convincing way for things of the spirit to appear.

2

Roger Cotes, the Plumian professor of astronomy at Cambridge, edited the second edition of Newton's *Principia*. In his opinion, the Newtonian philosophy is the most secure defense against the attacks of atheists because it enables us to perceive and contemplate the majesty of nature and induces us to worship and revere the Maker and Lord of all things. "He must be blind who from the most wise and excellent contrivances of things cannot see the infinite Wisdom and Goodness of their Almighty Creator, and he must be mad and senseless who refuses to acknowledge them." [12] Although what one recent writer has called "that peculiarly English phenomenon, the holy alliance between science and religion," [13] continued throughout the eighteenth century and gave rise to a great many observations similar to that of Professor Cotes, the first part of the century also brought a notable falling off both in the productivity of British science and in the intellectual and spiritual vitality of British theology. There is, however, no reason to suppose that these two developments were connected otherwise than coincidentally. In science all that declined was the rate of progress. This was a temporary phenomenon, the result partly of the magnitude of the achievements of the preceding century and partly of the accidental circumstance that the period from 1720 to 1760 or so produced no really great British scientists. The influences which by that time had dissipated the Puritan spirit were very different, and the character of religious life was fundamentally altered.

Puritan devotionalism flagged after the Restoration, and it failed altogether in the eighteenth century. Its disappearance weakened, if it did not destroy, the generally pietistic spirit in society, which revived only as the Methodist movement permeated the whole fabric of British life in the form of nineteenth-century evangelicalism. But evangelicals differed from their Puritan ancestors. Though not less devout, they placed their emphasis on emotions and good works and were not much interested in their formal theology, which in fact — apart from the doctrine of justification by faith — scarcely existed. The character of English society in the nineteenth century indicates that the decay of religious thought is not necessarily followed by the decay of religiosity, and it may conveniently be pointed out here that the scientists with whose religious problems the later chapters of this book will deal were living in an atmosphere which was pious but not theologically profound.

Except for the work of a few isolated writers, England produced no religious thought, as distinct from belief, of an order comparable to Puritanism until the Oxford movement of the 1830's, which, however different in spirit and doctrine, was (it may be) on an equivalent plane intellectually, though not nearly so profound or pervasive in its social effects. Bishop Butler's *Analogy*, the most impressive theological work of the eighteenth century, is usually described as a contribution to moral philosophy rather than to religion. Both Berkeley and Hume moved in higher reaches of philosophy than those which directly affected the subject of the present book, and the deist controversy of the early century seems in retrospect remarkable less for what it decided than for the philosophical ineptitude with which it was waged.[14] And although one of the issues was the degree to which the newly discovered order of nature permitted religion to dispense with revelation, natural philosophers themselves took almost no part in the discussion.

Despite the prestige of the idea of nature in the earlier part of the century, the only natural philosophers in England of a stature equivalent to even the secondary figures of the preceding generation were the astronomer royal, James Bradley, the clergyman-physiologist, Stephen Hales, and the mathematician and astronomer, Colin Maclaurin. This is not to say that there was no study of natural philosophy in England. Memoirs of researches continued to fill the volumes of *Philosophical Transactions*. Many of these were useful, and they reported valuable experiments and observations in all branches of science. Few of them rose above the level of detail, but the multiplication of detail is itself one aspect of the expansion of knowledge. Some, on the other hand, were not so fruitful. Dr. John Arbuthnot, for example, printed a memoir to prove that the regularity in the birth of both sexes, since it could not possibly result from chance, must be reckoned "Among innumerable Footsteps of Divine Providence to be found in the works of Nature . . . for by this means it is provided, that the Species may never fail, nor perish, since every Male may have its Female, and of a proportionable Age." [15]

This sort of thing was not as exceptional as might be supposed, and even important scientists put their attention on problems which now seem strange. Professor W. J.'s Gravesande of Leyden was so taken with Arbuthnot's suggestion that he wrote an entire treatise which subjected it to an intensive and confirmatory mathematical analysis.[16] But this is simply an illustration that it is time as well as genius which winnows the wheat from the chaff in scientific research. Even superior minds employ the conceptual schemes (like divine Providence) which, though rooted in tradition or in usage and not in facts, seem to explain phenomena. Edmund Halley, to take another instance, having brought comets within the pale of Newtonian astronomy, wrote a paper in which he proposed a collision between the earth and a comet as the device which God had used to unleash a deluge as powerful as Noah's had evidently been.[17] Since the flood was then thought to account for the occurrence of marine fossils on the dry land, it did not seem an inappropriate subject for papers in *Philosophical Transactions*.

Neither in *Philosophical Transactions* nor elsewhere were there published in England any really seminal contributions to science during this period. Apart from minor researches which pushed some topics further, natural philosophers were primarily occupied with assimilating Newton and with popularizing his system. The majority of the books on natural philosophy were designed for the intelligent public,[18] and of these two of the most authoritative and successful were translations of works by the Dutch professors Musschenbroek and Gravesande. The titles usually promise the reader a familiar introduction to, a compendium of, or a commentary upon the Newtonian system of the universe.[19] "The Thoughts of being oblig'd to understand Mathematicks have frighted a great many from the Newtonian Philosophy," as one of the best of the popularizers remarked,[20] and these works generally featured physics without tears and the *Principia* without mathematics. But they were good explanations — at least, the better ones were — and they were seriously conceived to fulfill a useful function. Many of them had originated as lectures, and the authors had devised a great variety of experimental demonstrations to illustrate points which Newton had derived mathematically. Some attempted to describe the necessary mathematical reasoning in words. Others introduced their readers to mathematical discussion by choosing illustrations of gradually increasing difficulty.

English natural philosophers were men of their time, though less so perhaps than French *philosophes*, and, as might be expected, their view of the religious implications of their work came to be expressed in the language of convention rather than of ardent conviction. Nevertheless, the convention was apparently sincere because divine Providence occupied an essential position in the literature of natural philosophy in the first half of the century. Colin Maclaurin, for example, is described as having undertaken the writing of his *Treatise of Fluxions*[21] with the object, among others, of refuting the charges of infidelity leveled against mathematicians by Bishop Berkeley.[22] Maclaurin's *Account of Sir Isaac Newton's Philosophical Discoveries* concluded with a chapter on "the Supreme Author and Governor of the universe, the True and Living God."[23] He was appalled at the rashness with which foreign philosophers like Descartes and Leibniz had dispensed with God. No small part of Newton's superiority, thought Maclaurin, lay in his correct and cautious views upon this most important subject. Maclaurin particularly emphasized the fact that "the Deity's acting and interposing in the universe, shew that he *governs* it as well as formed it," [24] and the circumstance that in many spheres He chose to exercise His control through subordinate agents and mechanical secondary causes, or through an ether, is no derogation from His power and no justification for substituting a blind, inanimate principle of order for a personal, superintending God. Maclaurin's discussion of this point makes one of the rare references to be found in Newtonian literature to the phenomena which later concerned geology, a subject that as yet had not even been given its name. The visible effects of revolutions and catastrophes in the crust of the earth are illustrations that "the Deity has formed the universe dependent upon himself, so as to require to be altered by him, tho' at very distant periods of time." [25]

Maclaurin was deeply impressed with how unsatisfactory the design of the universe would have been had it not included provision for a future life, to which our present existence is probationary. Our mortal intelligence and earth-bound perspective make possible only a very incomplete understanding of nature. In heaven, however, all will be made clear, and to Maclaurin this seems to have been the most attractive feature of the prospect for eternal felicity. He made the agreeable suggestion that after death it would be possible to compare notes with astronomers from other planets. The logical necessity that we should one day penetrate "farther into the scheme of nature" gives us, indeed, the strongest of reasons to feel confident of immortal life, for God could not have meant simply to tantalize us with the little we have been permitted to learn here. "It does not appear to be suitable to the wisdom that shines throughout all nature, to suppose that we should see so far, and have our curiosity so much raised concerning the works of God, only to be disappointed at the end." [26]

The intensity of Maclaurin's interest in the providential framework of natural philosophy was somewhat exceptional, but Newton's other expositors agreed with him in regarding God as the first cause of all the phenomena of the physical universe. "We must proceed cautiously in Physics," observed

Gravesande, "since that Science considers the Works of the Supreme Wisdom." [27] The Deity's role was axiomatic. As is the way with axioms, however, it was usually postulated in prefaces and, except in Maclaurin, not much discussed thereafter. "Physics do not meddle with the first Formation of Things. That the World was created by God, is a Position wherein Reason so perfectly agrees with Scripture, that the least Examination of Nature will show plain Footsteps of Supreme Wisdom." [28] There is, consequently, very little discussion regarding ultimate causation in this literature. The natural philosopher's business was rather to describe phenomena and to discover those uniformities of behavior which he calls laws and which may be described as causes, but causes only in the secondary sense that they explain appearances and not in the primary sense that they include within themselves the ultimate reason for their own existence.

The principle of gravity, for example, explains the movements of the solar system and permits calculation and prediction, but none of the philosophers pretended to understand the cause of gravity itself, and they always pointed out that there is a vast quantity of other things which are unknown and probably unknowable. Nevertheless, although the reason that divine Providence hit upon the law of inverse squares is inscrutable, this was not to say that the Newtonian philosophy, as critics charged, does not really explain the universe. Science describes its behavior, in part at least, and this is a great deal. Its reason for being at all must be referred to God, and though we cannot doubt that He had a purpose in creating the universe, natural philosophy cannot say what it was. Disclaimers of this sort were frequently accompanied by reflections upon the undistinguished position occupied by our earth in the solar system. Nevertheless, occasional remarks and habitual turns of phrase indicate that a very old and contradictory assumption was still widespread. Most writers on natural philosophy, except when they were making a conscious effort which was seldom sustained, agreed with Stephen Hales in thinking that "the beautiful Fabrick of this World was chiefly framed for and adapted to the Use of Man." [29]

Teleology was still too all-embracing a concept to be much discussed. The question of the Creator's purposes, like that of His existence, does not occupy a prominent place in Newtonian literature, which instead is concerned to exhibit the laws of nature. According to Gravesande, "A Law of Nature then is *the rule and Law, according to which God resolved that certain Motions should always, that is, in all Cases be performed. Every Law does immediately depend upon the Will of God.*" [30] Musschenbroek's definition is similar. Laws of nature are "those constant appearances, which are always the same, whenever bodies are placed in like circumstances." [31] They are discoverable only by applying our senses to the study of facts, and our only appropriate tools are observation, experiment, measurement, mathematical calculation, and induction. This, in Musschenbroek's view, is because the laws are divine and not simply reasonable.

The wisest of mortals could not have discovered any of them by reason and meditation, nor can pretend to have any innate ideas of them in his mind. For they all result from the arbitrary appointment of the Creator, by which he has ordered, that the same constant motions shall always obtain on the same occasions.

Hence plants and animals reproduce only their likes, all heavy bodies fall downwards with a constantly accelerated velocity, and an action is always accompanied by an equal and opposite reaction. There was nothing inherently necessary in this system of things, however:

All these things might have been otherwise constituted, if God had so pleased. And why he thought fit to constitute them in this manner, we can by no means apprehend. It is sufficient for us to know, that they are thus constituted, and to adore the infinite wisdom of the Creator, in this most admirable order and constitution of the universe. . .

By having recourse to these laws, we know when a thing falls out in a natural, and when in a miraculous manner. For those are *natural* phaenomena, which are constantly observed to happen after the same manner, when bodies are placed in like circumstances. And those are *miraculous* phaenomena, which happen contrary to these laws.[32]

Musschenbroek agreed with all the others that the laws of nature are by no means all found out, and he regarded this as a perpetual incentive to natural philosophers. Neither did he suggest, however, that miracles are simply natural events occurring in obedience to laws not yet understood. Gravesande might be construed in this latter sense — his discussion is not very clear:

> Also in respect to us, we call a Law of Nature every Effect which in all Occasions is produced after the same Manner; although its Cause is unknown to us. For we make no difference between a thing which immediately depends upon the Will of God, and what it produces by the Intermediation of a Cause of which we have no Idea.[33]

So far as laws of nature are concerned, the better commentators, who were still thinking in terms of motion rather than of time, did accept the invariability of the providential dispensations for the physical universe, but they did not altogether rule out the possibility that there might be other exceptional dispensations outside the realm of laws of nature.

The study of miraculous phenomena would not have been a subject for scientists, of course, but in the literature published in England, it is in Hume and not in the works on natural philosophy that there is to be found an explicit argument for the incredibility of miracles. The geological interpretations of the Neptunist and the catastrophist schools in the nineteenth century, which will be treated in detail in later chapters, make it apparent that the entire elimination of the idea of providential intervention in the physical universe was still a long way off. Many of the problems which bothered the geologists are foreshadowed in the eighteenth-century Newtonian literature, though in a different and fainter form since the history of nature was not yet much involved. John Rowning, for example, one of the less penetrating commentators, was troubled by the accusation sometimes leveled against natural philosophy that, "whereas it ascribes Effects to natural or *mechanical Causes*, acting by *fixed* and *unalterable Laws*, it therefore excludes a Providence and the immediate Care and Protection of the *supreme Being*, making him no other than an

Idle Spectator of things here below." Rowning was confident that he could prove this charge to be unfounded. His book was an attempt to explain the universe on the principles of attraction, cohesion, and repulsion.

It is to be considered in the first Place, that the Principles of the Philosophy which is now received, are so far from being mechanical Causes, at least those which are here made Use of, that . . . they are the very Reverse; and consequently can be no other than the continual acting of God upon Matter, either mediately or immediately. Consequently, Natural Philosophy, by endeavouring to account for the Phaenomena of Nature by those Principles, is so far from excluding the Deity from being concerned in the Affairs of this World; that it tends to shew that none are performed without him. Neither, secondly, does Natural Philosophy inculcate, that the Laws by which those Principles act, are *fixed* and *unalterable.*

Natural laws simply mean that things ordinarily happen after the same manner, not that they must do so.

Doubtless the Author, both of Matter and of those very Principles by which it acts, can, notwithstanding those Principles, cause it to act differently from what it would do in consequence of them alone, and so by that means produce Effects contrary to the common Course of Nature, whenever he shall think proper. That he has done so, when wise Ends require it, appears from History. . . Upon the whole therefore, to presume, that the ordinary and common Course of Nature is not sometimes altered, is *hasty* and *unwarrantable.*[34]

The Reverend Mr. Rowning was not a very profound philosopher, but if his definition of laws of nature is a little cloudy, his descriptive account of the Newtonian universe is well informed. It went through eight editions. And he is an interesting early example of the compulsion for empirical apologetics to have its cake and eat it too — to demonstrate the hand of Providence both in the course of nature and out of it.

Apologetics, however, was a by-product and not the purpose of the popular scientific treatises. To J. T. Desaguliers, whose extensive *Course of Experimental Philosophy* was less an exposition of Newton than a manual of applied physics, the business of experimental science was "To contemplate the

Works of God, to discover Causes from their Effects, and make Art and Nature subservient to the necessities of Life by a skill in joining proper Causes to produce the most useful Effects." [35] Desaguliers was a clergyman who occupied himself with physical science rather than with the affairs of the church. He devoted considerable attention to research and was the first to distinguish between conductors and nonconductors, or "supporters," of electricity, but popularization was his major interest. For a time he lectured on Newtonian physics at Oxford. After coming to London in 1713, he offered public and private courses in Latin, French, English, astronomy, and "all Parts of pure or mix't Mathematicks" for "Gentlemen who have a Mind to apply close to these Studies." [36] Like the other proponents of natural philosophy, Desaguliers urged on his readers the desirability of cultivating the elegance of mind which infallibly resulted from a comprehension of the true system of the universe. And besides pleading the intellectual advantages of natural philosophy together with the insight it gave into the divine attributes, he and the other authors also made a great point of the practical benefits which accrue to the individual and to society when the principles of mechanics, hydrostatics, and hydraulics are properly applied to the affairs of everyday life. Carriages, for example, would be kinder to the horse, the passenger, and the highway if the fashionable berlins and two-wheelers were replaced with vehicles rolling on four wheels of equal size. The utility of natural philosophy was similarly illustrated in a great variety of suggestions and demonstrations concerning the best design for pumps, stoves, steam engines, and water engines. On the whole, indeed, the utilitarian value of natural philosophy seems to have excited more real enthusiasm than its edifying aspects.

The various compendiums of natural philosophy seldom gave much space to the sciences which deal with organic nature and which, except as they bore on medicine, were usually lumped together as natural history. Martin's *Philosophia Britannica*, which covered physics, astronomy, and their practical applications, was offered to the public as a "Compleat System of Philosophy" and a "Physico-Mathematical Treasury of

Natural Knowledge." [37] Although the phrase "natural philosophy" in its general sense meant all the knowledge of nature which was based upon demonstrable fact, in common usage it seems to have been often employed to suggest simply Newtonian physics and astronomy. Many years later Professor Playfair of Edinburgh defined natural history as "the branch of knowledge which collects and classifies facts . . . Its objects are confined to what are called the three kingdoms, the Mineral, Vegetable, and Animal." [38] There is an allusion in Desaguliers which implies that natural history is an inferior sort of study, not admitting of certainty since experiment and mathematics cannot be applied to its subject matter. [39] This was, of course, an unduly derogatory and not altogether accurate remark. It was at this time that the Reverend Stephen Hales — of whom John Wesley remarked, "How well do philosophy and religion agree in a man of sound understanding" [40] — was laying the foundation of quantitative physiology and was very fruitfully applying Newtonian concepts to the study of plant and animal fluids. [41] But it is true that natural history was relatively far less advanced than physics, and that what distinguished it in method from the physical sciences was the degree to which it had to proceed by observation and classification rather than by experiment and calculation. So far as England was concerned, John Ray was still the great name in natural history, but important as the seventeenth-century advances in microscopy were, they had not been comparable to the Newtonian revolution, and no one towered over the descriptive sciences as Newton did over his field.

The dominant concept in the general understanding of organic nature was, in fact, not a product of scientific research at all, but was instead the ancient idea which Professor Lovejoy's *The Great Chain of Being* has traced from Plato, an idea which, with its attendant principles of plenitude, continuity, and gradation, reached its widest extension in the first half of the eighteenth century. [42] The organic creation in this conception was a chain of being, the links of which consist of all created forms stretching from the humblest and crudest types right up a graded ladder of perfection to the highest, God

Himself. The series was perfectly continuous and harmonious, without chasms or gaps, and the forms that made it up were thought to blend insensibly into one another. Since existence was a good, it would be incompatible with the Creator's power and benevolence to suppose him unable or unwilling to create any form of being which could possibly exist. In a somewhat circular fashion, it was often argued simultaneously that the plenitude of being was itself a proof of the Creator's benevolence. Along with many similar writers, William Derham, who was a Boyle lecturer, a minor scientist, and an enthusiast for the Newtonian philosophy, held that the other planets constitute so vast an arena for being that God could not have left them unpopulated.[43] There, thought Derham, would be found the forms not represented on the earth.

During the course of the eighteenth century, the obvious gaps in organic nature led to a movement in thought which Professor Lovejoy has described as temporalizing the chain of being. Instead of being a description of the universe as it is and always has been, the chain came to be conceived of as a process of creation occurring in time. The principle of plenitude became the program rather than the description of the universe — sooner or later all possible forms would have been created. In a very general sense this change of emphasis may be regarded as contributing to the development of evolutionary thought, but only in a speculative and not in an empirical fashion. By the end of the century, the idea of the chain of being had faded almost away. Echoes of it are found in the literature of natural history well on into the nineteenth century, more as a manner of speaking, however, than as scientific description. The interpretative problems faced by geology arose out of the actual facts discovered in the rock strata rather than out of the persistence of this ancient conception. After 1800 or so, geologists and zoologists were more impressed with the discontinuities and gaps in the animal kingdom than with any fancied continuity of forms. The *Essays and Observations* of John Hunter, for example, contain no allusions to anything like a chain of being.[44] But dissolution of the chain of being did not mean the elimination of the notion that the organic creation was peculiarly a theater for the observation of Providence in action. In 1822 the Reverend John Fleming published a *Philosophy of Zoology*, a work intended to be a summary of the science as then understood, and though his first pages explicitly refute the idea of the chain of being, he described zoology as a subject which considers "the wisdom of the plan of Providence." [45] The great chain of being had been simply one of the ways in which the conception of divine direction and divine purpose in nature was illustrated, and the conception survived this particular illustration as, indeed, it had survived many others.

Although the emotion and ardor of seventeenth-century religious feeling had disappeared out of the divine order of nature by the middle of the eighteenth century, the providential interpretation of the origin and purpose of the physical universe had not then been challenged in its essentials. Neither, however, was it illustrated in detail, and it should not be supposed that the general pattern of assumptions discussed in the last few pages was the major interest of the scientists who worked within them. They wrote their books to describe the content rather than the framework of natural philosophy. The Paley school of natural theology in the early nineteenth century displayed divine Providence in every nook and cranny of the physical system of things with far more insistence than its eighteenth-century predecessors. William Derham, although like a number of others he anticipated Paley in exhibiting the hand of God running through innumerable adaptations of means to ends in the material universe, was also one of the last writers whose work on natural philosophy expressed the religious enthusiasm of the seventeenth century. Like Paley, Derham felt that "inasmuch as every Workman is known by his Work," [46] both the existence and the perfection of God can be demonstrated in the creation, but unlike Paley, he attached primary importance to revelation.[47] *Physico-Theology* discussed the human soul as well as man's physical situation, and Derham concluded his book by outlining the duties of adoration, reverence, fear, and obedience which we owe to God. No one at this time gave the argument the characteristic twist by which Paley extracted a social message from the physical creation.

In Derham's generation the people who wrote on natural philosophy from first-hand knowledge seldom attempted to draw any social or political inferences from their subject. The conception of the universe as a chain of being was sometimes employed as proof that graded inequalities of rank and station in life were of divine origin and hence necessary, but the many writers who delivered themselves of variations on this theme were not usually scientists.[48] Desaguliers, who was a scientist, did compose a poem (as he described it) entitled *The Newtonian System of the World, the best Model of Government*, but this was simply a conventionally elegant *jeu d'esprit* celebrating the principles of limited monarchy in honor of the coronation of George II, an event so auspicious that it "makes us sensible, that Attraction is now as universal in the Political, as the Philosophical World." The annotations explaining the Newtonian system were more extensive than the poem, about which the author, being aware that "Philosophers are the worst of Poets," was somewhat apologetic. "Thus," he remarked in extenuation, "have I *tack'd* my Poetry to Philosophy, to make it go down; and tho' it should be thrown out by a *Majority*, I hope, by this Expedient, to gain a sufficient Number to keep it from being waste Paper." [49]

3

The study and interpretation of natural philosophy in the latter part of the eighteenth century exhibited a number of characteristics which, since they formed the immediate background for the later development of geology, are important for an understanding of the problems encountered in the growth of that science. After 1760 or thereabouts, the prosecution of scientific researches in England entered on a period of qualitative improvement and quantitative expansion. Oxford and Cambridge did nothing to advance science either by teaching or by facilitating research, but the functions that the universities might have performed were undertaken in scientific societies and private institutes which grew up in the last quarter of the century. The movement which gave birth to these organizations was carried much further after 1800, and from its beginning it had the effect of enlarging the area of intelligent public interest in scientific questions. Unfortunately, there is no way to measure the extent of this result in any very exact or satisfactory fashion. Nevertheless, the informed audience for scientific discussion must have been growing if only because of the increasing numbers of people who belonged to societies and who attended their meetings or read their publications.

This development reflects an interest in science itself, of course, and also a growing (though by no means an original) appreciation of the utilitarian and commercial potentialities of applied science. In the eighteenth century, the foundation of scientific academies was not occasioned by the necessity for specialization which gave rise to the nineteenth-century societies. This statement ought, perhaps, to be qualified to take account of the Linnaean Society, which dates from 1788, but the Linnaean Society was at first far from specialized in its objects: it was devoted to the cultivation of natural history in all its branches.[50] In general, the period down to the end of the century was still one of scientific universalism. Versatility was the most obvious common characteristic of people as different as Joseph Priestley, Benjamin Franklin, Henry Cavendish, Erasmus Darwin, and James Watt. With some few exceptions, of whom Joseph Black and Sir William Herschel were the most distinguished, those who were interested in science still took all of natural philosophy for their province. The most important advances were made in chemistry (apart from Herschel's astronomical work), but as with physics in Newton's time, it was the logical order inherent in the development of science itself rather than professional specialization among scientists which made chemistry the most fruitful field.

By the 1770's there had come to be three distinct centers of scientific research and discussion in Britain: in London, in Birmingham, and in Edinburgh. The Royal Society of London was still the most respected and the only formal forum. Most of the serious scientists and engineers in the provinces were fellows and kept in close communication with their colleagues in town. But the very informal Lunar Society in Birmingham encouraged, for a time, a greater intellectual vitality and certainly displayed a more gay and imaginative spirit than is usually associated with learned groups. In Scotland the savants surrounding the Universities of Glasgow and Edinburgh were considerably more sober. There the pursuit of natural philosophy was apt to shade imperceptibly into pure philosophy and even into political economy.

Colin Maclaurin had founded a Philosophical Society in Edinburgh in 1739, but after his death it had a chequered career and was threatening to become moribund when it was revivified under the presidency of Henry Home, Lord Kames, who took office in 1777. During his administration the society sought royal favor, which it received with little difficulty, and in 1783 one hundred and two members, divided into literary and philosophical sections, were incorporated as the Royal Society of Edinburgh.[51] In the same year, the Irish, not to be outdone, secured a charter for the Royal Irish Academy, a foundation for the cultivation of science, polite literature, and antiquities. It may have been a student of the latter subject who wrote the preface to volume I of the Academy's *Transactions*, which attributed Irish backwardness in science in large part to "the important changes in the government upon the invasion of Henry II," but in the future, the founders hoped, Ireland would yield precedence to no nation in the support and encouragement afforded to philosophy, literature, the arts, and commerce.[52] Both the Royal Irish Academy and the Royal Society of Edinburgh, like the Royal Society itself, were located in capital cities, and cultural nationalism played a part in their foundation. Dublin and Edinburgh, however, were not the first communities to feel the need of a society of their own. The Literary and Philosophical Society of Manchester was founded in 1781. It was the earliest and always the most distinguished of many similarly named societies in other towns. There was a resident membership of forty-three which the original by-laws limited to fifty, and no one was to be admitted who had not proved his seriousness and ability by literary or philosophical publications of recognized merit.[53] The society got off to a slow start. Dalton was the first member to achieve real eminence, and the earliest of his papers (on his color blindness) was read in 1794.[54] Before his time, the *Manchester Memoirs* do not contain anything of much importance.

The new foundations supplemented the Royal Society of London. They did not displace it as the central clearing house for discussion of all scientific subjects, and although there were beginning to be murmurs of complaint about its over-aristocratic administration before 1800, it was not until the 1820's that the society was generally accused of smothering the professional disciplines under the dead hand of fashionable amateurishness.[55] The range of the researches undertaken by Henry Cavendish, the greatest of the Royal Society circle, illustrates the pattern for his generation. His collected papers include original contributions to mathematics, chemistry, the physics of heat, optics, mechanics, electricity, magnetism, geology, meteorology, astronomy, aeronautics, cartography, and Hindu chronology. His most famous work was on the composition of air and of water, but he also clearly anticipated (though many of his results were left unpublished) the later formulations and determinations of electrical potential and capacity, of equivalent chemical weights, and of the density of the earth.[56] He was, in addition, a very odd man. His more normal colleagues, however — people like Sir Joseph Banks, Sir John Pringle, Richard Kirwan, and Samuel Horsley — differed from him in ability but not in diversity of interests.

Joseph Priestley, though he was a fellow of the Royal Society, spent most of his time with his Lunar Society friends in Birmingham. His activities almost defy summary. Priestley thought of himself as primarily a theologian and regarded his philosophical researches as occasional and auxiliary, though it is for them and not for his theology that he is remembered. Besides his scientific writings, he left behind him twenty-six volumes of miscellaneous works — theology, history, educational theory, general philosophy, politics, and psychology.[57] In natural philosophy he wrote on optics, electricity, botany, and pneumatic chemistry. Indeed, at one time Priestley felt "induced to undertake the history of all branches of experimental philosophy."[58]

The Lunar Society never had any formal organization. It consisted simply of a group of friends, sharing a passionate natural curiosity and considerable experimental skill, who met at one another's houses for philosophical discussion.[59] They formed a remarkably various group. Priestley was a nonconformist minister who was moving towards Unitarianism. The most vivacious member was Dr. Erasmus Darwin, whose spirit was peculiarly a product of the eighteenth century. In no other scientific milieu would anyone have attempted to capture the charm of experimental philosophy in verse; [60] in the nineteenth century books written in the form of didactic, moralizing conversations were the vehicles commonly employed for popularizing science on the lowest level. Darwin's evolutionary ideas were seldom remembered until his grandson's work awakened interest in them.[61] Unhappily, too, his verse was bad, and nothing is likely to recall it from oblivion. It is, however, a good example of a certain engaging naïveté which still suffused much of the scientific literature of the century. Priestley took an almost boyish pleasure in the appearance of his experiments, and he always liked to entertain his friends with the effects he got in collecting gas over water or mercury.[62]

James Watt and Matthew Boulton are the best known of the other regular members. Watt seems to have thought of himself less as an engineer than as a natural philosopher who had happened to invent a steam engine. Samuel Galton, a Quaker who manufactured gunpowder, was the group's most frequent host. James Keir, "a mighty chemist," [63] had once been an officer in the army, but he had become bored with a military career and had resigned his commission in order to devote himself to the manufacture of glass. Richard Lovell Edgeworth, a gentleman of leisure and something of an artist, had made himself an expert in agricultural improvement and in irrigation. The Reverend R. A. Johnson was vicar of Kenilworth, and Father Joseph Barrington was a Roman Catholic priest from Oscott.

There are fewer sources of information on the lesser Scottish scientists than there are on the Lunar Society. The correspondence of Lord Kames, however, conveys the impression that in Edinburgh the study of natural philosophy was the same all-embracing interest that it was in London and in Birmingham.[64] Far the most capable Scottish scientists were James Hutton and Joseph Black, who were close friends and lifelong companions. It is a curious coincidence that though both were doctors of medicine, neither practiced the profession. Hutton's work, which is often described as the foundation of modern geology, will be discussed in some detail in the next two chapters. Black's outstanding achievements were the discovery of "fixed air" (carbon dioxide) and the very fruitful investigations into latent heat which, besides their important long-run consequences, found immediate application in fields as different as Hutton's geological theory and Watt's steam engine.[65] James Watt had been one of Black's better students in the University of Edinburgh, where he was professor of chemistry. Black's approach to his work anticipated the modern emphasis on specialization. He is remembered only as a chemist. "Chemistry," he insisted, "is not yet a science. We are very far from the knowledge of first principles." His students were urged to confine their "attention to that body of knowledge which principally occupies and engages the chemist."

The chemist studies the effects produced by heat and by mixture, in all bodies, or mixtures of bodies, natural or artificial, and studies them with a view to the improvement of arts, and the knowledge of nature.[66]

Black looked forward to the day when chemistry would take its place in a unified hierarchy of the whole science of nature. He seems, however, to have been even more enthusiastic about the prospect for "the improvement of arts" and about the wealth and advantages which would accrue to his country if the traditional skills of the artisan — the pharmacist, the tanner, the blacksmith — could be informed by the philosophic principles determined in the laboratory. Like Boyle but unlike many of his contemporaries, he also appreciated the debt which science owed to technology. In Black's opinion, practical men, who had been spurred on to greater efficiency by economic competition, had been responsible for a larger share of even purely academic understanding than had natural philosophers.[67] Some day, he hoped, this situation would be reversed. Very likely the dramatic application of his ideas in Watt's steam engine had a decisive effect on Black's thought. That at any rate was the impression of the editor who, in the midst of the Napoleonic Wars, dedicated Black's published lectures to Watt — in form to Watt, in fact to the moral of the steam engine:

> By thus turning the reader's attention to Dr. Black's most illustrious pupil, I remind him of the important services derived from his discoveries: For surely nothing in modern times has made such an addition to the power of man as you have done by your improvements on the steam engine, which you profess to owe to the instructions and information you received from Dr. Black.
>
> When I contemplate the unparalleled state of prosperity of the British Empire, resulting from the skill, spirit, and activity of its inhabitants, and reflect on the imperious call, now upon us, for still greater exertions, that we may maintain ourselves in this our envied preeminence, I feel it my duty to hold forth every incitement that can animate to this honourable emulation: I shew to the Reader, in your example, that there is no preeminence in scientific attainment which he may not hope to reach, by rigidly adhering to the sober plan of experimental inquiry.[68]

Neither Black nor anyone else made the clear distinction between science and engineering which became one of the characteristics of specialization. In the eighteenth century there was a large community of interest between men who, in an industrial society, would be sharply differentiated as scientists, technicians, or manufacturers. Many of the Newtonian popularizations of the earlier part of the century were full of discussion of pumps, vehicles, water engines, and drainage arrangements. Later on, Watt and Boulton were founders of the Lunar Society. Watt always had in train purely scientific researches, and Boulton's house at Soho was a rendezvous for scientists, both English and foreign.[69] Josiah Wedgwood, who was very active in promoting the building of canals, often came to the

Lunar Society and used frequently to assist Priestley in chemical and electrical experiments.[70] The Royal Society also engaged the attention of the growing engineering profession. John Smeaton, who rebuilt the Eddystone lighthouse, began the Firth and Clyde canal in 1768, and constructed numerous bridges, was a member of its most exclusive club and a regular contributor of papers on mathematics, mechanics, astronomy, and scientific instruments. William Murdock, chief engineer of the Soho Works, won the Rumford medal for his researches into coal gas illumination.[71] Even the hard-bitten John Wilkinson, ironmaster of Wolverhampton, kept in close touch with the natural philosophers.[72]

"To promote the Arts, Manufactures, and Commerce of this Kingdom" was the intention of the Society of Arts, the largest and one of the most active of the eighteenth-century scientific organizations. Like the others, it was supported by private donations. The Society of Arts was founded in 1753, and by 1823 its directors had paid out more than £100,000 in awards to individual inventors and technicians.[73] Every issue of the *Transactions* printed a list of technological and agricultural problems and of needed inventions, and a reward was posted for the best solution of each, the method being very like that of a modern competition for advertising slogans. Premiums were also paid for unsolicited contributions in all branches of applied science, the only condition being that every recipient of a grant must permit the society to publish his discovery so that the public might have the benefit of it.

Encouraging practical science was also the original object of the Royal Institution, founded in 1799 under the leadership of Benjamin Thompson, Count Rumford. Whereas the Society of Arts concentrated its efforts on stimulating the ingenuity of the inventor, the founders of the Royal Institution set forth a comprehensive program of public education. Its *Prospectus* stated the two chief purposes to be "the speedy and general diffusion of the knowledge of all new and useful improvements, in whatever quarter of the world they may originate; and teaching the application of scientific discoveries, to the improvements of arts and domestic manufactures in this country, and to the increase of domestic comfort and convenience." [74] A journal was to be published and a "mass of instruction" made available by means of a library and a technical museum, the latter to contain a collection of working models of machinery so that engineers and workingmen might have access to the latest improvements while scientists and practical people of all classes would have the opportunity to profit from each other's achievements. The institution further proposed to furnish lectures by the most eminent men of science and to provide an auditorium complete with apparatus and all the facilities for popular instruction. [75]

The Royal Institution quickly began to take a somewhat different course from the one its founders had planned for it. Largely by reason of its accidental good fortune in securing the services first of Humphry Davy and then of Michael Faraday, its facilities contributed far more to the immediate advancement of science than to technology. Both happened to be excellent lecturers, so that the mission of popularization was carried out; but the scientific lectures were philosophical rather than practical in character, and after a few years the managers began to supplement them by engaging outside speakers to discuss topics of general interest — moral philosophy, literature, and political economy. Neither was knowledge disseminated to just the groups for whose welfare the founders had been solicitous. Count Rumford and his associates had originally been motivated in part by a spirit of philanthropy and had won the support of the Society for Bettering the Condition of the Poor. They hoped to raise the standard of living of the working classes by increasing productivity and lowering prices. Productivity, in turn, would be greater if artisans were taught to be skilled technicians, and then it could be expected that they would also be more contented citizens. [76] But the lectures to workingmen were never much of a success. They were not even seriously tried, and, not feeling bound by the founders' intentions, the board of managers soon forgot about "the usefullness of science to the poorer classes and to the common purposes of life." In 1804, one of the directors described the object of the institution as "great and important, not less than that of giving fashion to science." [77] A number of critics accused the institution of being only a showplace, but this policy succeeded on the whole, and instead of disseminating the principles of technology among artisans, the institution kept fashionable London abreast of the progress of science.

Nor were the provinces to be outdone. Facilities as elaborate as those of the Royal Institution were possibly only in the capital, but after the turn of the century a scientific society of some sort arose in almost every county and important town. Most of the societies established in London after 1800 grew out of the movement towards professional specialization. Those in the provinces, however, from the Royal Geological Society of Cornwall (1814) to the Orkney Natural History Society (1837), were more likely to reflect the prestige of the idea of science among the leisured classes and to be devoted to the cultivation of natural history.[78] Long after the physical sciences had turned into technical disciplines, it was still possible for a gentleman to set up as a naturalist and to experience the satisfaction of accumulating scientific information. This was a fashionable thing to do and a rewarding pursuit both socially and intellectually.

4

At the end of the eighteenth century, the word "science" was beginning to displace the phrase "natural philosophy," and though the older term was still occasionally employed until late in the nineteenth century, by 1845 or so "science" had become the more common designation for the study of external nature. This change in terminology was probably not of any concrete importance, and no doubt it is to be attributed to the imponderable shifts of usage rather than to any fundamental difference in subject matter or in method. Nevertheless, changes in usage, though they may be the result of fashion, often reflect alterations of attitude, and with the qualification that the remarks in the next two paragraphs are intended only as suggestions and not as definitions, it may be worth while to consider some of these differences in attitude. To the layman natural philosophy has a humane and comprehensive sound, and not only because it is in the past; the same was true at the time. Most of the new societies, for example, were literary and philosophical. The Society of Arts paid premiums to painters and sculptors as well as to inventors. Science, on the other hand, has taken on somewhat different connotations for the layman, who thinks of it as technical, abstruse, and even a little forbidding. Today the humanities are ordinarily set over against science — whether correctly or not — and are less often regarded as complementary to it.

Since the middle of the nineteenth century, it has become much harder to attach providential implications to the idea of science than it formerly was to discover God's hand in natural philosophy. Science is generally thought of as excluding from its scope any higher meanings. When it ceases to do so, it ceases to be science and becomes philosophy; whereas the older term described a pursuit which was itself part of philosophy and which could postulate Providence and elaborate a natural theology without discomfort. (Before this line of thought is carried too far, it should be recalled that providentialism is not the only general meaning that can be found in nature, that some late nineteenth-century physicists, for example, made almost a religion of materialism, and that there have always been scientists who wrote about various higher — or lower — meanings of science.) Nevertheless, in a rough sort of way, the decline of interest in elucidating providential implications from nature seems to have borne some relationship to the growth of knowledge and this in turn to have been accompanied by a shift in terminology from natural philosophy to science. It may be significant that the term "natural history" retained currency considerably longer than the more inclusive "natural philosophy" — its subordinate branches assumed the dignity of developed sciences later than physics and chemistry. And the arm of Providence played a part in natural history for some time after astronomers and chemists had ceased to invoke its aid in explaining their researches, even though many of them continued to regard the physical universe as divinely planned.

In any case, in England there was no attack on the idea of

divine Providence in nature until the nineteenth century was well advanced. In the late eighteenth century the reverse was true, and natural theology was widely represented as the higher meaning of natural philosophy. It is unfortunate that a number of accounts of the eighteenth century identify natural religion with rational religion or deism and then go on to describe the progress from deism to agnosticism as having been logically necessary. Such an interpretation can properly be applied to the growth of skepticism among rationalist *philosophes*, but it is not directly relevant to the bearing of natural philosophy upon religion. In France, many men of science did join the attack on Christianity. This, however, was not because they were scientists, but because they were part of a French intelligentsia which regarded religion as enlisted in the service of a social order that it wished to see changed. In England, on the other hand, most members of the intellectual class were well satisfied with the general system of society, to which they too may have regarded religion as useful, and even Priestley, the only important scientist who was a political radical, was an ardent Christian.[79] Paley was very unlike Holbach, and it was Paley, not Holbach, who epitomized the prevailing interpretation which English natural philosophers put on their own work.

It should also be remembered that a religion of nature as distinct from a religion of reason had always had some place in religious feeling. C. C. J. Webb wrote his *Studies in the History of Natural Theology* without ever coming closer to the *philosophes* than the middle of the seventeenth century. He quotes Bacon's definition of the subject:

> Natural Theology is rightly also called Divine Philosophy. It is defined as that spark of knowledge of God which may be had by the light of nature and the consideration of created things; and thus can fairly be held to be *divine* in respect of its object, and *natural* in respect of its source of information.[80]

This point of view was very widespread among English natural philosophers by the end of the eighteenth century; in fact, it was almost universal. The Reverend Dr. Samuel Horsley, for example, thought that every clergyman had an obligation to possess a knowledge of science and to encourage its development in the universities. Horsley himself was a mathematician, a physicist, an astronomer, and a pillar of Anglican orthodoxy who later became bishop of St. Asaph. He denied that a Newtonian approach to religion required the adoption of a mechanistic image of ultimate reality, and he regarded inertia and gravitation as proof of the primacy of spirit.[81] Richard Kirwan, an Irish chemist, geologist, and mineralogist, was a follower of Bishop Berkeley. He thought "the works of nature, as they are called," unreal. Nonetheless, they exhibit so perfect a design that they offer convincing evidence of an infinite intelligence behind them.[82] Jean André Deluc, a chemist, geologist, and physicist, was a Genevan Calvinist who had settled in London. He was seriously concerned about the loss of faith which followed upon rationalistic disbelief in revelation, but he was very optimistic about the potentialities of scientific study of nature as an instrument of Christian rehabilitation.[83] The religious convictions of Sir John Pringle, sometime president of the Royal Society, were an illustration that Deluc's idea actually worked in at least one case. Pringle's biographer and editor describes him as having resolved all his doubts about Christianity by applying rigorously Baconian methods to the evidence of scriptural revelation.[84] Sir William Herschel's doctrines regarding the condensation of nebulous matter were once described as tending to irreligion, and though his son thought the charge "contemptible," he took care to refute it:

> My Father, so far from contemplating such consequences, was a sincere believer in, and worshipper of, a benevolent, intelligent and superintending Deity, whose glory he conceived himself to be legitimately forwarding by investigating the magnificent structure of the Universe.[85]

Herschel never, it is true, committed himself in any detail on the subject. On one occasion, William Knox, a retired Under-Secretary of State, wrote him to inquire about the physical location of the "place of the Assembly of the 10,000 times 10,000 Angels who we are told surround the throne of the

Deity — We have local descriptions of Heaven and of Paradise . . . but in what part of Space are we to look for them?" Herschel's reply corrected some of Knox's astronomical calculations, but he was unable to answer the question: "An attempt to assign 'a space for the seat of bliss or the assembly of angels' does not fall to the lot of astronomers." [86] Of all the natural philosophers of this period, Erasmus Darwin is the one who has most frequently been called an atheist, but he was in fact a theist who, though he disbelieved in revelation, fully accepted God as the creator of the universe. In one of his odes he inquired:

> Dull atheist, could a giddy dance
> Of atoms lawlessly hurl'd
> Construct so wonderful, so wise,
> So harmonised a world? [87]

Indeed, the only contemporary scientist who seems not to have shared the conventional respect for the providential character of nature was Henry Cavendish, and he was simply indifferent.[88]

Bacon had never claimed more for his "Divine Philosophy" than that it could supplement divine revelation, from which, he had urged, it should be kept separate. As to revelation, natural theology followed Bacon rather than Erasmus Darwin, although the distinction between the two modes of attaining to knowledge of God sometimes became more blurred than Bacon would have altogether liked. The study of the divine was usually set out in the phrase "natural and revealed religion." The weight accorded to the natural and revealed aspects varied with the individual, but very few denied the importance of revelation even when attachment to it was a matter of lip service rather than of conviction. Priestley, for example, was a believer, a passionate believer, in revelation, but he allowed that it might be more convincing to begin the argument for a deity "a posteriori, finding that, in consequence of the *actual existence* of beings that must have had a cause, there must have been some being that could not have had a cause." [89]

With respect to both natural and revealed religion, all that we have to do is to consider whether *actual appearances* and known *facts*, can be accounted for on any other hypothesis. In natural religion the appearances to be accounted for are *the constitution and laws of nature*. In revealed religion, they are certain *historical facts*, as indisputable as any natural appearances. They are the belief of the miracles of Moses and of Christ, and that of his resurrection, in given circumstances.[90]

This was somewhat different from the devotionalism of seventeenth-century scientists. Priestley was unconsciously acknowledging that the persuasiveness of revelation was contingent upon the demonstrability of a divine hand in the laws of nature. In religion, thought Priestley — and with him many other people — the use of natural philosophy was to point to the universe and its creatures in order to demonstrate two things which, for a Boyle, would have needed no demonstration: first, the existence of a Creator, and second, the continued supervision of affairs by a divine intelligence. In Priestley's hands natural theology was more apologetic in tone than it had once been. The fact that materialistic and atheistic ideas existed had, of course, been realized for a long time in England. John Harris was worrying about it even before the end of the seventeenth century, and later both Cotes and Maclaurin rushed Newton into the breach against "the Efforts and Assaults of Atheists." [91] But the doctrines they were concerned about were so widely refuted in England that, if the literature were taken at its face value, it would seem that except for Hobbes — and in Priestley's time Hume and Gibbon, perhaps — all the atheists were French. On the occasion of a visit to Paris, Priestley describes himself as having been prepared for the state of unbelief among philosophers there; and, indeed, they seem to have been more shocked at his being a Christian than he at their skepticism.[92] He deplored the tendency they represented, however, and was relieved that it was not very strong in England.[93] The roots of unbelief, he thought, were "either a misunderstanding of the nature and object of revealed religion . . . or an inattention to the nature of its evidence." And summoning all natural philosophers, who already "attend with rapture to the voice of nature," further to "raise their thought beyond this, to the Author of nature," Priestley set out to establish revelation, "that religion which alone teaches the doctrine of *a future life*," by means of *"those rules of philosophizing* which have the sanction of all our experience." [94] His *Letters to a Philosophic Unbeliever* were calculated to reconvert rationalistic atheists to Christianity by applying the methods of natural science to the evidence. This did not seem an inappropriate project for a scientist in Priestley's generation.

In the late eighteenth century, utilitarianism was becoming, as Halévy says,[95] the language which clothed all shades of opinion in England. Priestley is frequently described as having provided Bentham with the inspiration for the greatest happiness principle, and though his religious convictions were very different from Bentham's and his political position the opposite of Paley's, Priestley often sounds like a compound of the two.

The more we see of the wonderful structure of the world, and of the laws of nature, the more clearly do we comprehend their admirable uses, to make all the percipient creation happy . . . And as true philosophy tends to promote piety, so a generous and manly piety is, reciprocally, subservient to the purposes of philosophy.[96]

And

Besides, the man who believes that there is a *governor* as well as a *maker* of the world (and there is certainly equal reason to believe both) will acknowledge his providence and favour at least as much in a successful pursuit of *knowledge*, as of *wealth*.[97]

In order to be convinced of God's moral excellence, we have only to contemplate the utility of his material beneficence, and our duty is to take advantage of both.

Archdeacon Paley did not originate the interpretation of nature with which he supplemented his *Principles of Moral and Political Philosophy*.[98] By the time he sat down to write out his *Natural Theology; or, Evidences of the Existence and Attributes of the Deity collected from the Appearances of Nature*,[99] all the ideas and values he set forth were already floating about among the religious assumptions of natural philosophers themselves. In his hands, however, natural theology became peculiarly insistent in its illustrations. Its apologetic character was fully developed, and large social inferences were drawn from the course of nature. In *Moral and Political Philosophy*, Paley had exerted himself to provide the greatest happiness principle with a providential sanction in order to bring utilitarian arguments to the support of the established structure of society. Like all utilitarians, he was scornful of the idea of a social contract. Instead, "rejecting the intervention of a compact, as unfounded in its principle, and dangerous in the application, we assign for the only ground of the subjects' obligation, *the will of God as collected from expediency.*" [100] Expediency, in the sense of planned contrivance, is the key to all of Paley's thought. The way to find out the will of God is to find out what works; since it works, God must have intended it to work, and it is, therefore, His will.

Paley described his *Moral and Political Philosophy* as a "work, that, in many of its parts, bears no obscure relation to the general principles of natural and revealed religion," [101] and he devoted a section to outlining man's duties to God. The most important, Paley thought, and the one most pleasing to God was "that silent piety, which consists in a habit of tracing out the creator's wisdom and goodness, in the objects about us, or in the history of his dispensations." [102] Accordingly, he spent his last years writing his *Natural Theology*. "As a divine," remarked one of his early editors, "the great aim of Dr. Paley's labours was to maintain the authority of the gospel, as an authentick revelation, and to enforce the practice of virtue by the sanctions of a future life." [103] *Natural Theology* was the keystone of Paley's entire philosophy. Morality being based solely upon the reward of happiness in heaven and the safety of civil society upon an appreciation of its providential basis, it remained only to demonstrate the existence of Providence itself, and this could best be done from the evidence of purposeful and benevolent contrivance in nature, evidence which Paley regarded as overwhelmingly convincing.

There cannot be design without a designer; contrivance without a contriver; order without choice; arrangement, without any thing capable of arranging; subserviency and relation to a purpose, without that which could intend a purpose; means suitable to an end, without the end ever having been contemplated, or the means accommodated to it. Arrangement, disposition of parts, subserviency of means to an end, relation of instruments to an use, imply the presence of intelligence and mind.[104]

Paley draws most of his particular illustrations from anatomy, and there is no need to follow him into detail, though it is sometimes tempting to do so — as, for instance, when he demonstrates the superiority of the divine over the human contriver's skill: "It is the most difficult thing that can be to get a wig made even; yet how seldom is the *face* awry!" [105] In substance, the argument runs that God must exist and must be good because the universe is itself one vast design, composed of an infinite complex of subordinate expedients, all intended to work just as they do work with the ultimate object of promoting, so far as may be, the happiness of created beings and above all of mankind. "Nor is the design abortive. It is a happy world after all. The air, the earth, the water, teem with delighted existence." [106] The only objection that occurs to Paley is that at first glance it might seem as if God had frequently made difficulties only in order to overcome them. Vision, for example, is a frightfully complicated process. Why could not the Deity have simply let animals see, without all the intricate apparatus now required? "Contrivance," Paley admits, "by its very definition and nature, is the refuge of imperfection." [107] There is, however, a reason even for this aspect of nature, and, when put in its proper light, it is a compelling one. God could have arranged things far more simply and directly, but part of the purpose of nature is to let us know that He exists. In order to convince us of His existence, He has often chosen to employ what might otherwise look like roundabout makeshifts. "It is in the construction of instruments, in the choice and adaption of means, that a creative intelligence is seen." [108] If things were too simple, we might not perceive the skill that had gone into them and the will that directed them, and we might attribute them to some self-sufficient principle of order instead of to a personal, planning intelligence. Astronomy, for example, is not the best starting point for natural theology because the movements of the planets are too perfect and complete in themselves, though once the existence of God is demonstrated from other materials, the mechanism of the heavens serves to give us a more exalted appreciation of His sublimity.[109]

As a machine, then, for the production of human felicity, the universe is the best advertisement possible for the existence and the character of its maker. There are, however, conditions which must be observed in order to secure the full measure of the product. The world is so constructed that perfect happiness is not possible on earth. The Malthusian law, for example, is inexorable. Equality of wealth or of station is as contrary to the nature of things as equality among the various species. Enjoyment of the blessings of property, the chief source of social well-being, is not equally available to all. Obviously, then, our mortal life is designed as a probationary period under the supervision of a ruling Providence, and in order to secure total and perpetual felicity, we must acquiesce in its dispensations. The role of Providence would, Paley felt, be meaningless if it were not connected with our immortal hopes. Indeed, it is the very imperfection of earthly existence which assures us that the opportunity for eternal enjoyment exists. The construction of nature proves that there is a God who intends our happiness, and since it is only partially provided for here below, it must be fully available in a future state.[110] All this, in Paley's opinion, makes the Christian message not only plausible but eminently credible. Once our contemplation of nature has assured us of the existence of God, we are well disposed to pay attention to His words:

The existence and character of the Deity is, in every view, the most interesting of all human speculations. In none, however, is it more so, than as it facilitates the belief of the fundamental articles of *Revelation*. It is a step to have it proved, that there must be something in the world more than what we see. It is a further step to know, that, amongst the invisible things of nature, there must be an intelligent mind, concerned in its production, order, and support. These points being assured to us by Natural Theology, we may well leave to Revelation the disclosure of many particulars.[111]

It is somewhat unfair to Paley to quote him. There have been few philosophers whose temper or intentions were better or whose honesty was more transparent. He had no exalted illusions about human nature, and — except for *Natural Theology* — his writings often display an incisive and arresting common sense. His explanation of the course of nature has been stood on its head so completely by the acceptance of evolutionary theories that it now seems almost a caricature rather than a sample of a framework of opinion, but this is partly because no one else had succeeded in making the explanation as clear and explicit as it was in Paley. His book highlights, it does not caricature, the essential features of the providential interpretation of the creation. Few scientists, it is true, were ever as literal in their theology or teleology as Paley was, nor were they as intent about such questions. Paley abstracted his attitude from a pattern of assumptions underlying the work of people whose own interests were concentrated primarily on the work itself, and his importance is that his elaboration of the pattern puts the assumptions common to his time in a peculiarly naked light. The lucidity of his interpretation was not beclouded by first-hand knowledge of the subjects on which he based it, and he was far from original — even the famous illustration of the watch and the watchmaker was not his own invention. Nevertheless, Paley's influence is apparent in the fact that his is the name most often attached to the view that everything in nature was designed as a means to the end we see it accomplishing. After his death he achieved, as someone has said, the distinction of becoming not a man but a subject, like Euclid or Cicero.

Like most contemporary philosophers, Paley based his arguments on the constitution of things rather than on their development. There is no historicism in his *Moral and Political Philosophy* and no geology in his *Natural Theology*; and the two books are good illustrations that a sense of history was as uncharacteristic of utilitarian political philosophy as a sense of evolution was of eighteenth-century natural philosophy. So long as natural philosophy was devoted to the construction of nature, natural theology emphasized design. Geology, still in its early infancy in Paley's time, was the first science to be concerned with the history of nature rather than its order, and the subject of the later chapters of this book, therefore, may be described as arising in part out of the attempt to render the Paley point of view historical. That its historical character made geology a different sort of science was appreciated from the beginning of its development. Doubts were sometimes expressed as to whether it could properly be called a science at all. Since the geologist, like the historian, had to rely largely on ancient relics and monuments of change, his conclusions were thought to be debatable in a way that those of the physicist, for example, were not.[112]

Not only was interpretation of the geological record an uncertain matter at best and hence a fruitful field for disagreement, but some of its larger implications also made the subject peculiarly liable to controversy in its early days. When the universe was thought of as having been much the same since its creation, the question of the Creator's control of events, though it occasionally arose, was not a very pressing one. When, however, the course of nature had to be considered as both a process and a blueprint, and when, therefore, the subject of science was the history of nature together with its structure, the issue of providential supervision became correspondingly more difficult for scientists who wished their work to bear continuing witness to the Deity's role. Elucidation of the divine plan now required a demonstration of how nature was governed and not simply of how it was balanced. The burden of this demonstration fell on the descriptive sciences which, with geology in the van, were emerging from natural history; and this happened at a time when the physical sciences were, in any case, passing over into the status of specialized disciplines neither suited to nor much interested in further elaboration of natural theology.

II

NEPTUNE AND THE FLOOD

EDWARD: Sea-shells, did you say, mother, in the heart of solid rocks, and far inland? There must surely be some mistake in this; at least it appears to me incredible.

MRS. R: The history of the shells, my dear, and many other things no less wonderful, is contained in the science called *Geology*, which treats of the first appearance of rocks, mountains, valleys, lakes, and rivers; and the changes they have undergone, from the Creation and the Deluge, till the present time.

CHRISTINA: I always thought that the lakes, mountains, and valleys, had been created from the first by God, and that no further history could be given them.

MRS. R: True, my dear; but yet we may without presumption, inquire into what actually took place at the Creation; and, by examining stones and rocks, as we now find them, endeavour to trace what changes they have undergone in the course of ages.

EDWARD: This will indeed be romantic and interesting.[1]

I

A GERMAN SCHOLAR once described the period from 1790 to 1820 as the "heroic age of geology," [2] because it was then that painfully organized observation began to take the place of original speculation. James Hutton's *Theory of the Earth*, published in 1795, is the earliest comprehensive treatise which can properly be considered a geological synthesis rather than an imaginative exercise.[3] For centuries, of course, people had been writing about the earth, its origins and its history.[4] But this literature was fanciful in content and probably in intent. Whatever observations it included were controversial and undigested and could be fitted well enough into whatever conceptual framework had captured the author's fancy. More often than not the details of the Biblical account of creation were corroborated and extended by collating them with natural appearances. Such an objective was not, however, the distinguishing characteristic. Buffon, the relation of whose system to Genesis was very attenuated, was often as imaginative as the generally orthodox Burnet. It was in its essentially speculative ends, not in the orthodoxy of its theological implications, that cosmogony differed from scientific geology.[5] Indeed, for a time geology was more authoritatively orthodox than its predecessor.

The cosmogonists did, to be sure, stimulate considerable interest, and they accumulated a great deal of incidental information. In addition, the eighteenth century had produced a few geological pioneers who had devoted themselves to amassing observations — men like Peter Simon Pallas, Horace Bénédict de Saussure, S. G. de Dolomieu, and John Michell.[6] Consequently, there was a reasonably extensive basis of knowledge when the science of geology emerged from the struggles of the Neptunists and the Vulcanists — the names taken by the contending schools which gave it birth.

It might be well to take a summary view of current opinion on what were to be the chief heads of disagreement not only in the Neptunist-Vulcanist dispute, but for the next half century or more. By this time, that is to say around 1790, the origin of fossils was no longer a matter of serious debate. These curiosities were recognized as the residues of living creatures, but they were not the object of any particular attention, scientific or otherwise. Noah's flood probably accounted for their presence in the mountain tops, and there the matter rested. There was no question about the historical reality of the flood. When the history of the earth began to be considered geologically, it was simply assumed that a universal deluge must have wrought vast changes and that it had been a primary agent in forming the present surface of the globe. Its occurrence was evidence that the Lord was a governor as well as a creator.

The flood, a conceivable event, loomed larger and more clearly than the creation. Yet, the notion of God's having brought the world into being in something like the fashion described in Genesis was not generally impugned. The accepted time span since creation was still around six thousand years, though there was beginning to be some doubt whether this was long enough. Whenever the question arose, however, it was supposed that this chronology might be referred to the deluge rather than to the origin of the world. In any case, the earth was allowed no very great antiquity. The antiquity of animal life depended on whether one postulated a single, all-sufficient act of creation or a series of special creations as the necessity arose for new forms of life. Both views were held, and the latter reserved mankind for a comparatively recent beginning. Animal and vegetable species, of course, were absolutely immutable and permanent, each created in its present image; suggestions otherwise were regarded simply as flights of fancy. All these points were inextricably involved in the differences of scientific opinion, however resolutely the early geologists might claim to have derived their theories from the rocks. In the Vulcanist-Neptunist debate, the antiquity of the earth was the issue that transformed a discussion among scientists into a dispute between zealots, even though the ostensible difference between the two schools centered around the primacy of heat as opposed to water in the formation of the crust of the earth.

The founders of Neptunist geology, or geognosy as they preferred to style it, were disciples and students of Abraham Gottlob Werner, professor of mineralogy at Freiberg in Saxony. The Vulcanists, who made little headway until after 1810 or so, owed the cast of their ideas to the theories of Dr. James Hutton of Edinburgh. Hutton insisted upon confining the attention of geologists to earth dynamics, and he deplored any attempts to account for the origin of the processes which could be observed in current operation. Werner's synthesis, however, seemed to explain everything that had happened since the deposition of the earliest rocks, and it did so in a fashion which could easily be referred to the supervision of a providential agent.

One of the curious features of the discussion was the comparative silence of the founder of each school. Werner himself published almost nothing and was so depressed at the thought of literary effort that he would not even answer letters, but he seems to have been a fine teacher whose generous enthusiasm and devotion to his students inspired their lifelong loyalty and affection.[7] In Britain the ablest of his pupils was Robert Jameson, professor of natural history in the University of Edinburgh, whose presentation of Wernerian thought was the focus of British Neptunist geology. Unlike Werner, Hutton did publish his ideas. His literary style, however, was so prolix and tortuous that his work might have fallen into neglect had it not been for the virulent opposition of the Wernerians on the one hand, and on the other the popularization of his theory by Professor John Playfair.[8]

The Neptunist synthesis explained stratification by postulating that all rock formations had been precipitated, either chemically or mechanically, from an aqueous solution and suspension. Originally this briny bath had covered all the earth, and even the highest mountains had been beneath it. Werner's classification of mineralogical observations led him to suppose that this deposition had taken place in five well-defined stages. The first formation suite had originated during the earliest period of earth history, when for some unexplained reason the "primitive" rocks — granite, gneiss, porphyry, and so forth — crystallized out of the chemical solution in which the primeval deep had held them. Next came "transition strata," some precipitated chemically (slates and shales), and some mechanically ("greywacke"). Fish were created in this epoch. In the third stage the waters began to recede, laying bare certain areas of the land and again inundating them. Disturbances alternated with quiet disposition. Mammals put in their appearance during this period. Many of the "Flötz" or "secondary" rocks (limestones, sandstone, chalk, basalt, and so forth) had been built up of fine particles torn from the slopes by receding torrents. In the fourth stage, these cataracts and the winds they produced gave rise to "alluvial," "derivative," or "transported" strata (clay, sand, pebbles). And lastly, in the fifth phase, after the waters had disappeared from the present continental areas, volcanic activity produced localized lavas, tuff, and other such deposits. Volcanoes were a late, post-aqueous phenomenon, incidental only and activated by ignition of coal deposits. In general, however, the earth was girdled in layers of rock as uniform as the leaves of an artichoke.[9]

The objections to this conception are so obvious that it is difficult to understand how responsible geologists could ever have accepted it. The facts which eventually overthrew it had not, of course, been studied as thoroughly as they have since been, but, even so, contemporary opponents were able to point to a mass of evidence which the theory could not satisfy. For one thing, Werner attempted to explain the entire surface of the earth in terms of what he had observed in the Hartz district around Freiberg. Elsewhere (and even in the Hartz in some instances) strata existed in which the mineralogical order simply was not in accordance with his sequence of deposition. Even more seriously, overthrust formations frequently exhibit older strata piled on top of more recent rocks, and this is true whether age is classified by Werner's mineralogical criteria or by modern paleontological indexes. The Neptunists could not explain why some strata should have been laid down at angles to the horizontal (as they held to have been the case), or why the strata inclined at angles of more than 30°, which they regarded as the result of secondary faultings, should have been folded up as well as down. Neither could they account for formations in which horizontal strata rest unconformably on bent and folded layers of rock. Since the foremost evidence for the theory was the crystalline character of primary rocks (it was then thought that materials solidifying from fusion never assume a crystalline structure), it was necessary to suppose that volcanic lavas and slaggy scoriae had originally been precipitated from solution and subsequently melted and ejected by volcanic action. There was no explanation of how or why they were melted or of how it happened that volcanic rocks, particularly basalt, occur in regularly defined formations far removed from any known volcano. Basalt, indeed, was the most inconvenient stumbling block Werner faced. Its presence in the volcanic districts of Auvergne, together with the fact that its frequently columnar structure argues solidification from a molten condition, was the crucial evidence which, once admitted, weakened the allegiance of many of his followers. Finally, it staggered the non-Wernerian imagination to think of the amount of water which would have been required to hold in solution all the practically insoluble rocks and ores of the crust of the earth. Even granting the water, however, where did it go? And once having gone there, why did it come back in successive inundations?

These objections were made at the time. The Wernerian system had certain advantages, however, not all of which were scientific. It was beautifully simple, and that, taken together with Werner's inspirational personality, attracted a large number of students to the subject. They were all imbued with Werner's own passionate delight in minute stratigraphical observation and classification. Like their master they were apt to be good mineralogists, however bad their geological theorizing, and their energetic interest sent them out from the mine school at Freiberg to accumulate a mass of information which outlived its faulty interpretation.[10]

The appeal of Neptunism is easier to understand than its acceptability. Its simplicity, of course, accorded well with the general theological argument from design. The Neptunists, moreover, dealt with the origins of the habitable globe if not of the earth itself, and they never denied the possibility of describing formative processes. Nor did they make excessive demands for time. Within reason one could suppose the rock strata to have been deposited as long ago or as recently as one pleased. There had been, obviously, a great deal of water indeed, enough for any number of floods. In fact the Flötz strata required successive inundations. Living forms postdated primary rocks, and when they appeared they did so in the order of Genesis: fish, mammals, man. Such tremendous fluctuations of the waters must have wiped out hordes of individuals and many species and genera, with the result that modern forms of life might well represent distinct creations.

The Vulcanist theory offered no such advantages. "We find," wrote Hutton in a moment of unwonted clarity, "no vestige of a beginning, — no prospect of an end." [11] His *Theory of the Earth* was almost a misnomer, for its outstanding features were a resolute refusal to speculate on origins and a rigorously empirical approach. Past events can be described only by inductive analogy to processes which we are able to observe occurring in the present and by the evidence of the resulting formations. The crust of the earth, declared Hutton, is composed of two sorts of rock, one of igneous and the other of aqueous origin. The primary igneous rocks (for example, granite, porphyry, and basalt) usually underlie the aqueous, except where upheavals have produced overthrust formations and where molten dikes have intruded from below. Weathering and erosion are constantly depositing a fine silt of sandstones, limestones, clays, and pebbles upon the ocean bed. There must always have been — there must still be — some agency which transformed these loose deposits into the solid rocks we see about us. Now this agency must have been heat; it could not have been water, because the material which cements sedimentary rocks is manifestly insoluble. On the other hand, most strata contain intermingled siliceous and bituminous materials which will fuse in a high heat. Hutton pointed to his friend Joseph Black's experiments which had demonstrated the abnormal effects of heat acting under high pressures. The intense heat of the subsurface, acting under the enormous pressures there prevailing, explained the consolidation of rocks which, had they been fused at atmospheric pressure, would have been altered in mineralogical composition by the loss of their carbon dioxide.

The expansive power of this same heat must have uplifted the present land areas after the consolidation of strata under the ocean floor. This hypothesis accounts, as the Wernerian could not, for bent and tilted strata and for the fissures into which molten rock and ores were extruded from below. Volcanic activity has always been an integral part of crust dynamics. Occasional eruptions are safety valves preventing too great an upthrust. Much of the primary rock had come from such volcanic action — subterranean lavas, which had never reached the surface, but had spread out and hardened under the seas or under other rocks. Hutton's process was not a past occurrence. It continued in operation. Even now rocks are being consolidated at vast pressures under oceans and beneath the bottoms of the seas. Even now some lands are rising while existing mountains are worn imperceptibly away.[12]

Hutton's theory accounted, on the whole, for phenomena which the Wernerians had to deny, ignore, or explain by postulating events that were at best improbable. Besides this, however, he and his followers offered a number of positive arguments. The unstratified character of many granitic accumulations indicated solidification from a molten condition; and the intermixture of limestone fragments in granite dikes was best explained by supposing the dikes to have been extruded into fissures while in a state of fusion. Rocks of similar, and often of identical, mineralogical character occur in widely separated strata. The existence of the remains of terrestrial vegetables and land animals in marine deposits argued that these materials had once been above the seas, and recent investigations disclosed undeniable traces of rising coast lines in Scotland, Sweden, and elsewhere. Most important was the current evidence for incessant denudation of land surfaces: atmospheric weathering, chemical decomposition, attrition of the soil by the mechanical and chemical action of water, the continuous transportation of detritus towards the sea, and the steady silting of the beds of seas, oceans, lakes, and rivers.

The wealth of evidence which Hutton and Playfair worked into their presentation must have made it very difficult for respectable geologists to resist a view that accorded so well with the facts.[13] Resist, however, they did, for more than twenty years. But more important in Vulcanism than particular points of evidence was the modern and forward-looking effort to conceive dynamics in accordance with observable fact and to restrict geology to no larger function. Certain consequences of Hutton's views became immediately apparent. Most obvious was the vastness of geological time which his theory demanded. No observed change had taken place in all of recorded history. Throughout how many inconceivable ages, then, must this endless rising and falling of continents have been proceeding! Dr. Hutton offered no evidence for a creation, and no denial of it either; he simply had nothing to say about it. Life, however, had to be very ancient, as old as the rocks which preserved its residues. And the whole concept hung upon the proposition that the cumulative effects of minute forces and infinitesimal changes can produce results equal to those of any sudden cataclysm and (though this last was never stated) superseding the necessity for any divine intervention.

Before this geological debate arose, Joseph Priestley had once remarked that it was needful to keep in mind "the great final cause [by which he meant ultimate purpose] of all the parts and laws of nature" in order to gain some clue by which to trace efficient causes. "This is most of all obvious," he had written, "in that part of philosophy which respects the animal creation." [14] The more passionate Wernerians were of Priestley's generation, and like him they took a large, universalist view of natural philosophy. A detailed account of two of them will bring out the aversion which the Vulcanist ideas inspired. Both Richard Kirwan and Jean André Deluc were able and respected naturalists. Both have real accomplishments to their credit. Kirwan, however, exhibited the extreme in theological obsession, while Deluc expressed an early and a limited attempt to come to terms with nature, although on his own conditions.

2

Richard Kirwan, president of the Royal Irish Academy from 1799 to 1819, was among the earliest and most widely read Neptunist geologists to take up the cudgels in opposition to Hutton's *Theory of the Earth*. In his day he was a well-known scientific figure, whose interests had led him into many fields.[15] As a young man Kirwan had conducted extensive determinations of the forces of chemical attractions, and, despite errors, his concepts turned out to be useful when experimental technique had developed sufficiently to make accurate measurements possible. In 1782 his researches along this line won him the Royal Society's Copley Medal.[16]

In those early years Kirwan had been one of the foremost proponents of the phlogiston theory. In 1787 he published his

Essay on Phlogiston, fondly imagining it the definitive work.[17] But he was capable of being dispassionate on a purely scientific matter. Madame Lavoisier translated his *Essay* into French in order to call forth refutations,[18] and it did so with such effect that even Kirwan was convinced.[19] He was, too, a recognized mineralogist, holding appointment as His Majesty's Inspector of Mines in Ireland.[20] Robert Bakewell, a Vulcanist whose scorn for Wernerian geology was exceeded by few, admitted that "Mr. Kirwan may be justly regarded as the father of British Mineralogy." [21] Kirwan's first geological venture was an article published in 1793 attacking Hutton's earliest outline of the Vulcanist views.[22] This at least served the purpose of eliciting Hutton's complete two-volume synthesis in 1795.[23] Kirwan's rebuttal, entitled *Geological Essays,* appeared in 1799 and fairly joined the issue.[24]

In view of Kirwan's respectably unspectacular chemical and mineralogical work, the transparent special pleading which characterized his geology is almost more surprising than the serious attention he received. To be sure, he possessed an Irish gift of clothing muddy thought in admirably lucid prose, in contrast to Hutton's genius for obscuring the essential simplicity underlying the *Theory of the Earth.* But even so, it is necessary to persuade oneself that the *Geological Essays* actually were propounded and accepted as a serious scientific exposition. So they were, however, and so they must be read. The function of geology, Kirwan announced, *"graduates* into religion, as this does into morality." [25] The science must of necessity concern itself with the origin and development of the globe, because the present state of things depends completely upon events gone by. "Moreover recent experience has shown that the obscurity in which the philosophical knowledge of this state has hitherto been involved, has proved too favourable to the structure of various systems of atheism or infidelity, as these have been in their turn to turbulence and immorality, not to endeavour to dispel it by all the lights which modern geological researches have struck out." [26] Kirwan, it may be remarked, shared Burke's distaste for the principles expressed in the French Revolution, though he seems to have thought

Hutton's views more likely to result in a British reënactment than Tom Paine's.[27]

Kirwan proposed to stick closely to the approved logic of inductive empiricism. He would attribute no effect to a cause "whose *known* powers are inadequate to its production." Nor would a cause be adduced "whose existence is not proved either by actual experience or approved testimony." [28] But, it soon turns out, by that "approved testimony," so casually introduced, hangs the tale. How absurd, thought Kirwan, to maintain that it is a philosophic necessity that we must remain ignorant of the origin of the earth. By the same argument — that is, by a refusal to accept valid testimony — northern Europeans would be unable to believe in the existence of earthquakes. Similarly, we could know nothing more of Greece than the broken remnants of her statues. When a man describes an incident, if one then discovers by an independent investigation that the incident happened, one does not care how the man got his information — one agrees that he is right. In like fashion there is no reason to suppose the circumstances surrounding the creation of the world unsusceptible of testimony, with the trifling exception "at the first blush sufficiently plausible, namely, that their existence preceded that of the human species." This is no real objection, however, for if in the sacred writings the "primary source cannot be human, it must have been supernatural, and most assuredly worthy of credit even in such instances as have not as yet been corroborated by observation, or perhaps are incapable of such additional proof." Independent geological investigation has derived so complete a picture of the creation that we must agree with any account confirming it, however deduced. "Now such an account of the primeval state of the globe and of the principal catastrophe it anciently underwent, I am bold to say Moses presents to us, and I make no doubt of demonstrating in the following Essays." [29]

The empirical part of the essay consisted of a rehash, in broad outlines, of the Wernerian sequence of formation suites, supported by an array of citations to the observations of obscure geologists, impressively intercalated in the text after the manner of a medieval bestiary. Having outlined the Neptunist succession in bold, sweeping strokes, Kirwan proceeded to its collation with "the Mosaic account of these events." A few samples will suffice to demonstrate the argument. "In the beginning God created the heaven and the earth" — that is to say, the first event was creation. "And the earth was without form and void." This statement is particularly significant, Kirwan felt, for:

> Therefore another terraqueous globe did not previously exist in a *complete state* out of the ruins .of which the present earth was formed, as some have lately imagined; *without form and void* the Hebrew has *Tohu* and *Bohu*. Ainsworth remarks that *Tohu* signifies a state of confusion, and *Bohu* a state of vacuity; see Pool's Synopsis. That is to say, that the earth was partly in a *chaotic* state, and partly full of *empty* cavities, which is exactly the state, which from the consideration of the subsequent phenomena, I have shewn to have been necessarily its primordial state.[30]

Moreover, all the cavities provided a reservoir to accommodate the retreat of Werner's primeval seas.

By similar reasoning, geological exegesis unfolds the Genesis story step by step. "Darkness on the face of the deep" signifies a globe-girdling aqueous miasma, particularly since David, "whose knowledge was derived from Moses, and who probably possessed a less abridged copy of Genesis than we do, expressly tells us that the earth was covered with water." The spirit of God moving on the face of the waters denotes "the great *evaporation* that took place soon after the creation, as soon as the solids began to crystallize." Though our shortened Genesis omits the fact, David mentioned that the waters covered the mountains, which geology has shown to have been precipitated from solution. Next day occurred the production of light, attested by our knowledge of the relatively late origin of volcanic action. And the "firmament in the midst of the waters" which served to "divide the waters from the waters" signifies etymologically an "expanded or dilated substance, than which a more proper name could not surely be chosen for the atmosphere," the function of which is "to separate and contain vapours." Hereupon the dry land appeared, the "fifth event which Moses places in the same order of succession that mere philosophical considerations assign to it." [31] And finally fish and land animals were created in proper sequence.

Here then we have seven or eight geological facts, related by Moses on the one part, and on the other, deduced solely from the most exact and best verified geological observations, and yet agreeing with each other, not only in *substance*, but in the order of their succession. On whichever of these we bestow our confidence, its agreement with the other demonstrates the truth of that other. But if we bestow our confidence on *neither*, then their *agreement* must be accounted for. If we attempt this, we shall find the *improbability* that both accounts are false, infinite; consequently one must be true, and, then, so must also the other.

That two accounts derived from sources totally distinct from and independent on each other should agree not only in the substance but in the order of succession of two events only, is already highly improbable, if these facts be not true, both substantially and as to the order of their succession. Let this improbability, as to the substance of the facts, be represented only by $1/10$ then the improbability of their agreement as to seven events is $1^7/10^7$, that is, as one to ten million, and would be much higher if the *order* also had entered into the computation. [32]

These curious paragraphs constitute the crux of the argument. For they establish "the credit due to Moses on mere philosophic grounds and abstracting from all theological considerations." Thus firmly established as a valid empirical and historical source, Moses can be referred to as a guide so "far as his testimony reaches" in tracing the subsequent events of earth history, particularly the circumstances of that "most horrible catastrophe," the flood. [33] In addition, criticism of recent geological theories must be referred to Mosaic evidence. Jean André Deluc, a "justly celebrated philosopher," had, for example, fallen into error by supposing the deluge to have consisted of the sinking of the present ocean areas, which had originally formed the continents, and the consequent exposure of the current terra firma. If Deluc were correct, how can one account for the rhinoceros carcasses lately uncovered in

Siberia? Moreover, Deluc's system was incompatible with that of Moses. For to what purpose would God have sent a rain of forty days to overwhelm a continent which was shortly to be immersed under a whole ocean? Moses informs us that the waters increased, rested, and returned upon the same ground, the rain having been pieced out by effusion from the Wernerian abyss. Since Noah himself did not believe the ancient continents destroyed, why should Deluc? For Noah took the olive branch to be a sign of waning waters — he must have supposed it to have grown somewhere on the ancient continents, since he could scarcely have expected it "to have shot up from the bottom of the sea." [34]

Deluc had suggested that the olive grew on an antediluvian island, one of a number which escaped the flood. Moses, however, clearly implied that there were no such. "If islands did exist, and were to escape the flood, so might their inhabitants also, contrary to the express words of the text"; one could scarcely accuse the Lord of engineering so inefficient a destruction. "It would surely be much more convenient for Noah, his family, and animals, to have taken refuge in one of them, than to remain pent up in the ark." [35] Deluc, Burnet, and Whiston, then, were all wrong. Only the Mosaic descriptive geology accords fully with phenomena now known. For only there is the deluge plainly ascribed

to a supernatural cause, namely the express intention of God to punish mankind for their crimes. We must therefore consider the deluge as a miraculous effusion of water, both from the clouds and from the great abyss; if the waters, situated partly within and partly without the caverns of the globe, were *once* sufficient to cover even the highest mountains . . . they must have been sufficient to do so a second time when miraculously educed out of those receptacles.[36]

The only real difficulty which this conclusion presents is the trouble Noah must have experienced in collecting and feeding all the species now known, all of them accustomed to such varying climates and diets. Kirwan was inclined to think, however, that a number of useless species had been left behind, and that others have been created since. And lastly, to those who objected that some areas must have been left unflooded in order to be available for the support of life when the voyagers disembarked from the ark, one may answer that the higher mountain tracts quickly became healthful again, particularly in the Far East. "Domestic disturbances in Noah's family, briefly mentioned in holy writ, probably induced him to move with such of his descendants as were most attached to him, to the regions he inhabited before the flood, in the vicinity of China, and hence the early origin of the Chinese monarchy." [37]

There is no point in following Kirwan into further detail; his method is sufficiently obvious. But much as he might deplore the way writers like Deluc and Burnet occasionally strayed from literal truth, the real enemy to morality was the atheistic teaching of James Hutton. Kirwan devoted his last few chapters to a thoroughly vicious attack on the Scottish geologist, to which he was led "by observing how fatal the suspicion of the high antiquity of the globe has been to the credit of Mosaic history, and consequently to religion and morality." [38] He ridiculed Hutton's literary style unmercifully. He accused the *Theory of the Earth* of being based on false evidence, of having manufactured observations whenever the real facts could not be misunderstood. So manifestly incorrect was the entire book that Kirwan had not even found it necessary to read it all. In order to point out Hutton's absurdities "we need only examine a few chapters of his work." [39]

To trace every one of Kirwan's refutations of Huttonian evidence would be a tedious and thankless task. In general, his technique was compounded of equal parts of ridicule and misrepresentation. After having knocked down a straw man or ignored a particularly inconvenient Vulcanist observation, he replaced it with reference to the applicable Wernerian interpretation carefully equated to a Mosaic counterpart. He readily admitted that his evidence was second-hand, but claimed authority to speak from his wide acquaintance with the observations of others. Surely his qualifications were greater than Hutton's, who had evidently traveled only in Britain, and there with his eyes shut.[40]

Kirwan presents, of course, almost too classic an example of the degree to which a perverse conception of natural theology could corrupt a scientific mind. His real objection to Hutton's theory never arose from the evidence. Hutton's sin lay in his failure to support a literal belief in Genesis, not in any denial of the Scriptures. He who is not with us, Kirwan would have agreed, is against us. If science is true, it must agree with revelation word for word. Basically the elucidation of such mutual confirmation comprises the noblest aim of scientific investigation, the only real reason for it. Therefore geology must concern itself with origins, with theories.

To be sure, the earlier cosmogonists had framed erroneous systems, based on insufficient geological experience and faulty interpretations. Their mistakes could not, of course, be accepted in an age which knew better, but Kirwan was able to criticize them, if not with tolerance, at least without rancor.[41] Burnet, Whiston, and Woodward had, after all, made properly directed efforts; philosophic success was denied them only by their lack of the requisite information. What a contrast their innocent ignorance presented to the subversive influence of James Hutton! How dreadful not to turn the vast accumulation of geological evidence currently available to sacred uses! And how much worse to insist that the nature of that evidence was intrinsically irrelevant to Scripture!

3

Jean André Deluc must have been distressed when Kirwan included his system of geology among those which had strayed from the straight and narrow way. For surely no one had labored more mightily in the Mosaic cause. Unlike Kirwan, however, Deluc had imposed upon himself the burden of serving two masters. To Bacon he accorded a sagacity as absolute as the veracity of Moses. Since he really did know Bacon's precepts well, he avoided the more obvious contradictions which flowed more eloquently from Kirwan's pen. It would be a fine distinction, but Deluc might well be awarded an intellectual position a cut above Kirwan's and be credited with a somewhat more subtle empirical exegesis. At least his writing expresses a terribly earnest and a mildly pathetic good humor. Deluc was more widely acquainted than Kirwan. Though he had been born and bred in Calvinist Geneva and usually wrote in French, he made his home in England after 1773.[42] Even Playfair had appreciative things to say about Deluc's innate ability,[43] and Hutton cited many of his observations.[44] His writings give the impression that he was a likable person, and they have the effect of making the reader regret that Deluc felt impelled to work so hard at unpromising projects. It seems unfortunate that he did not allow his reputation to rest upon his good investigations in electricity, chemistry, and meteorology. But he defined his life work himself, and must be taken at his word:

What can we determine with certainty respecting the *origin* and *nature of Man* without knowing his *history?* — How can we know anything of the *history of Man*, except we know sufficiently the *history of the planet*, without studying the *monuments of its revolutions*, and all that Natural Philosophy can discover to us of their causes?

To these questions, Deluc had, he wrote, "devoted near fifty years of my life," years which he thought well spent, for they had "demonstrated the conformity of geological monuments with the sublime account of that series of operations which took place during the *Six Days*, or periods of time, recorded by the inspired penman." [45]

Almost as discursive as Priestley, Deluc scattered his geology through many publications. His earliest synthesis, published in 1779, was entitled *Lettres physiques et morales sur l'histoire de la terre et de l'homme: Adressées à la reine de la Grande Bretagne.*[46] Then in 1790 and 1791, after having perused Hutton's early article with considerable alarm, he published four "Letters to Dr. Hutton" (he had a passion for casting things in the form of letters) in the *Monthly Review*, outlining his own system.[47] Deluc extended his ideas further in six letters, addressed for some reason to Professor J. F. Blumenbach, which collated in detail his own system with the account in Genesis.[48] In 1799 Kirwan reëntered the fray.[49] Playfair appeared with the classic *Illustrations* in 1802; and Deluc, abandoning his favorite epistles, fancied that he had erected *the* geology in the *Treatise* which, in 1809, summarized his earlier works and settled all the issues raised by the foregoing discussions.[50]

Deluc entertained the conviction that he had found natural "monuments" which, properly understood, enabled geology to begin its history of the earth at a very remote but distinct epoch.[51] What no one had appreciated, however — and this was the crux of his system, the point that made it original, complete, and scientific — was that this history must be divided between two intrinsically dissimilar eras, and studied so.[52] The first included the formative processes which eventually gave birth to our continents, the second the events which have since occurred:

> Until the importance of the distinction which I have pointed out between two classes of effects, one of those which had been already produced upon the earth's surface, *previously* to the birth of our continents, and the other of such as took place upon these continents, *subsequently* to that period, be fully understood, and those of the latter class accurately determined, we remain in the same labyrinth in which the first geologists wandered.[53]

Although the first class of causes has ceased operations on the globe, circumstances now being different, its effects, visible everywhere about us in static geological monuments, made it possible for Deluc to follow in detail the throes of continental gestation.[54] At some time before the fundamental revolution which produced our world, the earth's crust had been laid down in six successive stages. Though Deluc never acknowledged it, these stages present only minor modifications in the standard Wernerian formation suites. At varying intervals in the long-continued precipitation of strata from the primordial solution, light and the atmosphere appeared. The seas began to ooze down into the body of the earth eating out subterranean spaces into which originally level strata caved and folded. As the oceans subsided, releasing material from solution all the while, first islands and then the older continents appeared above the surface, the latter since inundated once again. Vegetation and fauna arose, and eventually man was created. Fishy life had already begun, as we know from the fossil residues in the oldest rocks. There is no telling how long all this went on, but its completion marked the end of the first era of world history, the era of creative forces.[55]

Four thousand years ago, however — using 1800 as the datum — there took place the notable event which produced the present state of the world. Previously our continents had been the bottom of the sea. Then quite suddenly, the ancient lands subsided in a catastrophic convulsion, the waters poured onto the newly sunken areas, and the modern continents were left exposed. Only a few primordial islands, now become mountain tops, escaped depression and preserved the continuity of vegetable and animal life.[56] Deluc had to spare these islands, because he was too honest to ignore the known deposits of terrestrial fossil forms overlying, here and there, marine remains. Fortunately for him no human relics had yet been found among them.

In the present era of earth history, entirely different kinds of geological causes are at work, causes which can be comprehended by observation of their operation instead of by induction from studying their finished effects. Such latter-day dynamics, however, must be considered incidental and not architectural: the earth's structure is now complete. The seas subside no more, the mountains are eternal. Some slight adjustments of the surface still find expression in earthquakes and volcanoes and in the minor silting of river basins, but the great revolution was final.[57]

"All this, I observe, is independent on any reference to the Book of *Genesis*," [58] and so indeed it seemed. In the presentation of his argument, Deluc nowhere bent any but physical observations to the erection of his geological synthesis. Nonetheless, when he had done with it, but not he thought until then, he was pleased to discover how he had "made it appear that the very facts upon which those systems seemed to rest, which assign an indefinite antiquity to our present continents, confirm, on the contrary, in the most satisfactory manner, the chronology of Genesis." [59] What were the six stages of construction in the prerevolutionary era, if not the six days of creation? It does not matter how long they lasted — a thousand years is as a day in the Lord's sight, and human memory runs not back so far. What was the great revolutionary catastrophe itself, if not the deluge? In the *British Critic*,[60] Deluc thus applied himself to detailed collation, equating the Mosaic account with the appropriate event in his system. Pagan mythology, the long life-span and memory of antediluvian man, Babylonian astronomical records, ingratitude among Noah's progeny, the optics of rainbows — all these considerations and many others were brought to bear upon the matter at hand in order to demonstrate the complete, literal credibility of the Biblical flood. Two examples will indicate how seriously he took himself.

Many of the unphilosophic faithful, Kirwan among them, had been distressed by Deluc's leniency with the islands and their resident fauna which escaped his flood. Deluc undertook to set their minds at ease:

"And God said unto Noah, the end of all flesh is come before me; for the earth is filled with violence through them: and behold, I will destroy them *with the earth*." The more literal translation of the latter part of the verse is, "I will *destroy them*, and the *earth with them*." We see that the term *earth* does not here signify the *terrestrial globe*, but the *land* inhabited by man; conformably to this we read in Chapter I, v. 10: "And God called the dry land *earth*." [61]

This left the surviving animals to be got over, however. Deluc managed to take care of them just as easily, while confounding the skeptics who discarded Genesis on the grounds that no boat could possibly hold two of every species or sufficient fodder for forty days and more:

Chapter IX, vv. 8, 9, and 10: "And God spake unto Noah, and to his sons with him, saying, and I, behold, I establish my covenant with you, and with your seed after you; and with every living creature that is with you, of the fowl, of the cattle, and of every beast of the earth with you; from all *that go out of the ark*, to *every beast of the earth.*" Does not this repetition of the words "with you," joined to the expression of "all that go out of the ark," corresponding with the order given to Noah, "two of every sort shalt thou bring into the ark, to keep them alive with thee," establish an evident distinction, between the species of *animals* which Noah had taken into the ark, and which had *come out of it with him* and "*all the beasts of the earth*"? [62]

Of course it does — the other beasts, having ridden out the deluge on a mountain top, spread downwards with the surviving vegetation onto the new continents. Their once temperate abodes became our Alpine peaks.

Many, many pages of this sort of thing boil down to a conclusion that if the Mosaic account were only a myth like any other, then its story could not now be explained in scientific terms. For Moses and Noah and all their contemporaries were totally ignorant of physics and geology. They could not have *invented* a formulation which still describes clearly recognizable physical and geological facts. Now that we do have, in the year of grace 1809, sufficient scientific knowledge to trace back from the evidence what processes must have occurred four thousand years ago, we find the picture so derived one which has always been available to men who perused Scripture. Therefore, since Genesis turns out to be a perfect description of nature set down by people who knew no science, its accuracy can be explained only as a divine revelation, taken these many years on faith, and now confirmed by completely independent collateral inquiry. [63]

All this being so, it might well be asked why scientists like Deluc should have troubled to go clambering about the Alps when they could have learned the same things so much more comfortably sitting properly at home over their Bibles? Part of the answer, of course, must be that their preconceptions did not lessen either the intensity of their natural curiosity or the vigor with which they pressed their inquiries. But partly, too, such men possessed different conceptions from ours of the basic function of scientific theory. Deluc, for example, pursued geological investigations not merely for their own sake but because of their "moral object . . . by the indissoluble connection which subsists between the history of the human race, and that of the earth." [64]

Unhappily, he gave away the weakness of his position by practically admitting that humanity's recent conquest of natural knowledge had been, in a sense, unfortunate. Geology had once been unnecessary since "the book of *Genesis* presented the history of the earth, and of mankind." [65] No essential information had been wanting. With the advance of philosophic learning, however, recent times had witnessed the promulgation of many pseudoscientific systems of cosmology which explicitly or implicitly contradicted particular incidents in Genesis, if not its total credibility. Some of these authors knew not what they did, but others were the intellectual heirs of infidels who in ages past had attacked the faith with pagan dialectic or with myth. Now this school had seized upon a weapon in geology — false geology, to be sure, but still geology. Theologians, then, must master the new instrument and turn it against the enemy. Errors in other branches of natural philosophy were not so serious. Such mistakes could be bothersome, of course, and regrettable, but hardly dangerous. [66] The geologist, however, if he was to be a friend to the best interests of humanity, must exercise particular caution. His inquiries were directed to a greater object than those of other scientists.

No general inference, indeed, drawn from the physical sciences, could be more important to men than that in which Genesis was involved; for to consider that book as fabulous was to plunge them into a final uncertainty, with regard to what it must concern them to know, viz. their origins, their duties, and their destination: it was sapping the very foundation on which the great edifice of society has always rested: it was, in short, abandoning men to themselves; and those must have been little acquainted with them, who did not foresee the fatal consequences which would inevitably ensue. [67]

In this crisis, Deluc's remedy was to bring Francis Bacon to the rescue of humanity: Bacon would reëstablish Moses' claim to be a source of unquestionable scientific authority. This project did not seem at all odd to Deluc. Since, fortunately or otherwise, the story in Scripture had become a subject for empirical investigation, the importance of sound method, defined once for all by Bacon, could never be sufficiently emphasized. Deluc convinced himself quite completely that he had arrived at his theory by a rigidly inductive route. Of all geologists, indeed, he, Deluc, was the only one who had presented truth, because only he had never faltered in his devotion to objective research.[68] In one installment of his endless public correspondence, he set himself to expose "what I believe to be the cause of that condition [the decline of religion], which seems to me to stem entirely from the abandoning of revelation"[69] — a desertion inspired by the presumption of those who usurped the name philosopher without knowing or caring anything for scientific method. Infidelity arose not from scientific inquiry, but from unscientific theories, from a failure to follow valid rules of philosophizing.

Deluc felt that people with good intentions and a very little knowledge, like Kirwan, were more dangerous than geologists who impugned details of Scripture outright. Naturalists of Hutton's class who first published systems contrary to Genesis "have already fallen, in consequence of the increase of knowledge; and thus is become obvious the imprudence of their attack on that, which a sublime tradition had established among men."[70] It was impossible, however, to apologize for those who, with no great information, brought forth various well-meant and chimerical systems so nonsensical as to discredit a great object in their own collapse.[71] Kirwan's *Geological Essays*, for example, could only be deplored. Their author knew no geology first hand, and he committed the unforgivable sin of reasoning *a priori* from Genesis itself. What was worse, he misconstrued the passages which would have been improperly used even had he understood them.

Deluc employed a rather more gingerly approach to criticism of Hutton and Playfair, against whose notions his *Treatise* was primarily directed. Somewhat consciously generous tributes to their talents, industry, and ingenuity preface passages of uncompromising opposition.[72] Playfair, in particular, had performed a great service in pointing out so forcibly how geology had recently possessed itself of sufficient factual basis for sound theorizing.[73] Unfortunately, however, the Scottish professor's arbitrary delimitation of the proper sphere of geology defeated the purpose of the science. If a student of the earth confines his attention to causes now operating, he can understand only the relatively incidental events which occurred subsequent to the diluvial birth of our continents. So partial a view of the sphere of geology must be considered very unscientific. More seriously, Playfair's definition denied the possibility of philosophically establishing a history of the earth, with all the moral benefits which could ensue. Indeed, any such narrow limits were "strange hypotheses." Playfair, in sum, had never grasped the Baconian conception of all knowledge as a rightful province.[74]

Apparently an accepted and almost expected feature of the scientific debating practice of the period was the conventional accusation that one's opponent had willfully forced his facts into line with his subjective delusions. Each of the forensic geologists made some such remark about every other. Deluc's basic objection to Hutton and Playfair arose, he said, from just this weakness in their thought.[75] He dismissed the mass of evidence Hutton had accumulated as specious and misinterpreted, too facile to stand. Nonetheless, it had best be refuted in detail, lest unwary laymen fail to perceive how the *Theory of the Earth*, with its artificial limitations upon geological knowledge, had sprung not from nature but from Hutton's brain. Actually, Deluc's strategy for counterattack seldom amounted to more than contradictory interpretation of evidence. Where Playfair saw a rising shore line, Deluc observed a sinking sea. If the Vulcanists pointed to a river system carrying detritus to the ocean, Deluc turned up a plain enriched by silt. When Playfair called attention to upthrust strata, the *Treatise* explained such contortions in terms of a once collapsing global crust — Deluc thought the earth had assumed its wrinkled surface after the manner of a drying prune. Rocks, of course, were straight Neptunist in origin.

More than anything else, however, the Vulcanist antiquity of the earth bothered Deluc, frightened him really. It was his King Charles's head. Remarks about it kept creeping into all his supposedly factual criticism of observational detail. Once, in the middle of a severely objective passage, he let himself go:

> According to the conclusion of Dr. Hutton, and of many other geologists, our continents are of indefinite antiquity, they have been peopled we know not how, and mankind are wholly unacquainted with their origin. According to my conclusions, drawn from the same source, that of *facts*, our continents are of such small antiquity, that the memory of the revolution which gave them birth must still be preserved among men; and thus we are led to seek in the book of Genesis the record of the history of the human race from its origin. Can any object of importance superior to this be found throughout the circle of natural science? [76]

Here, clearly, is the crux of the argument. In another place, one of the weakest sections of the *Treatise*, Deluc attempted to define how he had been able to use "natural chronometers" in fixing the date of the deluge at 2200 B.C.[77] But though he was ordinarily capable in purely descriptive passages, these chronometers were very vague. They were connected somehow with the rate at which currently observable causes operate. Here is the one point where the reader wonders whether Deluc really could have believed in his own objectivity. Probably he did, however. In any case, he had very little choice, for if the continents had been formed in time out of mind, obviously Genesis could not be historically true. The Pentateuch could still contain an authentic account of what men were miraculously told, but that was not good enough. In order to be susceptible of scientific confirmation, it had to be the record of what men had experienced, remembered, and set down. Its authors knew of creation from revelation, certainly — but they went through the flood themselves.

Quite obviously, of course, Deluc simply could not bear the thought that mankind should be "wholly unacquainted with their origin." He found no end of empirical objections to raise against the Vulcanists. Of all possible sources of infidelity, he thought, abandoning the literal sense of Genesis with regard to the deluge had produced the greatest number of unbelievers.[78] There is something rather pathetic in Deluc's interpretative gymnastics. For he really loved science as dearly as he loved the Lord. And he believed devoutly that any proper application of philosophic tools could only discover truth; therefore, any system which did not do so must have been reared upon false interpretations.

It can be said for him that he never impugned Hutton's motives. His tone throughout was sweetly reasonable and gently regretful about the Scottish geologist's great but misdirected talents. Occasionally Deluc seems over humble, always terribly serious, and quite remarkably discursive. In a sense, he made a fairly good step beyond Kirwan. He realized clearly, for example, the length of time required for the formation of rock strata, and allowed six allegorical days for his creative, antediluvian era. He refused, too, to blink away inconvenient mammalian fossils in what could more easily have been his primeval ocean bed. Occasionally, he abandoned symmetry for fact. And if his system was only a theological exercise, at least he never formally introduced his conclusions into the argument. The deluge, however, must be literal: man was represented as remembering it, and it had to be such that man could remember it.

Deluc once addressed a warning from the master to the people on his side: "Facts," Bacon had said, "will ultimately prevail; we must therefore take care that they be not against us." [79]

4

In Britain, the Wernerian forces were organized and led by Robert Jameson, regius professor of natural history and keeper of the museum in the University of Edinburgh. Jameson had deserted medicine for mineralogy about 1795, the year Hutton's book appeared, and he published *An Outline of the Mineralogy of the Shetland Islands and of the Island of Arran* shortly thereafter.[80] He was then only twenty-four and, so far as his work shows, not yet attached to any geological system. In 1800, however, he went to Freiberg to study under Werner. On his return home in 1804, he received his appointment to the chair he occupied for half a century. Like all the prominent Wernerians, Jameson was a good mineralogist, though his work suffered from the outlandish terminology his school employed. He acquired an enormous collection for his museum — forty thousand specimens of rocks and minerals, ten thousand fossils, eight thousand birds, and uncounted insects and botanical exhibits.[81]

The first two volumes of his chief work, *A System of Mineralogy*, were published in 1804. Encyclopedic in nature, they catalogue and describe in vast detail the whole range of mineral materials, employing Werner's nomenclature, of course. Four years later Jameson added Volume III, his first attempt at theoretical synthesis, under the subtitle *Elements of Geognosy*.[82] He did not claim any personal credit for theoretical originality — to do so would have been the rankest heterodoxy. In the introduction to the first volume, he let it be clearly understood that he was his master's voice:

This great geognost [Werner], after many years of the most arduous investigations, conducted with an accuracy and acuteness of which we have few examples, discovered the manner in which the crust of the earth is constructed. Having made this great discovery, he, after deep reflection, and in conformity with the strictest rules of induction, drew most interesting conclusions, as to the manner in which the solid mass of the earth may have been formed. It is that splendid specimen of investigation, the most perfect of its kind ever presented to the world, which I shall give an account of in the volume of my work which treats of Geognosie.[83]

This curious note of adulation carried through all of Jameson's earlier writing. Every conclusion, every definition, every classification, is Werner's. In the *Memoirs of the Wernerian Natural History Society*, nearly all of Jameson's papers open with some phrase such as "Werner observes" or "According to Werner." [84] Jameson was, as has been remarked, an indefatigable mineralogical observer, and he and his school professed to regard their geognosy as a subordinate feature of the main science, mineralogy.[85] In practice, however, he became so absorbed in defending Neptunist theory against

Vulcanist criticism that he found himself forever calling mineralogical observation to the support of Wernerian formation suites.

Other scientific influences than his first teacher's did, of course, interest Jameson as time went on. Cuvier's work attracted his attention, and he edited an English translation of the famous *Discours sur les révolutions de la surface du globe*,[86] thus linking, in a sense, the Neptunist school with the subtler catastrophists who later assumed its intellectual mantle. Biblical implications of Neptunism seem not to have interested him, however. The only reference to Mosaic matters in any of his writings lies in a casual note appended to the *Geognosy*, where he rather languidly points out that the deluge could not have been the primordial brine but must have come later.[87]

Jameson's happiest hours were spent in promoting the interests of his favorite project, the Wernerian Natural History Society, which he founded in Edinburgh in 1808. Since this Edinburgh group embraced the whole vague field of "natural history," its early publications included some useful papers in botany, zoology, paleontology, chemistry, and whatnot.[88] But the founder's concern lay with mineralogy — Jameson remained perpetual president until the society's demise some thirty years later — and in the Wernerian Society the Neptunists had a corporate vehicle for the perpetuation of theoretical error unusual in the history of scientific societies. The Vulcanists enjoyed no such monopoly of any propaganda medium.

The extent of the early appeal of Neptunism in respectable British scientific circles may be measured by the membership the society had attracted in 1811. There were then, the year the first volume of its *Memoirs* reached the public, three honorary, forty-three resident, seventy-nine nonresident, and one hundred foreign members. Of the honorary fellows, Werner's name was first, followed by Kirwan. Deluc appears in the roster, of course. Among general scientists are listed such prominent figures as Sir Joseph Banks, Humphry Davy, James Watt, W. Hyde Wollaston, secretary of the Royal Society, and James E. Smith, president of the Linnaean Society. University faculties, particularly the Scottish ones, were heavily represented.[89]

Jameson's followers cannot be dismissed as visionary cranks to whom real scientists paid no attention.

The first four volumes of *Memoirs*, published rather sporadically between 1811 and 1822, offer an outline of the decline and fall of Neptunist geology.[90] In volumes I and II, the emphasis fell upon articles dealing with mineralogy and geognosy (it was a point of honor with the group to use this word instead of geology). Volume II, covering the years 1811–1818, devoted twenty-one papers to these subjects, twelve to botany, zoology, and paleontology, and three to meteorology. But in 1822, by which time the whole controversy had died of inanition, only eleven contributions concerned themselves with geological subjects, twenty-nine with botany, zoology, and paleontology, and nine with miscellaneous items. Significantly, too, after 1813 not a single fellow of the Royal Society, and only two university professors, were included among the new members.[91]

The most frequent contributor to the first two volumes was, of course, Jameson himself: he had seven geognostical articles in volume I and five in volume II.[92] After the president, the Reverend John Fleming, minister of Bressay, the Reverend Thomas MacKnight, and a Lieutenant-Colonel Imrie were the most prolific members. Their articles, and indeed nearly all the articles, followed certain established conventions. Somewhere in the body of the material would be included a gracious tribute to the geognostical leadership of "our great President," without whose encouragement and inspiration the writer would never have succeeded in completing or comprehending his researches. Werner ordinarily received due acknowledgment from the faithful, but very few of them had been exposed to his teaching except as it filtered unalloyed through Jameson's example. Neither of the first two volumes contains a single geological paper which does not presuppose the Neptunist formation-suite dynamics in describing particular phenomena. By describing the rocks in the terminology Werner invented, all his followers began by admitting the very matter to be proved. Having started with the accepted mineralogical pattern, each author would triumphantly adduce his interpretation of whatever locality he was investigating as further proof of the beauty and truth of Neptunist geognosy. The Reverend Thomas Mac-Knight, for example, made an extended tour through the Highlands and reported that although "the object of these papers is to record facts without attempting to establish theory," nonetheless,

One remark more will not, I hope, be unacceptable in this Society. It relates to the satisfaction in surveying a country, afforded by the principles of Geognosy. Compared, indeed, with every mode hitherto proposed of viewing the mineral mass of the earth, the superiority of Werner's system can hardly, I think, be appreciated in its full value.[93]

By about 1820, however, the *Memoirs* appear to have gradually abandoned this rigorous Neptunism. There was no sudden change in outlook, no dramatic recantation. Rather the members seem slowly to have realized how vacuous such polemics had become, and after long exposure many of them had followed the general body of scientific opinion and had been converted in whole or in part to the doctrines of the opposite school. Part of the change may be ascribed to a shift in personnel; by 1825 only a minority of the 1810 members still belonged to the Wernerian Society. Whether as a cause or effect of Wernerian decline, the interests of the later group centered on the animate branches of natural history rather than on geology. Among the geological papers, certain contributions introduced opinions which would have been unthinkable ten or fifteen years before. Ami Boué, for example, writing in 1822, could quite casually "assert, that the Erzgebirge contains many interesting facts, and distinct appearances which might be adduced in support of the Huttonian theory."[94]

Even the Reverend James Grierson of Cockpen, whose voice had been one of the truest in the chorus during the mutual-admiration days of the Wernerian Society, eventually found himself impressed by the evidence. In volume V he published a general review of the history of the science. A great part of the errors characteristic of the "delightful romances" of Leibniz, of Descartes, and more lately of Buffon stemmed, according to Dr. Grierson, from the fact that these speculators had been guilty of "paying less attention, or we may say no attention at all, to the accounts we have in Scripture." [95] Their own society had, however, to a great extent remedied this unaccountable oversight. At the same time, it was important not to go to the other extreme represented by ardent and uninformed Biblical cosmogonists like Woodward and Whiston.

Nowhere, however, I think I may without an approach to flattery, say, have the Wernerian, or truly scientific methods of investigation in this department of nature, been followed with more ability, and attended with greater success, than in our own country; and when I say so, no one can fail to perceive that I allude to our President.

Nonetheless, writing this in 1824, Dr. Grierson also had appreciative things to say of the "truly sublime and beautiful doctrine" of Hutton and Playfair, and the usefulness of the idea of a central heat.[96]

Still, despite its defection from its godfather's tenets, the Wernerian Society did not wholly lack originality in these latter years. A frequent contributor to volume VI was the Reverend David Scot, whose field was scriptural zoology. He was particularly concerned with identifying the Saphan, a beast mentioned in Leviticus 11:5, Deuteronomy 14:7, Psalms 104:18, and Proverbs 30:26. "We are in suspense whether the rabbit or coney be the Saphan of the Hebrew Bible," or whether it be the fennec or pontic mouse of the Arabic Translation. The hedgehog was out of the question, though favored by some, because it does not chew its cud. So, after having considered a variety of animals described in the Chaldee Paraphrase (old Syriac version), Pliny, St. Jerome, the Septuagint, Philoxenus, and Cuvier, and traced the etymology of their names through Hebrew, Greek, Arabic, Chaldee, and Latin, the Reverend Mr. Scot concluded:

> We have no hesitation in agreeing with this illustrious naturalist [Cuvier], that there is but one species in the genus Hyrax, the Saphan of the Sacred Writings, the Webro of the Arabian, the Daman Israel of Shaw, the Ashkoko of Bruce, the Clip-Dass of the Dutch.

The result, then, to which we have come, after the most un-biassed consideration, is, that the Saphan of the ancient Hebrews, rendered "coney" in the English Bible, is a very different animal; that it has a nearer resemblance to the hedgehog, the bear, the mouse, the jerboa, or the marmot, though it is not any of these animals.[97]

The Wernerian Society had learned the virtues of scientific caution.

III

FROM VULCANISM TO PALEONTOLOGY

> . . . As when two black clouds
> With heaven's artillery fraught, come rattling in
> Over the Caspian: then stand front to front,
> Hovering a space, till winds the signal blow
> To join their dark encounter in mid-air,
> So frowned the mighty combatants, that hell
> Grew darker at their frown; so matched they stood:
> For never but once more was either like
> To meet so great a foe.

I

WHEN THE REVEREND MR. WHEWELL was writing his history of science, he decided that nothing less grand than the lines at the head of this chapter would serve to describe the stormy passions unleashed by the Neptunist-Vulcanist disputes.[1] The discussion did, in fact, produce an astonishing heat, most of which was given off by the advocates of water. Sir Henry Holland describes a performance in an Edinburgh theater when a play written by an ardent Huttonian was hissed off the boards by a house packed, evidently, with Neptunists.[2]

The partisans of fire were much less feverish. The chief of them, John Playfair (Hutton had died in 1797), was professor of mathematics and later of natural philosophy in the University of Edinburgh. He was a younger contemporary, a pupil, and a friend of leading Scottish philosophers. They were a cool, dispassionate circle — men like Joseph Black, Dugald Stewart, Adam Smith, James Watt, Lord Home of Kames, John Robison, and Hutton himself. Playfair became an able mathematician and naturalist, but he is not often remembered for his own work. His admirably lucid *Illustrations of the Huttonian Theory of the Earth* appeared in 1802, partly in answer to Kirwan's *Geo-*

logical Essays, which had threatened to sweep Vulcanist views into a misrepresented discard. Unlike Wernerian apostles, however, Playfair was neither unoriginal nor uncritical, and he was more than a popularizer.[3] He was Hutton's Huxley, and, like Huxley, his own contributions have been submerged in his advocacy of a larger cause.

Despite his impatience with unfounded speculation, Playfair's discussion of progressive scientific method did not minimize the importance of framing theories. He insisted, however, on limiting theories to the interpretation of observable phenomena. Mistaken hypotheses, he thought, had often performed useful service in stimulating further inquiry provided their supporters had been willing to modify or abandon their ideas in the light of further research. Horace Bénédict de Saussure and Dolomieu, however erroneous their notions, had much in common with Hutton because their theories were framed on honest scientific principles.[4] "I have already observed," wrote Playfair, "that there is a greater tendency to agree among geological theories, than among the authors of those theories."[5] This was so because properly derived scientific concepts always tended to complement each other in a few leading principles. The trouble with the Neptunists, then, was not that they had a theory of geology. Unhappily they did not have one; in its place they foisted off a cosmological speculation, and they did so inevitably because their system referred back to a state of terrestrial affairs which could only be imagined. To Playfair, this, and not the processes of rock formation, was the real point at issue.

> If it is once settled, that a theory of the earth ought to have no other aim but to discover the laws that regulate the changes on the surface, or in the interior of the globe, the subject is brought within the sphere either of observation or analogy; and there is no reason to suppose, that man, who has numbered the stars, and measured their forces, shall ultimately prove unequal to this investigation.[6]

The fundamental obstacle to the growth of geology lay precisely in the failure to understand its limitations. Anyone who attempted to carry back his inquiries "to a point prior to the present series of causes and effects" violated the very definition of inductive reasoning. But among all those who did so the most malicious were the critics who gratuitously injected religious controversy into the issue. Their faith served only to bring out the worst in people like Deluc and Kirwan, who "would have us to consider their geological speculations as a commentary on the text of Moses." Herein, thought Playfair, and not in Hutton, there found expression "a spirit as injurious to the dignity of religion, as to the freedom of philosophical inquiry." [7] The Holy Scriptures had not been revealed to mankind to teach them rock structure or any other science, and this would be true even if it were admissible to write, as Deluc had done, a scientific treatise on the history of the solar system before the appearance of the sun and prior to the establishment of the present laws of nature. Playfair deplored the philosophical ineptitude which had betrayed Deluc into so unpromising a project. But he described as even more serious the sacrilegious presumption of the Neptunists who sought to tear away the veil with which the Almighty had shielded His creative processes and had protected them even against the eyes of His prophets.[8]

As a matter of fact, however, Playfair probably resented the misrepresentations of Hutton more than the indignities offered the Creator. The injustice of such misrepresentations had wounded Hutton very deeply. It was not as if he had held that the world had never had a beginning and would never meet an end. All he maintained was that there is no mark of either in the economy of nature. To criticize the latter assertion for the former was uncandid, Playfair thought. To heap, on that account, reproaches for impiety and charges of atheism on Hutton's head was malicious. And to attempt to explain the means by which God established the present laws of nature was none of the geologist's affair and was in any case beyond the scope of his understanding.[9]

According to Hutton, the evidence, while it can never reveal the origins, does include indications which push the existence of the present order back to an antiquity exceedingly remote. Playfair admitted that a theological objection based on such grounds might have weight if the high antiquity in question were not restricted merely to the globe of the earth, but were also extended to the human race. That the origin of mankind does not go back beyond six or seven thousand years, is a position so involved in the narrative of the Mosaic books, that anything inconsistent with it, would no doubt stand in opposition to those ancient records.[10]

But geology has nothing to say about this subject. And the Scriptures actually seem not at all concerned with the mere antiquity of the earth itself. In any event, their language should no more be taken literally about the age of the earth than about its figure or its motion — which put Hutton on the same footing with Copernicus.

In fact, Playfair contended, properly understood, the Huttonian theory was far more conducive to reverent contemplation of the beneficence of natural order than were the incomprehensible convulsions put forward by the Mosaic critics. Natural theology had been strengthened by Newton's revelation of the interdependence, regularity, and cyclic efficiency of planetary motion. The same lesson was to be learned from the ceaseless rhythm of geological dynamics, forever building new substance and new worlds out of old and worn-out materials. This too testified to the skill of the Designer's hand.[11] To Dr. Hutton himself, the instances of design

which his geological system afforded, appeared . . . as its most valuable result. They were the parts of it which he contemplated with greatest delight; and he would have been less flattered, by being told of the ingenuity and originality of his theory, than of the addition which it had made to our knowledge of *final causes*.[12]

Hutton and Playfair, then, were not indifferent to the religious implications of their version of natural history. Playfair was himself a minister, and his defense of Vulcanist theory rests partly on the assertion that Huttonian order is more conducive to a properly worshipful attitude towards the divine plan than the misconceived Neptunist effort to demonstrate the geological credibility of every word of Genesis. Playfair never denied the importance of bringing the results of scientific research to the support of religious faith; he simply insisted on the impossibility of doing so by confusing theological problems with scientific ones. Science and theology were different spheres, and philosophic inquiry must proceed by its own laws and only in its own empirical domain. Nevertheless, Playfair thought, once theories were established in a properly objective fashion, natural philosophy could justifiably and creditably hold up for admiration those evidences of the Creator's design and purposes that fell within its realm.

In the contemporary state of knowledge Hutton certainly had valid grounds for asserting an absence of the sort of evidence which could support any theory of origins. Had Playfair confined his definition of the proper province of science to what geology could or could not describe in 1800, his consistency would be unimpeachable. But he went beyond that:

> The geologist sadly mistakes, both the object of his science and the limits of his understanding, who thinks it his business to explain the means employed by INFINITE WISDOM for establishing the laws which now govern the world.[13]

Playfair assumed that God had created the world, but that He had left no indications regarding when He had done so. So far as the evidence we can follow reaches, the geological process on earth and the celestial machine in the heavens have always been the same, and beyond that science cannot go.

> He has not permitted, in his works, any symptoms of infancy or of old age, or any signs by which we may estimate their future or their past duration. He may put an end, as he no doubt gave a beginning, to the present system, at some determinate period; but we may safely conclude, that this great *catastrophe* will not be brought about by any of the laws now existing, and that it is not indicated by anything we can perceive.[14]

The material universe, then, was not self-sufficient for Playfair. It was created, it runs, and (maybe) it will be abolished, but science can consider only the running. Playfair thought of the function of geology as comparable to that of astronomical physics and of Hutton's role as similar to Newton's. Astronomical observation offers continually more detailed illustra-

tions of the operation of gravitational laws. Astronomers, however, confine their attention to describing *how* the laws work;
why they should work is a question which scientists cannot
answer and into which, therefore, science must not inquire for
fear of degenerating into speculation. Playfair seems to imply
that scientists must not undertake problems which do not offer
some advance assurance of a successful solution. Theory will
necessarily fail if it goes beyond a generalized description of
appearances, but Hutton's system was not open to this objection. There was no more likelihood, thought Playfair, that it
would be superseded than that Newton would pass into the discard. To be sure, both had been preceded by earlier syntheses,
all of which had been overturned. But this gave no indication
that Newton's ideas would share the unhappy fate of Ptolemaic
or Cartesian notions because Newton, unlike his predecessors,
had at hand all the essential facts.[15] Hutton's case was entirely
analogous, and his theory was to be considered final:

> The outlines, at least, of geology have now been traced with
> tolerable truth, and are not susceptible of great variation . . . The
> mass of knowledge is in that state of fermentation, from which the
> true theory may be expected to emerge.[16]

Playfair, then, came close to assuming that the boundaries
of his understanding were the boundaries of possible understanding, and he assumed further that the proper function of
science is to describe phenomena without searching for the ultimate causes which, since they were divine rather than natural,
are unsuitable subjects for empirical investigation. These seem
odd positions for a champion of the untrammeled freedom of
scientific inquiry. So too does Playfair's admission of the importance of the recent creation of man, a point which he thought
essential for religion. All of this, however, is simply to notice
that Playfair was a product of his generation and that this
generation, as reflected in its most emancipated scientist, was
still a long way from Huxley's. Playfair was very far from regarding man, even in his physical history, as a natural object
like any other. For him, too, religious truth was served by the
process of suggesting final causes through an observation of

the current operations of nature. Playfair did, of course, clear the worst theological hurdles from the path of geological investigation. In order to eliminate religious obstructionism, he confined the scope of science to the consideration of the sort of phenomena which are observable in the present course of nature. But this definition of the function of science appears itself to have been determined by an unconscious adaptation to the needs of the moment of preconceptions arising from sources not altogether unlike the ones Playfair decried. Science, in Playfair's view, must push its inquiries only to the point where the Creator ended his direct activities.

2

Playfair and his fellow Vulcanists possessed no such exclusive vehicle for the interchange and propagation of Huttonian ideas as was afforded Jameson by the Wernerian Society and its *Memoirs*. Because of this, perhaps, as well as because of the essentially more scientific character of their geological system, the Vulcanists never became as doctrinaire as their opponents. After 1811 the publications of the Geological Society in London offered them an outlet. And on the layman's level the *Edinburgh Review*, to which Playfair was himself a frequent scientific contributor, was always friendly to their system. Vulcanist literature, however, is much less voluminous than Neptunist. Most of it is included in Hutton's own volumes, in Playfair's *Illustrations*, and in occasional papers in the journals mentioned. Until 1811 only the *Transactions of the Royal Society of Edinburgh* were particularly useful to the school, but the editors never devoted more than a fraction of their space to geological researches. Nor was that fraction reserved exclusively for Huttonian geologists, although the first volume carried Hutton's theory as it originally appeared in outline.[17]

The Huttonians expressed no sense of mission in their periodical literature. They adopted Hutton's general manner of thinking quite as a matter of course, and they made no difficulty about differing from him in detail. Since what they accepted from him was a method and an attitude rather than a body of truth, they were not, as the Wernerians were, "peculiarly fettered, by an ideal necessity of supporting the principles of their master."[18] Except for Playfair and Sir James Hall, Thomas Allen, the author of the opinion just quoted, was the most prolific Vulcanist contributor to the *Transactions*. His attitude towards Hutton exemplifies the difference in approach between the contending geological schools. In an article "On the Rocks in the Vicinity of Edinburgh," he remarked:

> This was the ground which, in all probability, first suggested the Theory to Hutton; and it was perhaps here, that his comprehensive mind originally laid the foundation, of the structure which he afterwards so successfully reared. But that theory, in itself so beautiful, and in many points so perfect, I am very far from embracing entirely. I am very far, indeed, from following him through his formation and consolidation of strata, or the transportation and arrangement of the materials, of which they are composed. There are other circumstances also, which, though totally irreconcilable with any other hypothesis, are yet imperfectly explained by his.[19]

Allen, in fact, disagreeing with Playfair, thought geology not yet ready for any comprehensive theory. And despite its terrible fallacies, he allowed Jameson's Wernerian Society credit for its accomplishments in the classification and identification of minerals, functions which were too much neglected by his fellow Vulcanists.[20]

Sir James Hall, much more instrumental than Allen in establishing Huttonian dynamics, also eventually expressed dissent from many fundamental features of the original theory though for reasons very different from Allen's. Among scientists Hall's solid experimental demonstrations of two essential assumptions of Hutton's formulation may well have weighed more heavily than Playfair's eloquent but essentially argumentative presentation of Vulcanist viewpoints. Sir James had originally viewed his friend's theory with considerable misgiving. Much of it came to seem convincing to him, however, and after Hutton's death he succeeded in devising experiments which demonstrated, first, that mixtures of melted minerals may be solidified either in crystalline or in slaggy form by varying the rate of cooling, and, second, that mineral carbonates retain their carbon dioxide when heated under huge pressures.[21] These experiments reproduced in miniature the processes which, according to Hutton, are responsible for the formation of rock strata under the conditions prevailing in the earth's crust. Sir James, therefore, performed Vulcanism a great service, and he himself subscribed to the ideas of the igneous formation of rocks and of the consolidation of strata by compression.

The mode of rock formation, thought Hall, was the essential part of the Huttonian theory.[22] He dissented emphatically, however, from the contention that current forces alone, operating over vast periods, could have brought about all observable geological changes.

> To this opinion I could never subscribe. . . I still believe, that vast torrents, of depths sufficient to overtop our mountains, have swept along the surface of the earth, excavating vallies, undermining mountains, and carrying away whatever was unable to resist such powerful corrosion. If such agents have been at work in the Alps, it is difficult to conceive that our countries should have been spared.[23]

In offering his diluvial views, Hall cited his own and Saussure's Alpine observations, and he expanded his conception in a later series of articles entitled "On the Revolutions of the Earth's Surface." [24] Here he reasserted his allegiance to what he deemed were the kernels of Vulcanist thought — subterranean consolidation and mountain uplift. The body of his material, however, was devoted to exhibiting evidence for a universal debacle, in the form of a cataclysmic torrent which had flowed high and deep over the Alps. He pointed to the architecture of river valleys and to the scoured appearance of inland basins. He made analogies to the tidal waves of Lima and Lisbon, and he referred to the old stand-by of Mosaic geologists, the bones of tropical dinosaurs found in Siberia. His continents, too, rose violently in sudden revolutions, not gradually and imperceptibly as Hutton had proposed.[25]

In all this, of course, Hall was anticipating the position of the later catastrophists, who would regard the *Theory of the*

Earth as the very foundation of modern geology while restating the Mosaic rationale in such a way as to take care of universally accepted conceptions. An intrinsic feature of all such systems would be a far more scientific presentation of Deluc's basic distinction between current causes and those which have ceased to act. Sir James himself had no intention of going over to his Neptunist opponents in making these qualifications:

> In thus controverting some of the collateral opinions of Dr. Hutton and Mr. Playfair, I venture to hope that my arguments, which have been founded on their principles, and which have led me to acquiesce in their most general and important conclusions, may tend less to weaken, than to confirm, the result of their immortal labours.[26]

Actually, however, the opinions which Sir James controverted were not collateral. He was proceeding upon principles the opposite of Playfair's when, having imagined a torrent sweeping out of the northwest, he searched about for its vestiges. The essence of Huttonianism lay not in specific details of weathering, denudation, or uplift, but in its attitude towards natural history. Sir James Hall's adherence to diluvial theories is an illustration of how the originally anti-Mosaic formulation of Vulcanism could be worked into a new providential synthesis. As yet no one questioned the historical credibility of the flood, and it was the flood which would eventually serve as the vehicle for catastrophist natural history.

3

During the more vehement moments of geological dispute, Edinburgh had been carried along on the crest of the Neptunist wave to heights of controversial passion never attained in London. In London the adherence of most inquirers to either school had been fairly well defined, to be sure, but what with distance and a more remote acquaintanceship with the leaders, the discussion was a rather pale reflection of the antagonisms developed in the northern capital. The Geological Society of London, therefore, founded in 1807, could unite the talents of

Neptunists and Vulcanists in an organized approach to further investigation. As Dr. Fitton pointed out in 1817, in reviewing the third volume of the Society's *Transactions*, they became

neither Vulcanists nor Neptunists, nor Wernerians nor Huttonians, but plain men, who felt the importance of a subject about which they knew very little in detail; and, guided only by a sincere desire to learn, they have produced, with a rapidity that is truly surprising, publications, of the greatest interest and importance, upon the subjects to which they have devoted their attention.[27]

The next fifteen years would show Fitton's view to have been overcheerful. He was writing in a lull between two storms, when geologists were engaged in mastering the details opened to them by William Smith's discovery of paleontological method, applied through an approach which, whether they realized it or not, was Huttonian. Controversy was to be renewed once the new material was sufficiently absorbed to afford a reasonable basis for restatement of the old, often unspoken issues underlying Neptunism.

Although William Smith was not the founder of a school of geological interpretation, his work was of far greater permanent value than the arguments of Vulcanists and Neptunists. An essential condition for the progress of a classificatory science is that it should employ a fruitful system of classification; and if geology owed many features of its dynamic theory to Hutton and his followers, who were also the first to approach it with a really scientific attitude, Smith provided the science with its descriptive methodology almost single-handed. Later on the attitude might waver when advancing technique threatened certain sacrosanct and originally unquestioned notions, but there was never again any doubt that the proper way to investigate, classify, and describe stratigraphical structure was by means of the characteristic fossil content of successive formations. Werner had already prepared the way for the organized study of stratigraphy by the emphasis his theory accorded the doctrine of geological succession, and in this respect he performed the science a service. But his deceptively simple chronology, based upon the mineralogical character of rock formations, could lead only to hopeless confusion. Hutton, on the other hand, had become absorbed in his endless cycles of degradation and upheaval to the exclusion of notions of sequence.[28] Neither school cast more than a passing glance at fossil remains. In France, meanwhile, the researches of the Abbé Giraud-Soulavie among fossil shells had attracted only slight attention. Lamarck's systematization of invertebrate zoology appeared between 1815 and 1822, and Cuvier's *Recherches sur les ossemens fossiles* in 1812.[29] Between them they established the basis for later biological developments in vertebrate and invertebrate paleontology, although Cuvier disapproved violently of Lamarck's evolutionary theory. In addition, Cuvier and Brongniart published in 1811 a memoir on the structure of the Paris basin, as clear a descriptive exposition of a universally regular succession of strata as had ever appeared.[30]

It was left for William Smith, however, an obscure drainage engineer, to discover in the fossil contents of rocks the clue with which to unravel the correct succession of strata. He formed his theories and multiplied his observations between 1791 and 1799, but a constitutional aversion to literary effort left their propagation to the conversations, correspondence, and publications of his not very prominent acquaintanceship.[31] In 1815 he finally got out his famous map of the strata of England and Wales.[32] Adam Sedgwick's presidential address to the Geological Society in 1831 summed up the impact of Smith's technique upon the next generation of geologists:

He saw particular species of fossils in particular groups of strata, and in no others; and . . . he proved (so early as 1791) the continuity of certain groups of strata, by their organic remains alone, where the mineral type was wanting . . . Having once succeeded in identifying groups of strata by means of their fossils, he saw the whole importance of the inference — gave it its utmost extension — seized upon it as the master-principle of our science — by help of it disentangled the structure of a considerable part of England.[33]

These remarks were intended as a belated recognition of Smith's contributions to the science. The importance of his researches was not widely appreciated before the 1820's. Smith himself had not been offered a fellowship in the Geological Society,[34] which at the time was concerned with consolidating the victory of Huttonianism in such a way as to smooth over the memory of what were generally felt to have been the discreditable Neptunist-Vulcanist controversies. In the decade between 1810 and 1820, the growth of the Geological Society of London paralleled the decline of the Wernerian Society in Edinburgh. Jameson himself eventually gave up the active publicizing of Neptunist interpretations. The second edition of his *System of Mineralogy*, published in 1816, no longer included the outline of Wernerian theory which had formed volume III of the original edition.[35] Its place was taken by a descriptive classification of the metallic minerals.

In the London group there was no single figure occupying a dominant position or exercising an influence similar to Jameson's in the Wernerian Society, though the early membership included many younger men later to be outstanding. George Bellas Greenough was the first president of the Geological Society and among his original associates were Humphry Davy, Dr. John Macculloch, Leonard Horner, William Phillips, author of one of the best of the early texts,[36] and, curiously, David Ricardo, a member of the first council. Fitton first appeared at a meeting in 1810, Buckland and Conybeare in 1811, Sedgwick in 1816, De la Beche in 1817, and Lyell in 1819. Corresponding fellowships were offered to Playfair and Hall, Kirwan and Jameson, and to the Reverend Joseph Townsend, who first fully publicized William Smith's researches. By 1820, the Geological Society had gathered the protagonists of both earlier schools into at least formal association with men of the succeeding generation who would lead new departures into catastrophism and uniformitarianism.

Inasmuch as the initial volumes of the *Transactions* assumed increasingly the character of purely descriptive compilation, they do not lend themselves to easy summarization.[37] The most common topics developed in the early papers were structural geology, lithology, mineralogy, and applied geology. Almost from the start the Geological Society manifested a conscious awarness of the economic utility of its members' investigations.

Nearly every contributor felt impelled to suggest possible economic consequences of the mineralogical characteristics of whatever district he happened to be describing. Some few of the articles were almost nothing but technological economics.[38] In commenting upon the happy results to be anticipated from coöperative research, the charter council remarked: "It would be superfluous to enumerate the many advantages which may be derived from geology: it is sufficient to observe that . . . practically considered, its results admit of direct application to purposes of the highest utility." [39] In the same connection, the society's gratifying and unexpected increase in numbers raised high its hopes for the immediate establishment of a geological museum, a library, and a central clearing house for advice on imperial mineralogical opportunities. Such worldly interests created before long an intellectual atmosphere very different from the proselytizing zeal characteristic of the Wernerian Society.

Though generally Huttonian, the Geological Society did not wish to identify itself as an organization with any particular system.

In the present imperfect state of this science, it cannot be supposed that the Society should attempt to decide upon the merits of the different theories of the earth that have been proposed. In the communications, therefore, which are now submitted to the public, every latitude has been allowed to authors, with regard to their theoretical inferences from the observations they record.[40]

The Council could consider itself fairly safe in according such license, for none of the contributors felt particularly inclined to take much advantage of it.

This changing emphasis in professional circles may be followed in its transmission to the readers of the *Edinburgh Review*. Since Playfair was an early associate of Sydney Smith and Francis Jeffrey and himself contributed a large number of scientific articles, the *Edinburgh* was never, of course, very sympathetic towards Neptunist literature.[41] Playfair, naturally enough, was inclined to use a book review as a vehicle for attacking the whole Wernerian school. His articles add little to his earlier publications.[42] Other writers were not personally involved in controversy to so great an extent, however. W. H. Fitton, for example, in reviewing volume I of the *Transactions*, described geology as originally

a species of mental derangement, in which the patient raved continually of comets, deluges, volcanos and earthquakes; or talked of reclaiming the great wastes of the chaos, and converting them into a terraqueous and habitable globe. This unreal mockery, however, though it has endured long and continued even to the present day, is now vanishing and melting into air.

And though Fitton was himself sympathetic to Hutton, he readily admitted "the theory of Werner, of all others the most in vogue at the present moment [1811]," to be "laid on foundations broader than any of the former" — broader, that is, than any other previous to Hutton's.[43]

Six years later, when he reviewed the succeeding volume of *Transactions*, Fitton no longer regarded theoretical questions as of any great significance. Instead, he felt confirmed in his earlier remarks "on the utility of such division of scientific labour, and on the probable advantages of this particular Institution."

In looking generally over the papers contained in the volume, we are struck by the collateral evidence they afford to one interesting fact in the present state of science: — we mean, the tendency, in all its branches, to assume a character of strict experiment or observation, at the expense of all hypothesis, and even of moderate theoretical speculation. . .

Matter-of-fact methods have lately been gaining ground in geology, as in other sciences: hypotheses are scarcely listened to; and even the well-organized theories which, a short time since, created so much controversy, receive in this day little attention or comment.[44]

The *Edinburgh Review* had taken a lively interest in the controversies which preceded this happy state of quiescence — nearly every other issue printed something about geology. The editorial policy of the *Quarterly Review*, on the other hand, illustrates the intellectual lag between a formulation of scientific attitudes and its comprehension by the public. Although it was much impressed with the persuasiveness of natural theology, the *Quarterly* was never so interested in science itself as the *Edinburgh*, and from its foundation until after Darwin's time it invariably adopted the obstructionist position in each successive interpretative controversy. In 1809, it made no doubt about the Neptunist leaders' acumen, genius, and accuracy. Only in their hands had "geognosy" become a science, its most faithful presentation to be found in the works of Jameson.[45] "His system is by far the most important which we have in our language: and indeed the only one by which the student can hope to investigate species." [46] With that, however, the *Quarterly* lapsed into a geological silence unbroken until 1823, when it hurled its hat into the air over Professor Buckland's newly published *Reliquiae Diluvianae*.[47] This work was the opening gun in the catastrophist controversy of the next two decades, but the *Quarterly* completely misunderstood its basis. The notice credited Buckland with having finally overthrown Hutton's atheistic and fallacious synthesis. The reviewer did not understand the way in which Buckland was reinstating Mosaic interpretations. Buckland had attempted, with considerable success, to build Vulcanism into his own paleontological approach solidly enough to serve as the foundation for a providential theory. To the *Quarterly*, however, geology still consisted of two schools. One had tried to bear out the Biblical account in a series of well-meant but unfortunately uninformed and ephemeral cosmogonies. The other school, the Huttonian, whose theory was "so extravagant, so gratuitous, so utterly unsupported by fact or testimony," had "boldly maintained opinions respecting the history of the globe, wholly incompatible with the truth of that volume in whatever way interpreted." [48]

In fact, however, in 1823 when these remarks were published, the Huttonian theory had not been a controversial subject for ten years or more. Among the geological publications of this period were four reputable manuals written to popularize the subject among intelligent laymen.[49] Although two of the authors, William Phillips and George Bellas Greenough, were professional geologists, the other two, Robert Bakewell and William T. Brande, were not. Geology was still not so technical that one need specialize in it in order to master the material well enough to write a good textbook. Bakewell was a free-lance land surveyor who undertook to restore impoverished estates to affluence by discovering mineral resources. Brande, the secretary of the Royal Society, was Davy's immediate successor as professor of chemistry at the Royal Institution, and he continued to lecture there on both chemistry and geology throughout the 1820's.[50] Davy himself had lectured on geology in his early years at the Royal Institution,[51] though he gave it up after the great success of his electrochemical researches had established his reputation and, with it, that of the Royal Institution. The manuals by Phillips, Greenough, Brande, and Bakewell enjoyed a steady sale. The four authors adopted Huttonian expressions and described rocks and ridges in a Huttonian manner without troubling to offer any comprehensive explanation. All of these writers were apt to be scornful of theorizing and to feel rather consciously superior to controversial questions. They expressed themselves as interested in other, more practical matters. Like the official publications of the Geological Society, their books implored the people at large to understand geology because at no time had there existed a more pressing necessity for the country to make the most of her natural resources. Geology, they agreed, like all sciences, had also a useful contribution to make to religion, but to fulfill this function it must keep clear of interpretative exegesis in order to concentrate on exhibiting material design.

The value of every science must ultimately rest on its utility; but in making the estimate we ought not to be guided alone by motives of narrow gain. The objects of nature appear destined to answer two purposes; the one, to supply the physical wants of the various inhabitants of the globe; and the other, to excite our curiosity, and stimulate our intellectual powers to the discovery of . . . the contrivance of the Divine Artist, and the ends and uses of the various parts.[52]

This was the general tenor of the literature, most of which was good, clear exposition. Partly because it did eschew comprehensive interpretation so relentlessly, there were certain traditional beliefs — notably the belief in the flood — which were never questioned. These implicit limitations upon scientific objectivity are most clearly apparent in the work of George Bellas Greenough, first president of the Geological Society and principal author of its geological map of England.[53] As a by-product of this endeavor, Greenough published *A Critical Examination of the First Principles of Geology*, which he intended for the general public and which appeared in 1819. His object was simply to show up the fallacies in all prevailing systems. He made no effort to replace them with any ideas of his own. Greenough devoted a chapter to each of the various classes of phenomena, stratification, for instance, or mineral veins, and pointed out how every theory failed to account for all the evidence. On the whole, the book was an ingenious and a well-informed performance.

By 1830, however, when Lyell's *Principles of Geology* appeared, Greenough was one of that writer's most bitter critics and was among the most doughty supporters of the cataclysmic theory. This is not so surprising a position for him as it might seem. Greenough's objectivity, like that of his generation of naturalists, was always a relative affair. To be sure, his *Critical Examination* had ruthlessly exposed the errors of observation and classification committed by Werner, Jameson, and their followers.[54] He had been just as severe about this as about the theoretical excesses of the Huttonians.[55] Leaders of both parties had been guilty of attempting an explanation of geological dynamics instead of simply describing what they had observed. Nonetheless, though Greenough made no conscious distinction, his criticism of the two prevailing schools failed to strike a balanced emphasis. For his objections to the Neptunists were almost always on the score of observation and definition, while his dissent from Vulcanism arose from its theoretical interpretations and seldom from erroneously described phenomena. The reason for this is quite simple. The possibility of there

never having been a universal deluge had not crossed Greenough's mind.[56]

He did not pretend to know himself how the flood had come,
or what its mechanism had been. A whole section was devoted
to examining and discarding the suggestions of those who
claimed to have explained it. Not a comet, not a resurgence of
Werner's primeval brine, not a collapse of ancient continents,
no one of these — nor any of the other popular causations —
was a sufficiently satisfactory agent.[57] Greenough showed very
easily what the flood was not. But about five or six thousand
years ago, long after the origins of the solar system and shortly
after the creation of man, all the continents had undoubtedly
been overwhelmed by a cataclysmic deluge. None of this had
to be presented controversially in the *Critical Examination*.
The flood itself was not a speculative matter in 1820.

4

Reading the geological literature of the 1830's and after,
writings not remarkable for originality of expression, one becomes a little weary of waiting for the inevitable tribute to William Smith as "the father of English geology." Since the treatises published before 1820 made no use of his methods, it is
apparent that for some time the child had not known its father;
and the nature of its upbringing is indicated in the fact that
the first complete account of Smith's researches reached the
public in a book by his friend, the Reverend Joseph Townsend,
entitled *The Character of Moses Established for Veracity as
an Historian, Recording Events from the Creation to the
Deluge.*[58]

Smith attained recognition as an engineer before anyone
was interested in his fossil researches. At a time when only
Townsend and a few close friends knew about the latter, he
was much sought after for his success with canals, mine and
swamp drainage, and water prospecting. Smith himself attributed his engineering success to his knowledge of the structure
underlying the waterways, the mines, and the fens.[59] Indeed,
in his view, the function of science was simply to facilitate just

such concrete results. Science had no other uses, no end in itself. He could, he wrote in 1799, "with ease trace each stratum of this country, from the chalk hills down to the coal," but he would not experience "the smallest wish whatever to appear in print, if it were not for a hope that some of the observations might be of service to the public." [60] Science ought primarily to promote manufacturing by discovering the most profitable utilization of natural resources. Only so could England increase her material and commercial wealth and maintain her hard-won preëminence among the nations. [61]

With such an objective, and in the very nature of his accomplishments, Smith's own interest in geology was purely descriptive. Although he worked out his methods during the height of the Vulcanist-Neptunist alarums and excursions, he paid no more attention to their theories than they to his fossils and drainage projects — of the former, indeed, they were necessarily ignorant for many years. Since speculative controversy concerned him so little, it is scarcely surprising to find Smith, in 1798, like most of his contemporaries, simply assuming the deluge as a historical fact. Its effects, he once remarked casually, "are very visible upon the surface of the earth, and to a great extent beneath." [62] He was referring to the evidence of unpetrified animal remains often found in alluvial deposits, the same evidence which Buckland later exploited as the basis for an entire system of geology. In the same fashion Smith sometimes permitted himself a conventional expression of approbation for the regularity, order, and utility of the Creator's arrangements. [63]

It may not, therefore, seem so surprising that the veracity of Moses should have been the first geological generalization to rest upon the new paleontological approach. Joseph Townsend's book enjoyed considerable success, sufficient to call forth a new edition in 1815, which included a second volume, *Recording Events Subsequent to the Deluge.* [64] Mosaic credibility in the postdiluvian epoch was established by comparative philology, but in the original, antediluvian volume, Townsend devoted the major portion of his scholarship to geological evidence. Nor was the work by any means entirely silly. Townsend and the Reverend Benjamin Richardson, Smith's other early patron, had won reputable amateur standings as naturalists. Townsend gave full acknowledgment to Smith's originality, claiming for his own descriptive chapters only that they were the result of "this extraordinary man's" researches.[65] Actually, Townsend presented the methodology for determining stratigraphical succession in a much more lucid fashion than Smith had ever managed to achieve.

Before proceeding to the argument, Townsend undertook to set forth the evidence. "My object in this part of my work is to enable my readers by means of extraneous fossils, to distinguish the several strata of our island." [66] In order not to obscure the picture in details, he confined himself to tracing the stratigraphical succession from Chichester northwest through Bath and South Wales to the Irish Channel. Then he compared this order of formations to that in other areas of England and in such parts of Europe as he had investigated in his travels. These chapters,[67] comprising the bulk of the book, are excellent scientific description. They were directed to the layman's understanding but without oversimplifying matters.[68] Except for vocabulary changes, the work affords, in the main, a perfectly valid delineation even today of the region he dealt with. Unlike Deluc, Townsend reported his observations as if he had never heard of the Pentateuch.

Because of the importance of his material, to scientists as well as to laymen, and his skill in handling it, Townsend's attitude towards the sciences of geology and natural history throws a particularly illuminating light upon the frame of mind characteristic of post-Neptunist investigation. Since he was one of Smith's pupils, the practical applications of the subject impressed him mightily. A whole concluding chapter urged the advantages of geological knowledge upon the cultivators of a large variety of economic enterprises — agriculture, civil engineering, drainage, land reclamation, the building trades, highway construction, brickmaking, sculpture, cloth manufacture, mining — and prospective benefits to each of these were illustrated in detail.[69] But this was no by means all:

The science of geology becomes of infinite importance, when we consider it as connected with our immortal hopes. These depend on the truth of revelation, and the whole system of revealed religion is ultimately connected with the veracity of Moses.

The divine legation of Christ, and of the Jewish Lawgivers must stand or fall together. If the Mosaic account of the creation and of the deluge is true, and consequently the promises recorded by him well founded, we may retain our hopes; but should the former be given up as false, we must renounce the latter.[70]

The surprising thing is that Townsend, with this dreadful fear in his heart, was able to separate his descriptions of physical fact from the conclusions he drew. There is none of Kirwan's breathless and ill-tempered piety in the descriptive portions of his book.

He would not, at any rate, take the easy Neptunist way out. On the evidence, Werner's formation suites would not do.[71] Townsend, however, was very much unhappier about the Vulcanists. "How wild! How unfounded are these suppositions!" [72] (He was writing in 1812, while the debate was still in progress.) Since he commanded a superior research methodology, Townsend was able to adduce some fairly acute objections to particular Huttonian details.[73] But he never pretended that these were his fundamental reservations, nor did he see any reason to conceal the difference between their theoretical attitudes. Hutton himself had, perhaps, not realized the consequences of his *"succession of worlds,* with no vestige of a beginning — no prospect of an end."

To religion in general this marvelous discovery is a matter of the most perfect indifference. It matters not how long the chain; we know where the first link must be suspended. . .

His object [Hutton's], therefore, in this work was not to establish atheism, but to justify his unbelief in Revelation and to make converts to his infidel opinions. He acknowledges, that there has not been found in natural history any document, by which a high antiquity might be attributed to the human race, the beginning of which, as he observes, the Mosaic history has placed at no great distance; but to the earth, in its present form, he gives millions of ages, and when he is speaking of the apparent disorder and confu-

sion in the solid parts of this globe, he says — there is no occasion
for having recourse to any unnatural supposition of evil — to any
destructive accident in nature — or to any agency of any preter-
natural cause in explaining that which actually appears.[74]

Here is particularly apparent the curious lack of confidence
which men like Townsend felt in their religion. It was not
enough that natural history should demonstrate the necessity
for a first cause, a point which Hutton admittedly did not
touch. What frightened Townsend, besides the threat to the
Scriptures, was the implication that God was no more than a
first cause. For Townsend to feel secure in his faith, God must
also be a direct participant in the physical processes He had
set in motion, and it must be possible to observe the evidence
of His activities there.

Though he agreed with Kirwan and Deluc about the pernicious character of Vulcanism, Townsend did not follow them
in offering a system of his own to replace it. Instead, like his
fellow members of the Geological Society, he fell in with the
emphasis of the school which had turned attention to the
multiplication of piecemeal observations, indifferent to the
formulation of theories. "It is yet too early in the day to think
of forming such a system, as may account for all the phenomena in nature." [75] All he could say was that obviously both
fire and water had played a part in constituting the earth,
though how he did not know. His deluge was an event, to be
sure, but not a cause. He did, however, accept from Deluc the
natural "chronometers" which determined its date.[76]

A complete theory was neither possible nor particularly
desirable. Townsend did not pretend to verify the Sacred Record
word for word, or even event for event. He only claimed the
geological evidence to be everywhere *consistent* with the more
detailed account of Moses. The rocks nowhere contradicted
revelation. "The veracity of Moses, as an historian, stands
therefore unimpeached by the natural evidence to be derived
from the actual condition of the globe." [77] That being so, no
one had any reason not to believe the Pentateuch. Provided
geology protected Genesis in the main positions, the point at
issue was established. Natural history had no need to make a

twice-told tale of Holy Writ. Once pseudoscientific theories which undermined Scripture were exposed in all their falsity, people would no doubt accept the Lord's word on its own authority, as they had these many centuries.

5

The progress of geology had created serious difficulties in the relationship of natural history to its larger implications in natural theology. By 1820, however, the issues appeared to have been resolved in satisfactory fashion. No one, not even the most liberal champion of scientific freedom, had questioned the propriety of the relationship itself. The age of the earth, to be sure, had been vastly extended, and the effort to connect Holy Writ directly to earth history was now felt to have been discreditable to all concerned. The actual origin of the earth's surface could no longer be identified with specific scriptural events. On such matters as this, and on the relationship of theory to observation, the Huttonian attitude had prevailed.

The main positions of providential natural history were still secure, however, at the end of this first round. No one denied the importance of the flood, nor its intimate connection with the history of the human species. No one had impugned the recentness of the creation of man. Mutability of other species was seldom if ever even mentioned,[78] and the Creator had still to be immediately responsible for the appearance of new forms of life.[79] Hutton's emphasis on the uniformity of geological dynamics had been allowed to sink into abeyance. Nearly everyone, even Vulcanists like Hall, implicitly accepted Deluc's distinction between the present order of causes and some former, more powerful ones.

Most important of all, everyone agreed that natural history must devote itself to exhibiting evidence of divine design and of material Providence. To be sure, science was also prized for another function: for its utility to commerce, industry, and economic welfare. But this, though it may have occasionally aroused more real enthusiasm, was always presented as complementary to the higher purpose.

This large area of peaceable agreement, however, persisted only until the exploitation of paleontological method presented new difficulties and a new basis for the old disputes about the character of divine design and providential supervision.

IV

CATASTROPHIST GEOLOGY

His eloquence rolled like the Deluge retiring
Where mastodon carcases floated;
To a subject obscure he gave charms so inspiring,
Young and old on geology doated. . .

Then exposed to the drip of some case-hardening spring
His carcase let stalactite cover,
And to Oxford the petrified sage let us bring
When he is encrusted all over;
There, mid mammoths and crocodiles, high on a shelf,
Let him stand as a monument raised to himself.

— *Elegy for Professor Buckland, 1820* [1]

I

FROM 1820 TO 1830, Professor William Buckland was the foremost English geologist, the chief architect of the catastrophist synthesis, and very probably the most talked-about scientist in Britain. Geologists, during these years, were very pleased with themselves.[2] By adopting Huttonian dynamics and by classifying their observations according to organized fossil remains, they had (they thought) put their science on a firm, unassailable basis. Just about this time, too, Cuvier's researches in comparative anatomy were being comprehended and were proving to be a powerful tool for further investigations in all branches of natural history.[3] Apart from his great popularity as a teacher and a publicist, Buckland owed his prestige to two things: he exploited and extended Cuvier's methods very ably, and he returned natural history to the explicit service of religious truth.

The writings of Georges Cuvier formed the scientific bible of catastrophism. Interest aroused by his startling success in the field of vertebrate paleontology directed the attention of most geologists towards the lessons to be learned from the bones of prehistoric monsters. Pursuit of these relics and the fascinating effort to reconstruct dinosaurs and flying reptiles made geology a subject practically identical with natural history. The more prosaic studies of petrography, stratigraphy, and volcanic action were relatively neglected during the years of Professor Buckland's greatest popularity.[4]

Cuvier's earliest statement of his views occurred in the paper he wrote with Alexandre Brongniart upon the structure of the Paris basin, published in 1811.[5] In the following year appeared the great *Recherches sur les ossemens fossiles*,[6] in which Cuvier set forth his completed theory of the earth in the *Discours préliminaire*. This preface, under the title *Discours sur les révolutions de la surface du globe*, was printed in numerous editions, many more than the parent work, though that too enjoyed a steady sale for thirty years and more. Jameson, significantly enough, emerged from his Wernerian obscurity to publish a translation of the *Discours* with explanatory notes of his own devising.[7] It went through four editions between 1817 and 1827. A much greater man than Werner, Cuvier has a permanent place in scientific literature; his argument is sufficiently well known and may be handily quoted in its essentials:

The lands once laid dry have been reinundated several times, whether by invasions of the sea or by transient floods; and it is further apparent to whoever studies the regions liberated by the water in its last retreat, that these areas, now inhabited by men and land animals, had already been above the surface at least once — possibly several times — and that they had formerly sustained quadrupeds, birds, plants, and terrestrial productions of all types. The sea, therefore, has now departed from lands which it had previously invaded. The changes in the height of the waters did not consist simply of a more or less gradual and universal retreat. There were successive uprisings and withdrawals of which, however, the final result was a general subsidence of the sea level.

But it is also extremely important to notice that these repeated inroads and retreats were by no means gradual. On the contrary, the majority of the cataclysms that produced them were sudden.

This is particularly easy to demonstrate for the last one which by a double movement first engulfed and then exposed our present continents, or at least a great part of the ground which forms them. It also left in northern countries the bodies of great quadrupeds, encased in ice and preserved with their skin, hair, and flesh down to our own times. If they had not been frozen as soon as killed, putrefaction would have decomposed the carcasses. And, on the other hand, this continual frost did not previously occupy the places where the animals were seized by the ice, for they could not have existed in such a temperature. The animals were killed, therefore, at the same instant when glacial conditions overwhelmed the countries they inhabited. This development was sudden, not gradual, and what is so clearly demonstrable for the last catastrophe is not less true of those which preceded it. The dislocations, shiftings, and overturnings of the older strata leave no doubt that sudden and violent causes produced the formations we observe, and similarly the violence of the movements which the seas went through is still attested by the accumulations of debris and of rounded pebbles which in many places lie between solid beds of rock. Life in those times was often disturbed by these frightful events. Numberless living things were victims of such catastrophes: some, inhabitants of the dry land, were engulfed in deluges; others, living in the heart of the seas, were left stranded when the ocean floor was suddenly raised up again; and whole races were destroyed forever, leaving only a few relics which the naturalist can scarcely recognize.[8]

The two main lines of evidence which catastrophists called to witness for their views are indicated in these paragraphs.[9] The first of these, the symptoms of mechanical violence on a very large scale, had, of course, excited the attention of observers long before the rise of paleontological method. By their comprehensive generalizations from phenomena of this sort, theorists like Élie de Beaumont worked the permanent contributions of Vulcanism and Neptunism into the completed doctrine of geological cataclysms. Forces which have raised the continents and hurled great mountain chains into the clouds must have been very different from any agencies currently in operation. Similarly, evidence of erosion and denudation led to a fairly universal agreement that such great upheavals had been followed by vast, torrential deluges of world-wide scope.

Complementary to this older sort of argument, and much more interesting to Buckland and his school, were the conclusions derived from evidence of complete changes in the living things which have tenanted the fickle surface of the earth. Here the essential tool, of which Cuvier was both the inventor and the most productive technician, was the new science of comparative anatomy, with emphasis upon the great vertebrates. This was the only method, thought Cuvier, by which one could successfully investigate the past, the number and order of global revolutions, and the history of creation.[10] Morphological evidence disproved the Lamarckian contention that existing forms are derived from a gradual modification, or indeed from any modification, of earlier ones. Limited variations within a species have occurred (like Airedales and dachshunds), but specifically characteristic features have been constant since creation. In stratigraphic successions, fossils occur in the chronological order of creation: fish, amphibia, reptilia, mammalia — the older the strata, the higher the proportion of extinct species. No human fossils have turned up anywhere.[11] Therefore, mankind must have been created at some time between the last catastrophe and the one preceding it.[12] It was probably not possible to determine the exact date of the most recent revolution, but data derived from the rate of increase of deltas, sand dunes, and peat deposits made a reasonable approximation feasible:

If there is any circumstance thoroughly established in geology, it is, that the crust of our globe has been subjected to a great and sudden revolution, the epoch of which cannot be dated much further back than five or six thousand years ago; that this revolution had buried all the countries which were before inhabited by men and by the other animals now best known . . . that the small number of individuals of men and other animals that escaped from the effects of that great revolution, have since propagated and spread over the lands then newly laid dry; and consequently, that the human race has only resumed a progressive state of improvement since that epoch, by forming established societies, raising monuments, collecting natural facts, and constructing systems of science and learning.[13]

Read out of context, this sounds as if Cuvier had not advanced very far beyond Deluc. Such an impression would be misleading. Cuvier was a scientist of major importance. As against his permanent contributions to the biological sciences, his theory of intensive global revolutions is of only incidental importance. This chapter, however, will be concerned with the uses to which this theory was put in the hands of scientists who were less gifted, who were less cautious, and who had a very high respect for so convenient an authority.[14]

2

In the 1820's the popular conception of geology was practically synonymous with the doctrine of catastrophes,[15] and the reason for this was the success with which Buckland and Conybeare, Sedgwick and Murchison, and a host of amateur naturalists in the provincial scientific societies exploited and extended the avenues Cuvier had opened. The Geological Society was very conscious of its debt:

The beautiful conclusions drawn from unexpected facts; the happy combination of mineralogical and zoological evidence; the proofs of successive revolutions, till then unheard of in the physical history of the earth — all these things together, not merely threw new light on a subject before involved in comparative darkness, but gave new powers and new means of induction to those who should in after times attempt any similar investigation.[16]

The idea of cataclysms, of course, was not new, but neither had it ever been scientific. It was the achievement of catastrophist geology to describe the essential cataclysm as the last of "successive revolutions" (the notion of succession was already persuasive) and hence to invest it with the prestige of inductive respectability.

Professor Buckland, much of whose work has survived the interpretation he put upon it, made his reputation as a teacher and a publicist before he had accomplished anything remarkable in the way of original research. His collaboration with Greenough secured him Oxford's readership in mineralogy in 1813; at that time Oxford had no teaching post in geology.

He was, apparently, a distinguished teacher. His lecture room, a terrible jumble of rocks, skulls, and skeletons, was famous all over the university. Buckland emphasized field work, and he would meet his classes in caverns and mud banks, where his habit of appearing always in top hat and academic robe added that touch of idiosyncrasy which often contributes to pedagogical success. Almost all of Buckland's professional colleagues in the 1820's, including Lyell, regarded themselves as his pupils. They had either studied under him at Oxford or had been introduced to geological investigation under his patronage.[17] In 1819 his admirers in the Royal Society bestirred themselves to secure the endowment of a professorial chair in geology, a post which, wrote Sir Joseph Banks, "No one in England is so competent to fill." [18]

Professor Buckland had never been indifferent to the more sublime implications of his studies. Upon his elevation to professorial rank, a sense of the fitness of things and a warm admiration for his "noble subterranean science" persuaded him to attempt to dispel the suspicions about it which an undercurrent of theological opposition had kept alive.[19] He published his inaugural lecture, therefore, under the title, *Vindiciae Geologicae; or, the Connexion of Geology with Religion Explained*, the objective being "to shew that the study of geology has a tendency to confirm the evidences of natural religion; and that the facts developed by it are consistent with the accounts of the creation and deluge recorded in the Mosaic writings." After contending that the physical sciences should be "admitted to serve at least a subordinate ministry in the temple of our Academical Institutions," [20] Buckland urged that the study of our earthly abode had pressing claims to be included among the recognized moral and intellectual disciplines. "What are its pretensions to this honor, and what its utility?" What, indeed? Not primarily its economic applicability, though geology need not shrink from other sciences in this important respect, for

such views should be altogether objected to *in limine* as unworthy and unphilosophical. The claims of Geology may be made to rest on a much higher basis. The utility of science is founded upon other and nobler views than those of mere pecuniary profit and tangible advantage. The human mind has an appetite for truth of every kind, Physical as well as Moral; and the real utility of Science is to afford gratification to this appetite. . .

Now when it is recollected that the field of the Geologist's inquiry is the Globe itself, that it is his study to decipher the monuments of the mighty revolutions and convulsions it has suffered, convulsions of which the most terrible catastrophes presented by the actual state of things . . . afford only a faint image, (the last expiring efforts of those mighty disturbing forces which once operated;) these surely will be admitted to be objects of sufficient magnitude and grandeur, to create an adequate interest to engage us in their investigation.[21]

The interrelations of geology with botany, zoology, chemistry, astronomy, physics, and mathematics were obvious enough to require little laboring, but "as any investigation of Natural Philosophy which shall not terminate in the Great First Cause will be justly deemed unsatisfactory, I feel no apology to be necessary for opening these Lectures with an illustration of the religious application of Geological science."[22] Buckland's argument here outlined the pattern on which the whole generation of scientific theologians, or theological scientists, did little more than ring a remarkably uninspired set of changes. First, the indications of the power, wisdom, and goodness of the divinity would be demonstrated from the evidences of design in his works, and particularly from the happy dispensation of coal, iron, and limestone by which the Omnipotent Architect, or the Divine Engineer, had assured manufacturing primacy to his British creation.[23] Paley's argument may be somewhat sterile spiritually, but if the tastes of a reading public can be measured by the books it buys, an endless elaboration of the motif of divine "contrivance" satisfied a steady demand in the 1820's and 1830's. Buckland, in his inaugural lecture, slanted this part of his thesis towards bringing out the beneficent relations subsisting between stratigraphical structure and mineral resources, the interdependence of animal and vegetable creation, and the cleverly arranged situation of the earth in the solar system:

In all these we find such undeniable proofs of a nicely balanced adaptation of means to ends, of wise foresight and benevolent intention and infinite power, that he must be blind indeed, who refuses to recognize in them proofs of the most exalted attributes of the Creator.[24]

This sort of argument contained, of course, the seeds of its own destruction. For four decades prior to the publication of *On the Origin of Species*, the British public had enthusiastically bought up volume after volume by one or another of the fellows of the Royal Society, each one tying additional illustrative knots in the web which knitted the existence of a God to the unity of design exhibited in His works. But if the infinity of physical adaptations on which this popular theology rested turned out to stem from their own interactions and not from a managing Providence, what became of the Supreme Lawgiver? However the question later developed, this stage of the difficulties between science and orthodox Christianity cannot be described as the protest of the spiritually-minded against materialistic arguments. Actually, the notably unspiritual school which had fastened the Creator to His material creation was the one most bitterly opposed to His removal from manifestations in every detail thereof, and this had been the case for many years before evolution was an issue. In the stream of popular literature, this point of view had become a way of looking not only at the physical universe but also at society, a way which found in the existing adjustment of every detail of natural and social relations the evidence, and hence the sanction, of divinely ordained natural necessity.

Still, on the surface, the arguments centered around natural history. Buckland himself sensed some of the difficulties he might encounter, though scarcely in the way they actually developed. Without the assistance of the descriptive sciences, natural philosophy had, he felt, accomplished much, but not enough:

The evidences afforded by the sister sciences exhibit indeed the most admirable proofs of design and intelligence originally exerted at the Creation: but many who admit these proofs still doubt the continued superintendence of that Intelligence, maintaining that the system of the Universe is carried on by the force of the laws originally impressed on matter, without the necessity of fresh interference or continued supervision on the part of the Creator. Such an opinion . . . nowhere meets with a more direct and palpable refutation, than is afforded by the subservience of the present structure of the earth's surface to final causes; for that structure is evidently the result of many and violent convulsions subsequent to its original formation. When therefore we perceive that the secondary causes producing these convulsions have operated at successive periods, not blindly and at random, but with a direction to beneficial ends, we see at once the proofs of an overruling Intelligence continuing to superintend, direct, modify, and control the operations of the agents which he originally ordained.[25]

Once it is put together, a clock has no reason to fear, to respect, or to obey its maker. It must, then, be the purpose of science to exhibit the continuing and immediate supervision of divine Providence. The Creator must be shown to have moved the hands backward and forward from time to time and to have replaced the works when they misbehaved. This was the province of natural history, and in this connection revelation was not at all irrelevant. It was, indeed, a necessary complement to natural religion. All the difficulty had arisen from the effort to treat Genesis instead of the rocks as the source of scientific evidence. Like everything else, Scripture requires interpretation, thought Buckland, and the Wernerian contentions had been uncritical. The six days, for example, were to be taken figuratively. Thousands of ages may well have intervened between each act of creation and the next, and tens of thousands have preceded the deluge. Since wholly unconnected with the human race, these epochs had been passed over in silence by the sacred historian who, for moral purposes, had only to let us know there had been a beginning.[26]

Buckland repeated — and immediately disregarded — Bacon's warning lest his readers "unwisely mingle or confound" the book of God's word with the book of God's works. Having disposed of the difficulties of an earlier, cruder generation, he pointed out how the literal credibility contended for by Kirwan was unnecessary because the empirical evidence does indeed confirm the Mosaic records on the two *essential* matters:

The evidence of all facts that have yet been established in Geology coincides with the records of Sacred History and Profane Tradition to confirm the conclusion, that *the existence of mankind* can on no account be supposed to have taken its beginning before that time which is assigned to it in the Mosaic writings. Again, the grand fact of *an universal deluge* at no very remote period is proved on grounds so decisive and incontrovertible, that, had we never heard of such an event from Scripture, or any other authority, Geology of itself must have called in the assistance of some such catastrophe, to explain the phenomena of diluvian action which are universally presented to us, and which are unintelligible without recourse to a deluge exerting its ravages at a period not more ancient than that announced in the Book of Genesis.[27]

Actually, Buckland had completed his empirical theology before he stumbled upon the evidence which won it the most widespread support, and which, incidentally, remains an enduring contribution to the progress of scientific knowledge. In 1821 some miners came upon a large cavern at Kirkdale in the Vale of Pickering in Yorkshire, in the recesses of which were deposited a tremendous quantity of assorted bones. Buckland heard about the discovery and hurried thither to investigate it. The spectacular productivity of his researches created such an impression both upon Buckland himself and upon the interested public that he devoted all his professional energies in the next few years to seeking out similar caverns and exhuming their skeletal contents. The majority of the bones found in the Kirkdale cavern were those of hyenas, but a number of birds and a total of twenty-three other species were also represented in the underground graveyard, among them lions, tigers, elephants, rhinoceroses, and hippopotamuses.[28] All the bones and skulls were cracked in the same way, and Buckland came to the conclusion that he had come upon a den of hyenas. He published his results in the *Philosophical Transactions* for 1822 [29] — the paper won him the Royal Society's Copley medal. His magnum opus, an idyll of the caves which he entitled *Reliquiae Diluvianae,* appeared late in 1823. It met with a paean of critical praise. Even the few who were opposed to his theoretical conclusions admitted the excellence and the value of his researches.[30]

It would be easy to smile at Buckland's argument, except for two things. In the first place, it was widely accepted; and secondly, the *Reliquiae,* despite its thesis, presented scientists as well as the general public with a new and illuminating account of the past fauna of the European continent. In little more than two years, Buckland and his colleagues had explored more than twenty caves in England and on the Continent and had identified and classified the osseous remains buried in diluvial detritus. The sheer volume of the work attests his command of the principles of comparative anatomy and his ability to conceive and to execute so large a research project. His descriptive inferences as to the identity of specific relics are reasoned with painstaking validity. He went so far as to import a hyena in order to observe whether its behavior in its cage would reproduce the phenomena he had observed at Kirkdale and was delighted, according to Lyell, when he received "a letter from India about modern hyaenas whose manners, habitations, diet, etc., are everything he could wish, and as much as could be expected had they attended regularly three courses of his lectures." [31] At the end of the century, Buckland's books were still being used as college texts, even by so mundane a geologist as Boyd Dawkins.[32]

Anyone who browses in the monuments of early nineteenth-century natural history learns, however, not to be surprised at the unlikely vehicles chosen for the description of important discoveries. The full title of Buckland's book ran, *Reliquiae Diluvianae; or, Observations on the Organic Remains Contained in Caves, Fissures, and Diluvial Gravel, and on Other Geological Phenomena, Attesting the Action of an Universal Deluge.* And the dedication to Shute Barrington, Bishop of Durham, permitted itself to suggest how the work, "by affording the strongest evidence of an universal deluge, leads us to hope, that it will no longer be asserted, as it has been by high authorities, that geology supplies no proofs of an event in the reality of which the truth of the Mosaic records is so materially involved." [33]

There would be very little profit in following Buckland into the details of his proofs, even though, as such proofs go, he managed to make them fairly convincing. In general, he sums up his description of each cave with an illustration of how it attests the universality and uniqueness of a deluge. The argument falls into a pattern predictable after the first cavern: Most of the bones are from species now extinct in Europe. They are never found in alluvial accumulations of peat, sand, and silt. There is no human testimony to these animals having existed in Europe since the flood. Therefore, they were interred in the caves prior to Noah's time. Further, the top layers of bones have been so perfectly preserved in mud and silt that they must have been buried suddenly and, judging by the quantity of postdiluvial stalactite covering the mud, not more than five or six thousand years ago. That such relics turn up only in caverns illustrates the violence of the last revolution and its total destruction of the face of the earth — though one wonders how Buckland could have thought his caves would themselves have been able to survive such a cataclysm as their contents indicated. And lastly, there has been only one flood since the hyenas died, inasmuch as the mud encrusting the deposits is uniform throughout. [34]

Buckland had, of course, brought his researches into line with the two essential points set forth in his inaugural lecture of four years earlier: the reality of a flood and the recent creation of man. In the latter connection, Buckland and his colleagues were probably relieved not to discover any human remains which could not be referred to postdiluvial accumulations. One sometimes feels him to have been a little arbitrary here. In the cave of Paviland, for example, near a Roman encampment, he dug up what he took to be a woman's skeleton, dyed a rusty red and adorned with bits of ivory. She need give no cause for concern, however, for she was obviously a relic of a period later than that of the animals which were buried more deeply in the mud. In any case, whatever her value as evidence, she was not, Buckland feared, a wholly respectable discovery:

The circumstance of a British camp existing on the hill immediately above this cave, seems to throw much light on the character and date of the woman under consideration; and whatever may have been her occupation, the vicinity of a camp would afford a motive for residence, as well as the means of subsistence, in what is now so exposed and uninviting a solitude.[35]

3

Buckland's books have been treated in some detail, not because he was the only diluvial naturalist — far from it — but because he was the most widely read and the most successful in identifying Cuvier's ultimate cataclysm with the Biblical flood. In doing so, he exploited primarily a single line of research and one with considerable romantic appeal. There has always been something intriguing and mysterious about caves. But during this same period, the publications of the various learned societies gradually worked the whole of natural history into the same framework. The result was that prevailing interpretations, whether derived from paleontological, petrographical, or stratigraphical researches, generally required the architectural agency of a torrential deluge to explain the present appearance of the surface of the earth. A summary of the evidence will be sufficient: the sluicelike conformation of hills and valleys; the pattern of drainage basins; the occurrence of gorges, ravines, and water gaps torn through mountain masses, and of buttes and mesas separated from the parent formation by valleys of denudation; immense deposits of gravel, carried from distant regions, on hills and slopes where no river ever could have drifted them; the nature and condition of organic remains in diluvial gravel; the consistency of similar phenomena all over the world; the impossibility of referring such vast effects to the puny forces of weather and erosion; the harmony of the rate of changes now going on (delta-building, coral reefs, lava accumulation, the formation of ravines, silting in lakes and rivers) "with the hypothesis which dates the origin of all such operations at a period not more ancient than that which our received chronologies assign to the deluge." [36]

Diluvial geology, unlike its Neptunist ancestor which arose with the explicit mission of confounding Huttonian infidelity, succeeded in winning, for a time, nearly unanimous assent both to its assumptions and conclusions, though these were practically the same thing. Buckland came out right where he went in, with the ark, but he brought with him a lot of new information picked up in the course of his circular progress. Serious uniformitarian objections date chiefly from 1830, when Charles Lyell published the first volume of his *Principles of Geology*, paying, incidentally, respectful tribute to his former teacher's contributions to the science by dedicating it to Buckland. As late as 1826, Lyell's correspondence indicates no divergence from the prevailing mode of interpreting diluvial phenomena. Nor, of course, did the surviving leaders of the older generation, men like Greenough or Macculloch, make any difficulty about accepting the empirical verification of their own presuppositions. In 1826, to be sure, George Poulett Scrope attacked the diluvial theory in a book about volcanoes,[37] a treatise which was important in shaping Lyell's more comprehensive uniformitarian views. But Scrope's book seems not to have aroused much comment from the catastrophists who, in any case, could easily grant his demand for "almost unlimited drafts upon antiquity" [38] from the ample reserve of antediluvian time which their own theories required. Even W. H. Fitton, perennial geological contributor to the *Edinburgh Review*, who of all English geologists was the most consistent in his suspicion of attempts to frame comprehensive theories from inadequate data, did not oppose the Buckland-Cuvier interpretations in the twenties.[39]

These were the years when Adam Sedgwick and Sir Roderick Murchison were laying the foundation of the collaboration which resulted in unraveling the entire Paleozoic system, still vaguely dismissed with such descriptive appellations as "primitive rocks" or "greywacke." In conjunction with his friend, Sir Humphry Davy, Lady Murchison had persuaded her husband, at the age of thirty-two, to become a scientist. Until then he had devoted his energies chiefly to fox hunting. Since geology was the most outdoor of sciences, he elected to become a geologist and went up to Oxford in 1824 to take lessons from Buckland.[40] As it turned out, Murchison possessed very great ability indeed, and Buckland inspired him with an enthusiasm to match it. His early communications to the Geological Society were meritorious, if not important, and illustrated his attachment to the catastrophist theories which introduced him to the science,[41] and particularly to the doctrine of progressive creations.

Murchison's colleague and, until an unfortunate estrangement, co-worker, the Reverend Adam Sedgwick, entered upon his career in an even more haphazard fashion. A fellow of Trinity College in Cambridge, Sedgwick knew nothing about geology until after his election as Woodwardian professor of the science in 1818. "I had but one rival, Gorham of Queens'," Sedgwick wrote later, "and he had not the slightest chance against me, for I knew absolutely nothing of geology, whereas he knew a good deal — but it was all wrong!" [42] Though he was then thirty-three, Sedgwick passed rapidly through a Wernerian phase to a real command of the subject he taught, a command based upon arduous personal investigations in the field. He was elected president of the Geological Society in 1828, succeeding Buckland and Fitton, with the former of whom he was particularly congenial. Like Buckland at Oxford, Sedgwick placed great emphasis upon the moral lessons to be derived from scientific studies in general and geology in particular, and upon the value of these subjects as intellectual discipline. Both Sedgwick and Buckland were anxious that science should occupy a more prominent place in the universities — in neither Cambridge nor Oxford did the curriculum or the examinations for the degree offer any incentive for attendance on the lectures of professors, who had to rely wholly on the charm of their personalities and on the intrinsic interest of their subjects to attract hearers. In 1825, Sedgwick published his own collation of the two great kinds of truth. He embedded it in an article on diluvial formations, in the form of an answer to those timorous and bigoted few who still shrank from the dangers of philosophic investigation:

It must . . . at once be rash and unphilosophical to look to the language of revelation for any direct proof of the truths of physical science. But truth must at all times be consistent with itself. The conclusions established on the authority of the sacred writings may, therefore, consistently with the soundest philosophy, be compared with the conclusions established on the evidence of observation and experiment. . . The application is obvious. The sacred records tell us — that a few thousand years ago "the fountains of the great deep were broken up" — and that the earth's surface was submerged by the water of a general deluge; and the investigations of geology tend to prove that the accumulations of alluvial matter have not been going on many thousand years; and that they were preceded by a great catastrophe which has left traces of its operation in the *diluvial detritus* which is spread out over all the strata of the world.

Between these conclusions, derived from sources entirely independent of each other, there is, therefore, a general coincidence which it is impossible to overlook, and the importance of which it would be most unreasonable to deny. The coincidence has not been assumed hypothetically, but has been proved legitimately, by an immense number of direct observations conducted with indefatigable labour, and all tending to the establishment of the same general truth.[43]

The career of the Reverend William Daniel Conybeare did not result in the permanent additions to scientific knowledge which Sedgwick and Murchison made, but in the years of their apprenticeship he was, next to Buckland, the most widely read geologist. Buckland and he were very friendly. After marrying a lady whom he described as "an admirable fossil geologist," Buckland even had his first child christened Adam Conybeare Sedgwick. In 1822, Conybeare and William Phillips published *Outlines of the Geology of England and Wales*, a text which was often referred to as the standard introduction to its subject. The book went through a number of editions in the next few years, and it offers, perhaps, the best illustration of the way in which a paleontological approach to Huttonian conceptions discarded the crude formulations of Neptunism while re-

taining the flood and the revolutionary agency of divine interventions in the course of nature. Murchison described the
volume as his "scientific Bible." [44] Conybeare's later researches were devoted to sustaining the orthodox views upon
the structure of river valleys and upon the destruction of fossil
species.[45] He began to fade into obscurity after having vigor-
ously headed the catastrophist attack upon Lyell's *Principles
of Geology*.[46]

In the period before 1830, the paleontological evidence for
the flood, though it was the chief resource of the providentialist approach, was not the only line of argument employed
to demonstrate that the Creator had often exercised an immediate control over the course of natural history. Dr. John
Macculloch, for example, who prepared the first geological
map of Scotland, would never admit the superiority of the new
paleontological over the older mineralogical emphasis in geological research. Despite this, however, and despite the resulting estrangement from his colleagues, he had been one of the
most productive members of the Geological Society ever since
its foundation, a scientist of the second rank if not of the
first.[47] Macculloch spent the last years of his life writing
three enormous volumes to prove

that God does exert a perpetual government, over the physical
world at least; that it cannot proceed without His immediate action,
or personal interference, and that no appointment of deputed
"laws," of modes of motion originally impressed on matter, will
account for the phenomena of the universe.[48]

Macculloch regarded the positive demonstration of God's association with His works as the ultimate purpose of science.

To believe justly in the existence and nature of God, is, first, to
know Him as the creator of the world, in wisdom and goodness; and
next, as the governor and disposer, first of the physical universe, and
then of the moral world, as the end and purpose of that.[49]

Much of the language of Macculloch's treatise is Huttonian —
in his description of the processes of rock formation, for example. His attitude, however, was thoroughly providentialist,

and he makes particularly clear the degree to which this sort of interpretation of science was thought to serve a moral and hence a social purpose. God, he argues, chose to operate by occasional deviations from general laws not because He was incapable of making arrangements that would hold, but in order to convince us of the immanence and continuing nature of His immediate supervision.[50] To fix this point, indeed, was the chief purpose of the book. "If the Deity governs the physical world, governing therefore its events, so must He, of necessity, govern the moral one." [51]

The reviews, during the 1820's, devoted more space to keeping the educated reading public abreast of the progress of natural history than they did to all the other sciences put together. The *Westminster*, to be sure, was too absorbed in pushing the Benthamite creed to waste any articles on even so innocent a distraction as the cataclysmic theory of the earth, but the *Edinburgh* and the *Quarterly* found themselves in the surprising position of offering a common interpretation. Articles in the *Edinburgh Review* usually included a congratulatory survey of the state of knowledge in the science, in which the reviewer would find occasion to commend the editors for having been staunchly and objectively Huttonian during the wilder days of geological disputes. *Reliquiae Diluvianae* was greeted with great enthusiasm, for, despite apprehensions which the title might arouse, Buckland had quite properly detached his observations from his theoretical inductions.[52] The *Edinburgh* pointed up Buckland's superiority by a lengthy and scornful review of "Geology of the Deluge" from Burnet through Kirwan, followed by a full and appreciative précis of the *Reliquiae*. A year or two later, Charles Daubeny's comprehensive treatise on volcanoes [53] was described as the sort of work which had rescued geologists "from the reproach so justly cast upon their predecessors, of being little better than visionary theorists." Daubeny, "by far the most accurate and scientific inquirer into the whole range of volcanic phenomena, who has yet laid the result of his labours before the public," suggested in the course of his description of active and extinct volcanoes that just as the Deity had chosen to employ a flood as the physical instrument to effect the general destruction of the human race, so also He had worked His will against Sodom and Gomorrah by means of volcanic action.[54] In neither case, thought Daubeny, had God resorted to other than natural causes. Daubeny was professor of chemistry at Oxford, and as a scientist he liked to think that he kept science and religious belief in their proper relation to each other. He classified volcanic works, for example, according to whether they were ante- or postdiluvian, the former having been deposited before the valleys were formed and the latter afterward, but he refused to offer an opinion as to whether the deluge in question was to be identified with "the particular deluge recorded in Mosaic history."[55]

In 1830, the *Edinburgh Review* set out to sum up in thirty popularized pages all it had published on the science of man's past.[56] The article speaks of "animals of the present creation," and refers to the extinction of large numbers of species "in the last retreat of the sea but one, and during that state of the world which preceded its last eruption." Buckland, who remains "one of the most zealous and successful cultivators of geology of modern times," has placed the deluge in its scientific setting by means of animal relics.[57] This, however, was the year in which Lyell published *Principles of Geology*.

The *Quarterly Review* had ignored geology during the years of tacit Huttonian triumph. In the 1820's, however, the periodical was very enthusiastic about the science, a shift in attitude which is not surprising because, as Buckland once observed, "The general attachment of the *Quarterly Review* to the cause of Revelation is so decided."[58] The reviewer hailed *Reliquiae Diluvianae* as ecstatically as if the book were the *Principia Mathematica* of earth sciences.[59] For Buckland had seized upon the essential key, implicit in Deluc, and applied it properly to the vexed question of the scientific soundness of the sacred records. That is, in the past a series of causes, different in nature from any now acting, had molded the globe. The possibilities inherent in this approach would remove the religious stumbling block which had made the history of geology a record of discord unparalleled in scientific discussion. By

1826, the *Quarterly* felt, natural history was well launched upon a career of sober progress.[60] "Its chief claim to our estimation is founded on the new impulse imparted by its discoveries to minds engaged in prosecuting various philosophical pursuits."[61] Working in the wake of Cuvier and Buckland, an army of observers had conclusively demonstrated how geology, of all pursuits, is the best suited to bear out Bishop Butler in his truly inspired analogy between the constitution of the natural and moral worlds.[62]

By 1827, however, the scientific editors of the *Quarterly* began to sense trouble. Scrope's *Geology of Central France*, published in that year, argued that rivers working over limitless centuries had cut their own valleys, and it rejected Daubeny's diluvial classification of volcanoes.[63] The *Quarterly* had become wary, however. Let not an ignorant and narrow philosophy regard such views as derogatory to the dignity of man, for if they turn out to be true, they will be more derogatory to the dignity of the opposition. "We hope, above all . . . that none will fall into the error of imagining that the truth of the sacred writings is in the least implicated." Evidently the sacred writings had not been so very much beside the point since Buckland's magnum opus as the *Quarterly* had thought. At any rate Lyell, the author of this review, felt impelled to warn off a "certain class of writers who have lately appeared before the public," and who, "wholly destitute of geological knowledge derived from personal observation," threatened to defend the Scriptures in the fashion of Kirwan again:

> While they denounce as heterodox the current opinions of geologists [meaning Buckland's school, oddly enough], with respect to the high antiquity of the earth and of certain classes of organic beings, they do not scruple to promulgate theories concerning the creation and the deluge, derived from their own exposition of the sacred text, in which they endeavour to point out the accordance of the Mosaic history with phenomena which they have never studied, and to judge of which every page of their writings proves their consummate incompetence.[64]

Deluc's old vehicle had also become considerably more moderate in the decade or so since it had carried the last of his letters. In 1825, it turned itself into a quarterly and from 1827 frankly called itself *British Critic, Quarterly Theological Review and Ecclesiastical Record.* The first issue pledged the periodical to "the great object" of maintaining "those principles connected with the Church or State, which have always been associated with the name of the British Critic." [65] The editors planned to continue its tradition of keeping up with the world of science.

> In fine, their work . . . will still be in essence, as well as name, The British Critic; a *Review* undertaken and conducted upon British principles and for British objects, and consulting in its speculations the morals and religion of Englishmen, as much as their information and amusement. [66]

The *British Critic* had missed the more important geological developments, but it unwittingly anticipated future problems in an enthusiastic review of James C. Prichard's *Researches into the Physical History of Mankind*: [67]

> The reader is no where insulted by any of those startling theories as to the origin of certain varieties in the human species, whether of form or color, which have threatened to degrade man to the rank of an ape, and to confine his destiny to the changes and chances of this mortal life. [68]

At the time this was written, however, the *British Critic* was not antagonistic to the scientifically accepted interpretation of earth history. It deplored Andrew Ure's "unwise and unsuccessful" *New System of Geology*, [69] which attempted a literal and rather blatant reconciliation of the geological with the Mosaic records. Ure was an extremist who denounced Buckland's views for infidelity. The reason, though — and significantly — that the reviewers in the *British Critic* thought it impossible for any theory of the earth ever to succeed completely is that geology is the *one* science which labors under

> the appalling difficulty connected with the undeniable fact, that the principal phenomena of geology have been produced by a partial deviation from the ordinary laws of nature; by violent disruptions; by the bursting asunder the adamantine zones of the earth; by a

supernatural elevation of its waters; and even, it is supposed, by a temporary suspension of its astronomical properties. In short, we have *revolutions* to account for by means of ordinary laws and principles.[70]

Science can describe the results of the methods employed by "Infinite Wisdom in arranging the mineral substances which form the outer strata or crust of the earth, at that early period which preceded the creation of animals, and the epoch even of Sacred History itself." [71] In all branches of science, of course, the ultimate causation of phenomena must be explained as the will of God, but astronomers and physicists, more fortunate than geologists, can nevertheless discuss general laws governing the behavior of matter because in their fields God has chosen to employ uniform methods of directing His creation. In the sphere of geological action, however, God has seen fit to vary the character of the forces which have produced the effects studied by geologists who, therefore, can never hope to arrive at a completely consistent or sufficient explanation even of secondary causation.

Of all the periodicals, the *Philosophical Magazine* was probably the nearest thing to our own *Popular Science*, though without resorting either to dilution or sensationalism. It featured short articles and abridged reprints from the professional journals, the whole designed to transmit to the public the editors' view of the state of the sciences. The selections were seldom controversial. Its files offer probably the best gauge of the contemporary layman's comprehension of scientific theory. Each number presented brief notices of all new books, accounts of meetings in the learned societies, and descriptions of their publications. Every volume in the 1820's contained three or four geological notices, all descriptive. There would be a stratigraphical section of the cliffs of Devon, for example, or a three-page outline of the natural history of Sumatra, but the majority of the articles reflect the current fascination with prehistoric monsters. All such contributions simply assumed a diluvial framework — the deluge *had* happened; it was not a matter for much discussion.[72] Evidences were everywhere, though no one labored the point.

The *Philosophical Magazine* found itself so enthusiastic about *Reliquiae Diluvianae* that it published continual excerpts from it, lest the remarkable importance of the book be overlooked. Buckland ran a great many abstracts and reprints in the magazine,[73] and his colleagues did their part in keeping the school's interpretation in the public eye. Conybeare's "On the Discovery of An Almost Perfect Skeleton of the Plesiosaurus" drew very nice, and perfectly predictable, conclusions from the situation of that interesting beast.[74] And Adam Sedgwick's report upon a lengthy dike of trap rock in Yorkshire is a typical example of the way in which religious orthodoxy had absorbed the Huttonian proofs of igneous origins into devoutly catastrophic interpretations.[75]

4

By 1830, then, the descriptive sciences were again enlisted in the explicit service of natural theology. Revealed truth and scientific truth coincided in a number of points. There was always the fundamental argument from design, of course, but beyond that the progress of zoology, paleontology, and geology now offered new and specific evidence for the recent creation of mankind and for the historical reality of the flood. These were the essential points, both in Genesis and in geology. The flood was particularly convenient because it linked the sacred records with the doctrine of global revolutions and of cataclysms which transcended the ordinary course of nature. This interpretation seems to have been of greater moment, really, than the Biblical story. The flood was the latest of the great catastrophes, and it was the primary concern of these scientists to prove that nature itself was sometimes supernatural.

V

THE UNIFORMITY OF NATURE

We now propose to examine those changes which still take place on our globe, investigating the causes which continue to operate on its surface. . . This portion of the history of the earth is so much the more important, as it has been long considered possible to explain the more ancient revolutions on its surface by means of these still existing causes. . . But we shall presently see that unfortunately this is not the case in physical history; the thread of operations is here broken, the march of nature is changed, and none of the agents that she now employs were sufficient for the production of her ancient works.

— Georges Cuvier [1]

When we are unable to explain the monuments of past changes, it is always more probable that the difference arises from our ignorance of all the existing agents, or all their possible effects in an indefinite lapse of time, than that some cause was formerly in operation which has ceased to act. . .

Our estimate, indeed, of the value of all geological evidence, and the interest derived from the investigation of the earth's history, must depend entirely on the degree of confidence which we feel in regard to the permanency of the laws of nature. Their immutable constancy alone can enable us to reason from analogy, by the strict rules of induction, respecting the events of former ages, or, by a comparison of the state of things at two distinct geological epochs, to arrive at the knowledge of general principles in the economy of our terrestrial system.

— Sir Charles Lyell [2]

I

IF BUCKLAND FEARED that without cataclysms there was no God, Lyell was as fundamentally apprehensive lest, without uniformity, there be no science. He could feel no reverence for a lawgiver who kept amending the constitution of nature. For some reason or other, however, the catastrophist controversy never became so acrimonious as the Vulcanist had been. Professor Sedgwick might disagree profoundly with Lyell — in fact, he was almost certain to — but they remained fast friends. Perhaps the incidental fact that the catastrophist-uniformitarian debate was carried on within the Geological Society instead of by conflicting academies contributed to its air of scholarly good humor. Then too, Lyell's followers, and he with them, had once been diluvialists and could display a certain amused and superior tolerance for the error of their own past ways.

One may, perhaps, deplore the disappearance of subtitles in the twentieth century, for it is convenient to know what a book is going to say before one reads it. Like Buckland in the *Reliquiae*, Lyell firmly staked out his subject on the title page: *Principles of Geology, Being an Atttempt to Explain the Former Changes of the Earth's Surface, by Reference to Causes Now in Operation.* Unlike Werner, Hutton, and Cuvier, Lyell was more the critic than the original investigator. A younger contemporary later remarked, "We collect the data, and Lyell teaches us to comprehend the meaning of them." [3] Even before Lyell removed the flood from its accepted place in geological dynamics, however, a few scientists had begun to express reservations about its universal efficacy. Next to paleontological research, a field more popular with the diluvialists, the phenomena of volcanic action and the structure of valleys were the subjects most interesting to geologists during this period. A number of points began to seem very dubious as a result of continually extended observations. In the first place, it became increasingly difficult to refer the commencement of all so-called alluvial deposits to a single event or even to any one period. Rivers, too, appeared in many cases to have cut their valleys through successive strata and through lava flows of many different epochs, some of which were postdiluvian even by the catastrophist chronology. It was difficult to describe gently winding river beds as the result of the scouring action of a single torrent, which could more easily be supposed to have cut straight gorges in its violent retreat. Nor could mixtures of fresh and salt water deposits be explained as the kind of uniform succession which a single flood, either salt or fresh, would have produced. Moreover, there was an increasing comprehension of the proper chronological classification of "primitive" and "transition" rocks and of the vast ages which must have elapsed between their formation. Such suggestions were scattered, however, among a number of memoirs through which it would be profitless to chase them. It would be even less profitable to develop the arguments with which diluvialists met the difficulties.[4]

Although these scattered objections were not pulled together into an integrated attack upon catastrophist assumptions in natural history until the publication of *Principles of Geology*, there were a few obscure critics who raised strident voices of dissent in the chorus of mutual congratulations which Buckland had touched off among geologists. Perhaps the Reverend John Fleming, a zoologist member of the Wernerian Society, set forth the closest approximation to an anticipatory statement of uniformitarianism. He had to admit Buckland's success:

> This work [*Reliquiae Diluvianae*], like the "Theory" of Cuvier, has greatly contributed to render the science of geology popular, by bringing it into favour with the Church, and even securing the countenance of the drawing-room. The general reader has been charmed with the novel scenes which it discloses, while the Christian has hailed it with joy, as offering a valuable testimony to the authority of revelation.[5]

Such easy popularity was not sufficient excuse for error in the stern, Calvinist eye of the Reverend Dr. Fleming, however. For Buckland's geological deluge was contradicted both by the evidence of revelation and by that of the rocks. In developing the latter objections, Dr. Fleming anticipated in outline the major points which Lyell expanded into his three-volume *Principles*: the gradual excavation of river valleys; the artificiality of referring "alluvial" detritus, whether sediment or organic remains, to a single source; the philosophic gratuitousness of supposing that a different order of forces had ever been called into play. Oddly enough though — in view of the attitude uniformitarians were to profess towards such reasoning — it was also on the ground of Mosaic testimony that Dr.

Fleming took severe exceptions to Buckland's flood. For Cuvier and Buckland destroyed every species; Moses saved two individuals from each. They substituted the antediluvian sea floor for the old land surfaces; Moses summoned and dismissed the waters from a never-changing earth. They described a sudden, transient, and violent torrent which left marks on every valley and gorge; Moses left word of a gentle stand of water rising placidly for forty days. And the true flood left no traces except a rainbow, the only empirical sign God has ever given us.[6]

It was chiefly, however, upon the work of George Poulett Scrope, who had published his views in 1825 and 1826, that Lyell relied for much of the new factual material included in the *Principles of Geology*. Scrope had devoted his descriptive talents to the investigation of extinct and active volcanoes. His theoretical conclusions demolished the "craters of elevation" conjured up by Werner's younger followers in their belated appreciation of the widespread incidence of volcanic formations. Scrope emphasized the continuous nature of volcanic deposits, their presence in strata of every epoch, and the impossibility of classifying volcanoes according to whether they had been eruptive before or after a flood. Given time enough, one could account for all lava formations by volcanic action of an intensity no greater than that of the present, and Scrope explicitly suggested that the same thing was true of every aspect of geological change.[7]

Lyell, then, did not pull his method of interpretation out of thin air, nor single-handed revive the Huttonian attitude. In the quotation at the head of this chapter, Cuvier remarks that "it has long been considered possible to explain the more ancient revolutions . . . by means of these still existing causes," and he regarded this as a doctrine which his work had overthrown. In 1825 Constant Prévost had dared to challenge Cuvier's authority, though no one paid much attention to him, and between then and 1830 he and Lyell undertook a number of extensive geological tours on the Continent, a type of journey very fashionable at the time among laymen as well as among scientists. Lyell's ideas seem to have formed rather suddenly. In 1825, for example, he knew Scrope only slightly and referred to his *Considerations on Volcanos* merely as "a very creditable work." [8] He did not then see in it implications which would upset diluvialist assumptions. "I was," he later wrote, "taught by Buckland the catastrophical or paroxysmal theory," and not until 1827 does his published correspondence begin to mention the existence of a definite "liberal" camp in geology.[9] By the end of that year, however, he had delivered the manuscript of his first volume to the printer, who must have become a little annoyed with uniformitarianism, because, what with several more continental tours and continual changes in detail, Lyell did not get the book through the press until January 1830, though he later declared the main points of his theory to have been fixed before he wrote his first draft.[10] For so single-minded a work, the *Principles* came out in remarkably haphazard fashion. Originally Lyell had planned two volumes. The counterattacks of the opposing school compelled him to modify his tactics, and he altered his plan so that each volume would not only cover its phase of physical history interpreted in terms of the present but would also meet the objections raised by the preceding installment. In the end, volume II appeared in January 1832, a second and revised edition of volume I in June 1832, and volume III in April 1833.

2

The time had come, announced Lyell, for a proper science of the earth and of its inhabitants, and he proposed to set it forth. It was now for the first time possible to do so. The suspension, since around 1810, of all attempts to form cosmogonies had been a salutary reaction against the excesses of Neptunism. A host of industrious toilers had accumulated a great new body of data, and, by avoiding generalizations, "they in a few years disarmed all prejudice, and rescued the science from the imputation of being a dangerous, or at best but a visionary pursuit." [11] They also provided Lyell with the raw materials for a book. What is the good, asked Lyell, of describing results, if their causes be necessarily a matter of indeterminate speculation? There had, of course, been considerable progress. But instead of hearing that fossils are sports of nature, or rock strata the result of aqueous precipitation, we now hear of sudden and violent revolutions of the globe, called in by scientists more anxious to cut the Gordian knot of knowledge than to unravel it.[12]

Whoever would unravel the tangled skein of phenomena which the face of the earth presents to view and discover a single, intelligible thread therein must accept this doctrine:

that all former changes of the organic and inorganic creation are referrible to one uninterrupted succession of physical events, governed by the laws now in operation. . . The principles of science must always remain unsettled so long as no fixed opinions are entertained on this fundamental question.[13]

Hutton, indeed, had approximated the uniformitarian position, and as a result the study of the earth as a science dates from his work. But although Hutton had properly remarked that science could study only causes of the same kind as those observable in the dynamics of present changes, he had fallaciously allowed for a difference in intensity of operation because his theory of thermal uplift postulated alternating periods of disturbance and repose.[14] Later generations had unfortunately taken advantage of this loophole to neglect the Huttonian attitude, and to bring in changes so catastrophic as to differ in kind.

Lyell's strong insistence upon the distinctiveness of his own approach laid him open to charges of plagiarism levied by opponents who protested that, however infidel his system, it did not possess the merit of an original heresy. Even a reviewer who was sympathetic towards Lyell's general attitude made this point,[15] and indeed much of uniformitarianism was implicit in Hutton. For Lyell, too, science could not concern itself with origins of the universe, "a metaphysical question, worthy a theologian."[16] He built his synthesis on the methodological limitation that the past could be studied only by analogy to what natural agencies can accomplish in the present. Such theoretical originality as uniformitarianism possessed lay in its pushing the analogy to an identity, in its rigorous, undeviating insistence that existing forces, given time enough, account for the observable state of man's habitat.

The three skillful and lucid volumes of the *Principles of Geology* were devoted simply to marshaling the evidence in support of this simple thesis, and since the contention required that there be no exceptions, the result came very close to being a *Summa Geologica*. But first, it was necessary to point out why geologists had been so long in finding out what their subject was, and why their work had so often been ill received. The inherent difficulties of the science, Lyell thought, had rendered it peculiarly susceptible to the interpretations of ancient miraclemongers and their modern successors. The most ubiquitous stumbling blocks were popular preconceptions in regard to the extent of past time. If one had to produce our world out of a hat only six thousand years old, one obviously must call upon extraordinary deviations from the normal course of events, even though one might admit that nature now proceeds according to uniform laws. Aside from the authority of the Mosaic chronology, further obstacles arose from our unfortunate position as land animals, a situation eminently unfavorable for geological observation. Human beings inhabit only about a quarter of the globe, and that quarter the one which is the theater of decay. We know of, but cannot observe, the progress of new formations under the land and beneath the seas. A race of fish with human intellects, thought Lyell, would have built a proper, sound natural history much sooner than we have done.[17]

Having stated his thesis and, as he thought, exposed the popular and theological prejudices against it, Lyell set himself and his readers to inquiring how the vicissitudes which the earth's surface obviously had experienced "can be reconciled with the existing order of nature."[18] He did not, of course, deny the reality of change, but he insisted that all change had been uniform, proceeding in cycles in time rather like the orbits in space through which the planets swing. The climatic conditions of any given spot, for example, had varied with the continual shifting in the relative proportions of land and sea in that particular portion of the globe. Volume I devoted itself to describing the geological dynamics which occasioned such changes. Familiar examples of the mode in which the various agents behave were pointed out — the action of the atmosphere and of living organisms, of volcanoes and earthquakes, and above all of water. After each contemporary or historical illustration the point was made that the cumulative effects of such common forces had produced the phenomena which Cuvier and Buckland referred to cataclysms of an essentially miraculous character. In similar fashion, the second volume dealt with changes now in progress in the animate creation and showed them to be the only kind ever to have occurred. The last volume, in spite of the necessity for a number of digressions occasioned by objections to the first two, was largely descriptive. It incorporated the latest developments in chronological stratigraphy, paleontology, and physical geography, and it included Lyell's most important constructive contribution to the science in his identification and separation of the Pliocene, Miocene, and Eocene epochs of the tertiary period.[19]

Lyell professed to have derived his theory entirely from appearances, and no doubt he thought he had done just that. A crudely additive inductive approach still enjoyed an almost exclusive methodological vogue in 1830, and though the chance that a hypothesis may be deduced from a brilliant intuitive flash would damn it out of hand no longer, such an admission would have killed it then, even for its originator.[20] Actually, however, after abstracting the central idea implied by Hutton and Playfair, Lyell simply universalized the principle of uniformity and then arranged the facts in accordance with it. The process necessarily involved some incidental special pleading.

Lyell was, of course, perfectly aware that the flood was his chief enemy, because to many minds the diluvial theory alone seemed capable of affording an explanation of natural phenomena in accordance with scriptural history.[21] And being chary of disturbing religious convictions unduly, he impugned the deluge explicitly in only one passage, and that one rather in the nature of a digression. Generally, he preferred the method of draining the flood of its influence incidentally to the development of his larger interpretation. And where he does allude to the flood, what he objects to is its universality and its geological efficacy, not its existence.

It had long been a question among the learned, even before the commencement of geological researches, whether the deluge of the Scriptures was universal in reference to the whole surface of the globe, or only so with respect to that portion of it which was then inhabited by man. If the latter interpretation be admissible, the reader will have seen, in former parts of this work, that there are two classes of phenomena in the configuration of the earth's surface, which might enable us to account for such an event. First, extensive lakes elevated above the level of the ocean; secondly, large tracts of dry land depressed below that level.[22]

That is to say, a lake like Titicaca, far above sea level, might burst its banks and flood the neighboring lowlands, or a very depressed land area, like the Valley Jordan, might be inundated by a break in the barriers surrounding it. Such, Lyell implies, was the Mosaic deluge. He admitted it to be undeniable, however, that recent naturalists had followed Buckland almost to a man in picturing the flood as violent, universal, and a primary geological agency.

But we agree with Dr. Fleming, that in the narrative of Moses, there are no terms employed that indicate the impetuous rushing of the waters, either as they rose or when they retreated, upon the restraining of the rain and the passing of a wind over the earth. On the contrary, the olive-branch, brought back by the dove, seems as clear an indication to us that the vegetation was not destroyed, as it was then to Noah that the dry land was about to appear.[23]

It is somewhat surprising to find the evidence of the olive branch in Lyell as well as in Kirwan, though one suspects that when Lyell introduced it, he had his tongue in his cheek. Lyell, however, never questioned the accuracy of the Pentateuch in its own realm, which was historical and religious. He did not even intend to discredit it as the description of an actual geological event, provided the event was interpreted simply as an incident in the regular course of nature, but he hoped the issue would not be pursued. "We have been led with great reluctance into this digression, in the hope of relieving the minds of some of our readers from groundless apprehension respecting the bearing of many of the views advocated in this work." [24]

The subject of volume II, however, was not a digression. The whole of it was devoted to a discussion of the animate creation and the vicissitudes which species undergo. "To Geology . . . these subjects do strictly appertain"; [25] and the basic question is, "First, whether species have a real and permanent existence in nature; or whether they are capable, as some naturalists pretend, of being indefinitely modified in the course of a long series of generations?" [26] Lyell offered his readers an admirably clear and dispassionate exposition of Lamarck's theories. He was perfectly fair and perfectly sure that they were wrong, and his refutation of the doctrine of progressive development of life took the form of an equally clear précis of Cuvier's arguments.[27]

Each species "was endowed, at the time of its creation, with the attributes and organization by which it is now distinguished." [28] Only limited variations within a type have ever occurred. Each species, itself immutable, probably takes its origin from a single pair, such pairs having "been created in succession at such times and in such places as to enable them to multiply and endure for an appointed period, and occupy an appointed space on the globe." [29] Linnaeus had been mistaken in supposing that one corner of the globe had once been set aside as a divine incubator; instead, life had obviously originated in a number of "foci of creation." Races of animals have, of course, become extinct and the globe repopulated by new creations from time to time, although it is somewhat unsettling "that so astonishing a phenomenon can escape the observation of naturalists." [30] As to the most important point, Lyell agreed with Bishop Berkeley, who "a century ago . . . inferred, on grounds which may be termed strictly geological, the recent date of the creation of man." [31] But neither the appearance of man nor the disappearance of other species is to be considered a break in the uniformity of natural variation.

We cannot conclude this division of our subject without observing, that although we have as yet considered one class only of the causes (the organic) whereby species may become exterminated, yet the continued action of these alone, throughout myriads of future ages, must work an entire change in the state of the organic creation. . . The mind is prepared by the contemplation of such future revolutions to look for the signs of others, of an analogous nature, in the monuments of the past. Instead of being astonished at the proofs there manifested of endless mutations in the animate world, they will appear to one who has thought profoundly on the fluctuations now in progress, to afford evidence in favor of the uniformity of the system, unless, indeed, we are precluded from speaking of *uniformity* when we characterize a principle of endless variation.[32]

It has often been suggested that Lyell was on the verge of hitting upon an evolutionary theory of organic nature, and it is true that, with benefit of hindsight, uniformitarianism in geology seems almost to cry out for evolutionism in biology. In this general and important sense, Lyell undoubtedly prepared the way for Darwin. Lyell did not have the benefit of hindsight in the 1830's, however, and at the time he was forced to reject the idea that organic life had developed through modification of species, because the conception of a progressive approach to the present order of things, which Lyell referred to as "the ancient doctrine,"[33] was relied on very heavily by his opponents. This is not surprising when it is recalled that "progressive" is not necessarily the same as "evolutionary" — it all depends on how the progress comes about, whether by providential interventions or by natural laws.

Lyell did not perceive the possibility of amalgamating progress with uniformity by substituting transmutation of species for successive creations. Instead, he tended to deny the progressive character of earth history. The more subtle of the Mosaicists, on the other hand, urged that extraneous fossils and extinct vertebrates exhibit a continued development of organic life from the simplest to the most complicated forms. Sir Humphry Davy, and with him nearly everyone else, thought that "there seems, as it were, a gradual approach to the present system of things, and a succession of destruction and creation preparatory to the existence of man." [34] Lyell thought the recent creation of man to be indisputable, but the remainder of the proposition, "though very generally received, has no foundation in fact." [35] The argument was a little weak here, and Lyell seems not to have been entirely comfortable with it. His theory had to account for the absence of the remains of mammalian quadrupeds in the more ancient rock formations. Lyell's explanation was not that species like lions and elephants had appeared only in recent ages, but that in the successive metamorphoses of older rocks, all traces of these larger, softer, and less durable terrestrial forms had been destroyed. [36] This fact, since we know how present causes destroy such relics, offers further proof of uniformity in the past population of the globe.

One might well wonder why the absence of relics should be proof both of the uniform antiquity of other species and of the recent date of man's creation, but Lyell never noticed the inconsistency. His purpose was to demonstrate that our creation had not been an event so exceptional as to constitute a break in the continuity of nature:

> The introduction at a certain period of our race upon the earth, raises no presumptions whatever that each former exertion of creative power was characterized by the successive development of *irrational* animals of higher orders. [37]

Comparison between men and animals strains the bounds of valid analogy. Though it was a new departure for the creative power to link "moral and intellectual faculties capable of indefinite improvement, with the animal nature," that it did so does not justify the assumption of any corresponding steps in a hypothetical progression of purely physical forms. [38]

It might be thought that uniformitarians would be more uncompromising opponents of Darwin than catastrophists, but it did not fall out so in the event. Attitudes are more lasting than theories, and in any case Lyell was not likely to achieve a prestige as imposing as that of Moses. In later times, when Lyell ranged himself by Darwin's side, his earlier writings did indeed supply their opponents with a limited store of obsolete ammunition. But if anything is more damaging than a Pyrrhic victory, it must be a Pyrrhic defeat; and though providentialist critics of uniformitarianism did not prevail in the 1830's, they seized avidly on its inconsistencies and gave a suggestive airing to notions of progressive development. It would not be too difficult to substitute natural selection for providential cataclysms and divine creations.

For all that his attack upon scriptural geology was oblique, Lyell was thoroughly aware that his chief enemies would be "the ancient and modern physico-theologians." [39] The real purpose of his book was "to sink the diluvialists, and in short, all the theological sophists." [40] He had before him, however, a horrid example of what might come from such an effort, and he was most anxious not to reawaken an uproar similar to the one which had greeted Hutton's theories.

The mind of the English public was at that time in a state of feverish excitement. A class of writers in France had been labouring industriously for many years, to diminish the influence of the clergy, by sapping the foundations of the Christian faith, and their success, and the consequences of the Revolution, had alarmed the most resolute minds.[41]

Lyell, like most British scientists, never thought of himself as having anything in common with the tradition of rationalist skepticism. Quite the reverse, for Voltaire, who in Lyell's view had misinterpreted physics in order to ridicule the Scriptures, had also poked fun at the cultivators of geology, "regarding the science as one which had been successfully enlisted by theologians as an ally in their cause." [42] No good would come of this sort of thing, either for science or religion, and Lyell desired each to return to its proper sphere, before they had hopelessly compromised one another once again.

If ever Mosaic natural history could be set down without giving offense, thought Lyell, it would be in a historical sketch,[43] and he very much wanted to avoid giving offense. His letters began to express worry about the reception his volumes would meet with before he started writing them. He may, he fears, have to sustain the episcopal wrath of the whole bench of bishops, newly roused to ire by the Reverend Mr. Milman's *History of the Jews*. On the other hand, there is a hopeful chance that the furor over unfrocking Milman may create a diversion in his favor.[44] Tact, he urges his friends Mantell and Scrope, tact. Let them not run "unnecessarily counter to the feelings and prejudices of the age." [45]

Lyell attached great importance to preparing public opinion to accept his views. The traditional orthodoxy of the *Quarterly Review* made it the key organ in his campaign, and Lyell discovered in advance that Scrope would be his reviewer therein. A series of letters, written before the *Principles* appeared, briefed Scrope on what to say. "If Murray has to push my volumes, and you wield the geology of the *Quarterly Review*, we shall be able in a short time to work an entire change in public opinion." [46] The resultant article was, not unnaturally, eminently satisfactory; it turned one of the enemy's main batteries against him.[47] Lyell was not an unduly sensitive person, but he had a bad case of literary apprehensiveness as he saw his pages through the press. His concern cannot be laid to his temperament; it can only have arisen from his appreciation that, however carefully his argument sought to ignore the issue, its implications ran directly counter to a deep current of accepted opinion.[48]

The question naturally arises, what of Lyell as a scientific thinker? It is, indeed, obvious that he did protest too much. All his opponents immediately pointed out that the "attempt to explain the former changes of the earth's surface by reference to causes now in operation" was intrinsically no more objective than the effort to explain them by reference to a comet, a flood, or whatever catastrophes might be indicated. Lyell gave himself away, they said, by his frequent use of the word "reconcile" and achieved only a patent over-reconciliation.[49]

Geologically, of course, Lyell's critics were right. No one now holds such extreme views upon the uniform course of nature. As early as 1840, although the immediate issue as to the universal efficacy of contemporary causes was not settled,

neither did the problem taken simply as a geological one pro-
voke much discussion. Sir Roderick Murchison's *The Silurian
System*, which was published in 1839, and which after Lyell's
Principles was the next major contribution to the science to
appear in England, seldom even alludes to the uniformitarian-
catastrophist debate or to any theoretical controversies.[50] But
the question had become very much more than a geological
one, and the root of Lyell's ideas lay outside the bounds of
that science, wide though they then were. By 1830, he wrote,
in all branches of natural knowledge, and even in enigmas of
the moral world, the advancement of learning was presenting
more and more of the phenomena which an ignorant past had
attributed to miracles, to demons, to divine interventions, or
to other extraordinary agencies as merely manifestations of
larger laws, more perfectly understood.

The philosopher at last becomes convinced of the undeviating
uniformity of secondary causes, and guided by his faith in this
principle, he determines the probability of accounts transmitted to
him of former occurrences.[51]

Uniformitarian presuppositions, then, were simply those of
optimistic materialism. It would take time, and Darwin, to
demonstrate how hopelessly Buckland's school was out of key
with the times — witness Lyell's apprehensiveness and the
Principles' inclusion of certain Mosaic details. But however
pervasive the hold of catastrophism in 1830, materialistic
science had almost cut the ground from under materialistic
theology, even then. Gratuitous Lyell's assumption may have
been, but it opened the way . for scientific progress, while
Buckland's blocked the very path he sought to tread. After
1859, the surviving catastrophists, although they had toyed
with ideas of organic progression in the 1830's, were to be
found solidly behind Wilberforce; while the uniformitarians
who were still alive supported Darwin and Huxley, despite
volume II of the *Principles*.

3

The uniformitarian thesis was launched with considerable éclat, and it became immediately the object of widespread attention.[52] It did not, however, win the universal and enthusiastic assent which had hailed Buckland's magnum opus seven years earlier. Lyell's arrangement of the evidence, as it flowed from the press, wore the opposition down instead of overwhelming it, and chipped away the catastrophic positions in somewhat the same fashion as that in which his rivers produced a gradual, if much less rapid, degradation of land surfaces. Even his opponents extended the work their hearty approval insofar as its purely descriptive features were felt to be the most skillful and interesting presentation of the subject ever set before the public. Before attacking its conclusions, most of them injudiciously and somewhat ostentatiously welcomed the opportunity to discuss theoretical first principles.[53]

Adam Sedgwick, before attacking all of Lyell's main points, felt constrained to express his appreciation of "the instruction I received from every chapter of his work, and of the delight with which I rose from the perusal of the whole."[54] The effort, too, to disarm religious opposition had been fairly successful, at least to the extent that no reputable scientist exploited the whirlwind of theological outrage which was blowing up on a cruder level of criticism. Lyell even attributed his election to a chair in King's College, London, to Conybeare's intervention with the bishops who controlled the appointment and who were told that Lyell's doctrines were "startling enough, but not . . . come by in otherwise than a straightforward manner" or "from any hostile feeling towards revelation."[55] The bishops were uneasy, but they managed to master their qualms.

Publishers hastened to take advantage of the renewed interest in natural history aroused by Lyell, and a host of new titles, or of new editions of old titles, were rapidly bought up as soon as they appeared on the book stands. Macculloch, Mantell, Conybeare and Phillips, Jameson, Bakewell, and Brande got out revised versions of their commentaries. Granville Penn, Andrew Ure, Bishop Copleston, and John Faber, among others, appeared with the latest refinements of scriptural geology. Lyell's volumes, too, went through a number of editions.

As the debate developed, the most prolific of Lyell's supporters was Gideon Mantell, a competent geologist who was not of an original turn of mind and whose work, therefore, was abreast of his time but never ahead of it. His books are useful as examples of the adoption and popularization of Lyell's ideas by the uniformitarian school. Mantell's discovery of the iguanodon was his major claim to fame. He was a surgeon by profession, a highly successful popular lecturer — receiving as much as twenty-five pounds for lectures at charity benefits [56] — and something of a social climber. He evidently hoped to emulate Sir Humphry Davy in realizing his social ambitions by achieving scientific eminence, and like Davy he was also sincerely interested in research for its own sake. Science even cost him his wife, who left him when his collection of specimens and fossils grew so large and so popular that it crowded the family out of their home, which had become virtually a public museum.

Mantell got out a number of geological works written for the general public.[57] *The Geology of the South-East of England*, the expansion of an earlier work,[58] appeared in 1833. At this time Mantell's interpretations showed little evidence of uniformitarian influence. In his general sketch of the science he referred in conventional fashion to causes still in operation which date "from the period when our continents and islands assumed their present form," and he distinguished between the alluvial and diluvial deposits overlying the tertiary formations — though he refused to commit himself as to whether the Biblical flood was responsible for diluvium.[59] In the *Wonders of Geology*, however, first published in 1838, Mantell gave a précis of Lyell's description of contemporary causes and asserted them to have been sufficient for all time. Formations were now classified as metamorphic, secondary, and tertiary, and the tertiary period was broken down into Eocene, Miocene, and Pliocene. Mantell still used the word "alluvial"

for loose, water-borne accumulations, but "diluvial" no longer
appears.

There are a number of passages in the *Wonders of Geology*
which illustrate how uniformitarianism seems (to the modern
reader) almost to have demanded an evolutionary explanation
of organic phenomena. If, for example, "naturalistic development" were substituted for "the Creator" in the following
sentences, they would read like a vague anticipation of
Darwin:

The fluctuating state of the earth's surface, with which our
previous inquiries have made us familiar, will have prepared us for
the disappearance of some species of animals; — and here another
law of the Creator is manifest. Certain races of living beings,
suitable to peculiar conditions of the earth, appear to have been
created; and when those states became no longer favourable for
the continuance of such types of organization, according to the
natural laws by which the conditions of their existence were determined, the races disappeared, and were probably succeeded by new
forms.[60]

For the uniformitarian school in the 1830's, however, the activities of the Creator still supplied a satisfactory hypothesis
covering the evidence later explained by evolutionary theory.
Mantell even refers to human skeletons which had been discovered in Guadeloupe encased in limestone and to human
footprints found in a block of the same material in Missouri,
but he regards this as proof that the formations were recent
and not that man is ancient. The point is simply stated, not
argued.[61]

The Wonders of Geology was a uniformitarian text for
laymen, and Mantell attached considerable importance to
quieting the uneasiness of people who might have been misled
by the hostility of uninformed theologians. When science and
religion are properly understood and their spheres kept distinct, there is, he assured his readers, no conflict between
them. There were very few scientists in Mantell's generation
who did not make this point at some time or other, and like
the great majority of them Mantell did not perceive that his

position logically required the rejection of the whole framework of conventional natural theology. Rather than attempt any original contribution to the well-worked subject himself, he preferred to disarm suspicion by stating the views of the "eminent philosophers and divines" whose central opinions were so widely accepted that they had rescued geology from the "absurd and unfounded" charge of being inimical to Christian piety.[62] The philosophers and divines he relied on were, most of them, catastrophists like Whewell, Buckland, and Sedgwick. While rejecting their particular theories regarding the course of nature, Mantell did not hesitate to adopt their fundamental interpretation of the meaning of nature.

The new page in the volume of natural religion, which Geology has supplied, has been so fully illustrated by Dr. Buckland, in his celebrated Essay,[63] that I need not dwell at length on the evident and beautiful adaptation of the organization of numberless living forms, through the lapse of indefinite periods of time, to every physical condition of the earth, and by which its surface was ultimately fitted for the abode of the human race.

It is enough to point out that "we must believe, that every physical phenomenon which has taken place, from first to last, has emanated from the will of the Deity." [64] Although Mantell's reader is repeatedly told that geology had nothing to do with the Bible, this does not seem to have meant that science had no religious implications. All it meant was that Scripture had no scientific implications.

Mantell adopted uniformitarian geological theories somewhat uncritically, but he never rose above the more general presuppositions of the period. Henry de la Beche, on the other hand, in spite of many reservations about the specific thesis of *Principles of Geology*, came much closer to accepting Lyell's central attitude towards science. De la Beche was the first director of the Geological Survey, founded in 1835, and like Mantell he wrote several popular texts and elementary manuals designed to assist the amateur observer towards a constructive enjoyment of his hobby.[65] Though not a uniformitarian, neither had De la Beche ever been a scriptural catastrophist.

He represents, in fact, the tendency to ignore all questions of the sort — a tendency not yet very marked. For De la Beche, "The difference in the two theories is in reality not very great; the question being merely one of intensity of forces, so that, probably, by uniting the two, we should approximate nearer to the truth." [66] He did, it is true, assume that there must have been successive creations of species, but in this he was simply expressing the current hypothesis. He did not relate it to the Biblical account.[67] De la Beche's own interpretations of the geological evidence were closer to the catastrophist than to the uniformitarian pattern, but entirely without Mosaic allusions or overtones, and as a result his writings were both temperate and, compared to the rest of the discussion, rather dry.[68]

The orthodox opposition was more excited and, after an initial period of disorganization, took up its positions on lines of argument so well defined as to indicate careful staff planning. The catastrophist high command centered in the universities. Buckland and Sedgwick still held the chairs of geology at Oxford and Cambridge. Daubeny was professor of chemistry at Oxford, Conybeare a fellow of New College, and Whewell senior tutor and later master of Trinity College, Cambridge. Nearly every meeting of the Geological Society appears to have resolved itself into a debate between Lyell's supporters and this "Oxford School of Geology." [69] In general scientific circles, the Oxford school seems to have been thought the more reputable and the safer of the contending groups. Buckland was elected second president of the British Association for the Advancement of Science in 1832, and Conybeare the chairman of its geological section.

One thing the *Principles of Geology* unquestionably accomplished. The book administered the *coup de grâce* to the deluge. Few denied that Moses had indeed described an impressive flood, but as a primary, universal geological agency, it was abandoned. It is, of course, interesting that Lyell felt required to find a humble niche for it in his picture of a uniform past, and that he specifically comforted Bishop Copleston of Llandaff by assuring him that there was "no objection to his drowning as many people as he pleased on such parts as

can be shown to have been inhabited in the days of Noah." [70]
But the speed with which the ecumenical flood evaporated is
startling. As late as 1829 the period at which a flood operated
was still regarded as central to chronological classification.
Daubeny, it is true, did attempt to preserve some scope for
violent aqueous action, but only in the formation of volcanoes
and of valleys and not as a unique, world-wide event. He
made this point in the course of a general argument to the
effect that catastrophes greater than any we now see could be
produced by present causes acting more intensely, and that he
and Lyell, therefore, differed only on a question of degree.
Although he thought it possible that "a doctrine in science
may be true, although involving questions that cannot be reconciled, at the time, to the statements of Scripture," he also
felt that his position, as opposed to Lyell's "has the further
advantage of rendering the accounts of such catastrophes,
which are handed down to us on the authority both of history
and tradition, consistent with probability, instead of opposed
to it . . . and thus, if not directly confirming the Mosaic history on this particular point, removing at least those obstacles
to its reception that might exist, if we considered the event
related as out of the course of nature." Scripture was not a
source for science, of course. In the case of conflicting theories,
however, Scripture may, Daubeny held, appropriately be used
to tip the balance of probability one way or the other.[71]

The faithful were unable to take much satisfaction in so
limited a catastrophe as Lyell's deluge allowed them, and
most of them either lost interest in it or hastened to abandon
it. Whewell, who, according to Lyell, "has more influence than
any individual, unless it be Sedgwick," [72] now contemptuously
dismissed "those who have framed their geology by interpretations of Scripture." He still, however, allowed a limited validity
to those

geological speculations in which the Mosaical account of the deluge
has been referred to; for whatever errors may have been committed
on that subject, it would be as absurd to disregard the most ancient
historical record, in attempting to trace back the history of the

earth, as it would be gratuitously to reject any other source of information.[73]

But Whewell no longer felt inclined to introduce this particular evidence into the argument.

Conybeare backtracked even more hastily, though less unreservedly. He had been so impressed with the *Principles*, and so disturbed by their implications, that he prevailed upon the editor of the *Philosophical Magazine* to run a series of pieces in which he took issue with all of Lyell's interpretations and with many of his specific illustrations.[74] These articles furnish the most complete statement of the catastrophist counter-offensive. Conybeare professed to adhere to the diluvial theory, but "only in a general and philosophical sense. Theologically, I am well contented to let the Scriptural narrative rest on its appropriate moral evidence, and should only fear to weaken that evidence by mingling it with my own crude scientific speculations." This was a new fear with Conybeare, and he seems to have mastered it fairly rapidly, because his next sentence illustrates nicely the distressing necessity for reconciliation which arose from his religious beliefs — or were they doubts?

I hold indeed, that Science, by exhibiting to us the independent evidence of analogous convulsions, may well be cited, as removing from that narrative all objections arising from alleged antecedent improbability: but whether the diluvial traces we still observe geologically, be the vestiges of the Mosaic deluge, or whether that convulsion was too transient, etc., to leave such traces, is quite another question.[75]

Upon the deluge itself, Adam Sedgwick's apostasy was even more uncompromising and his recantation as president of the Geological Society almost ostentatiously manly:

Having been myself a believer, and, to the best of my power, a propagator of what I now regard as a philosophic heresy . . . I think it right, as one of my last acts before I quit this Chair, thus publicly to read my recantation.

We ought, indeed, to have paused before we first adopted the diluvian theory, and referred all our old superficial gravel to the action of the Mosaic Flood. For of man, and the works of his hands, we have not yet found a single trace among the remnants of a former world entombed in these deposits.[76]

The implication is significant. If relics of humanity had been found in the debris of a destroyed world, then we would have evidence that the destruction had been wrought by the Mosaic flood which, as we know, drowned a great many human beings. Sedgwick never abandoned the idea of sudden and universal geological catastrophes even though the Biblical deluge could no longer be one of them.

Buckland, at this time, was preparing to meet the uniformitarian challenge in his contribution to the *Bridgewater Treatises*. Much was hoped for from him by the trustees and devotees of that once popular series, and in the meantime rumors of the course his thoughts were taking were eagerly seized upon in scientific circles. Even his opponents never doubted Buckland's original sincerity. "Although I am convinced," wrote Lyell, "he does not believe his own theory now, to its full extent, he believed it when he started it." [77] And later, Lyell hears that Buckland has changed his plan again, and that his "mode of reconciling geology and Genesis in his B. Treatise has been approved of by the Oxford Professors of Divinity and Hebrew!" [78] As it turned out, Buckland never mentioned the deluge in his treatise. Sedgwick, indeed, made an abortive effort to account for it as a product of the paroxysmal earthquakes postulated in Beaumont's mountain-uplift theories.[79] But uniformitarians had no difficulty in blocking this new tack of the diluvialists.[80] The deluge was finished.

All this meant, however, was that catastrophism had been deprived of its most popular catastrophe. Upon the larger question of the relations between scientific theory, natural causation, and religious truth, the attitudes which had given rise to diluvialism remained stubbornly unaffected by the demise of that specific interpretation. Sedgwick, for example, worked up to his criticism of Lyell by way of some general remarks on the laws of nature and the comprehension of them. He was then president of the Geological Society. His attack, wrote Lyell, was the "severest," and the one against which he must put forth all his energies in the second volume of the *Principles*.[81] "I believe," declared Professor Sedgwick, "that . . . all the primary modes of material action, are as immutable as the attributes of that Being from whose will they derive their only energy." The basic laws of nature, the law of gravitation, for instance, or of atomic affinity, are few and simple and not yet all discovered. Uniformitarianism confounded imperfectly comprehended appearances with some such basic law. It was a Ptolemaic view of earth history. "It assumes, that in the laboratory of nature, no elements have ever been brought together which we ourselves have not seen combined; that no forces have been developed by their combination, of which we have not witnessed the effects." [82] It circumscribes, in other words, God's operations by our ignorance of them. At this level, Sedgwick was a penetrating critic.

As an irreducible minimum, catastrophists required that theories of natural causation admit of direct providential application. In this demand, never explicitly formulated, lay the root of all the troubles, and to satisfy it the Oxford school followed Sedgwick onto very treacherous ground. Conybeare had calmed down a little by 1832, when, as first president of the new British Association's geological section, he delivered his annual charge:

> No real philosopher, I conceive, ever doubted that the physical causes which have produced the geological phenomena were the same in kind, however they may have been modified as to the degree and intensity of their action, by the varying conditions under which they may have operated at different periods. It was to these *varying conditions* that the terms, a different order of things, and the like, were, I conceive, always intended to have been applied; though these terms may undoubtedly have been by some writers incautiously used.[83]

Conybeare continued to feel fundamental reservations about the identity of causes in degree and in intensity, while admitting that the Supreme Lawgiver always moved in similar ways His wonders to perform. These reservations ultimately prevailed, to be sure, though scarcely in the way Conybeare presented them. Still, he painted an impressive and persuasive picture of a progressing global surface, of a progressive set of creations, each more complicated than the last. Sciences even had developed in a logically necessary order of succession, from astronomy to geology. Gradually the globe had changed from a fluid spheroidal mass to a solid crust, itself still cooling in paroxysms less and less intense. This globe bore a different aspect in every age. As natural forces degenerated from age to age, the planet was inhabited by successively more advanced animal creations.

Sedgwick too had discovered in his meditations upon the organic creation the most insuperable objections to uniformitarianism.

And I ask you, have we not in these things some indications of change and of an adjusting power altogether different from what we commonly understand by the laws of nature? Shall we say with the naturalists of a former century, that they are but the sports of nature? Or shall we adopt the doctrine of spontaneous generation and transmutation of species, with all their train of monstrous consequences? [84]

Lyell, to be sure, devotes a chapter to combating successfully the latter speculation. "A doctrine may however be abused," thought Sedgwick, "and yet contain many of the elements of truth."

I think that in the repeated and almost entire changes of organic types in the successive formations of the earth — in the absence of mammalia in the older, and their very rare appearance (and then in forms entirely unknown to us) in the newer secondary groups — in the diffusion of warm-blooded quadrupeds (frequently of unknown genera) through the older tertiary systems — in their great abundance (and frequency of known genera) in the upper portions of the same series — and, lastly, in the recent appearance of man on the surface of the earth (now universally admitted) — in one word, from all these facts combined, we have a series of proofs the most emphatic and convincing, — that the existing order of nature is not the last of an uninterrupted succession of mere physical events derived from laws now in daily operation: but on the contrary, that the approach to the present system of things has been gradual, and that there has been a progressive development of organic structure subservient to the purposes of life.[85]

This weighty sentence took Sedgwick onto very thin ice indeed, but William Whewell in the *British Critic* skated even closer towards the final catastrophe of the cataclysmic creed:

It is clear . . . that to give even a theoretical consistency to his system, it will be requisite that Mr. Lyell should supply us with some mode by which we may pass from a world filled with one kind of animal forms, to another, in which they are equally abundant, without perhaps one species in common. He must find some means of conducting us from the plesiosaurs and pterodactyls of the age of the lias, to the creatures which mark the oolites or the iron-sand. He must show us how we may proceed from these, to the forms of those later times which geologists love to call by the sounding names of the paleotherian and mastodontean periods. To frame even a hypothesis which will, with any plausibility, supply this defect in his speculations, is a harder task than that which Mr. Lyell has now executed. We conceive it undeniable (and Mr. Lyell would probably agree with us,) that we see in the transition from an earth peopled by one set of animals, to the same earth swarming with entirely new forms of organic life, a distinct manifestation of creative power, transcending the known laws of nature: and, it appears to us, that geology has thus lighted a new lamp along the path of natural theology.[86]

So there the question stood. It could not have been more clearly stated. Deluc, Kirwan, Conybeare, Sedgwick, and Buckland might almost be described as having written the last chapter in a historical interpretation to which Orosius and Gregory of Tours had contributed the early volumes. Their approach to natural history in the half-century of their scientific leadership disguised its lust for the catastrophic and the miraculous more successfully, perhaps, than the *Seven Books Against the Pagans*, but the compulsion to exhibit examples of divine intervention was strong.

Neptunists and catastrophists set themselves a task which ultimately proved self-contradictory. They accorded complete philosophic validity to whatever results Baconian induction might bring them; and they also required these results to display the structure and development of the material world as the history of an intending Providence with a moral purpose, as physical evidence not only of God's power but of His will and His immediacy. However firmly they might insist that Genesis was not designed to teach the truths of science, or the Geological Society to teach the truths of morality, still truth, as Sedgwick felt, could not be inconsistent with itself. The central thread of interpretation became finer and finer. One by one its strands were broken and the weight of demonstration put upon those remaining — the six days of creation, the six-thousand-year span of earth history, the birth of our present globe in a primeval diluvium, the antiquity and original parentage of species, the dynamical efficacy of divinely ordained cataclysms, the flood itself. Finally, the conception of a divinity who must continually interfere with his arrangements in order to prove himself a governing force depended upon the immutability of different manifestations of life. This was the one remaining strand. Publicists of the school of theological science rushed to hang upon it, and of course they hanged themselves with it. In Sedgwick's view,

Geology, like every other science when well interpreted, lends its aid to natural religion. It tells us, out of its own records, that man has been but a few years a dweller on the earth; for the traces of himself and of his works are confined to the last monuments of its history. Independently of every written testimony, we therefore believe that man, with all his powers and appetencies, his marvellous structure and his fitness for the world around him, was called into being within a few thousand years of the days in which we live — not by a transmutation of species, (a theory no better than a phrensied dream), but by a provident contriving power. And thus we at once remove a stumbling block, thrown in our way by those who would rid themselves of a prescient first cause, by trying to resolve all phenomena into a succession of constant material actions, ascending into an eternity of past time.[87]

Lyell, said the catastrophists, by dramatizing the necessity for getting from one form of life to another and for explaining the unique character and recent appearance of man, had offered the final proof for the incessant and ubiquitous application of God's creative powers to a universe which He had ordained, and the natural laws of which were few, perfect, and simple; beneficent when properly understood; and unchangeable (except by God).

In the 1830's, however, no one, not even Lyell, pressed the argument to its logical conclusion. It will have been noticed that the anti-Mosaic schools also labored under the conventional obligation to point out how their larger understanding put God's works into a more sublimely necessary focus than the puerile and unscientific approach of Neptunist or catastrophist. Further, there were certain received empirical boundaries which Huttonians and uniformitarians themselves never thought to question. Playfair and Smith admitted a flood; Lyell's 1830 man was recently created and his animal species unique and more permanent than the progressive creative installments on which Sedgwick took insecure refuge. Even the attacks, then, upon the theories of religious materialism did not spring from a point of view fundamentally opposed to the idea of apprehending the divine through the sort of manifestations which guide an engineering project. Vulcanism and uniformitarianism were simply further stages in the retreat from the rigorous fundamentalism of Kirwan and from the philosophic inspiration of Priestley.

VI

THE VESTIGES OF CREATION

The idea, then, which I form of the progress of organic life upon the globe —
and the hypothesis is applicable to all similar theatres of vital being — is, *that
the simplest and most primitive type, under a law to which that of like-pro-
duction is subordinate, gave birth to the type next above it, that this again
produced the next higher, and so on to the very highest,* the stages of advance
being in all cases very small — namely, from one species only to another; so
that the phenomenon has always been of a simple and modest character.

— *Vestiges of the Natural History of Creation* [1]

I

It would have been impossible not to understand the *Vestiges of Creation,* however full of nonsense the first few editions
were. Robert Chambers had anonymously taken up the challenge which Adam Sedgwick, William Whewell, and the catastrophists had presented to Lyell: how to explain the progression
of organic forms in view of the uniformitarian requirement
of an unvarying natural law. The answer, plausible and unscientific as it was, provoked a pitch of popular excitement
seldom paralleled in the annals of scientific controversy.
Sedgwick, even though he had originally put the question so
that it almost begged the answer, had never seriously imagined
the matter would come to this. He was horrified:

The world cannot bear to be turned upside down; and we are
ready to wage an internecine war with any violation of our modest
principles and social manners. . . It is our maxim, that things must
keep their proper places if they are to work together for any good.
If our glorious maidens and matrons may not soil their fingers with
the dirty knife of the anatomist, neither may they poison the springs
of joyous thought and modest feeling, by listening to the seductions
of this author; who comes before them with . . . the serpent coils

of a false philosophy, and asks them again to stretch out their hands and pluck forbidden fruit — to talk familiarly with him of things without raising a blush upon a modest cheek; — who tells them — that their Bible is a fable when it teaches them that they were made in the image of God — that they are the children of apes and the breeders of monsters — that he has *annulled all distinction between physical and moral* (p. 315) — and that all the phenomena of the universe, dead and living, are to be put before the mind in a new jargon, and as the progression and development of a rank, unbending, and degrading materialism.[2]

This was a cry from the heart of a scientist upon whom had suddenly flashed the full implications of his own endeavors, and who refused to understand them. The very framework of society seemed threatened, and this was one of the basic points at issue though it was not always made explicit since the question was ostensibly a scientific one. But there appear in Sedgwick's outburst certain words and phrases of which the conceptions and unspoken definitions turn up again and again in the literature, and which carry the debate beyond the bounds of scientific disagreement into the sphere of social values: modest principles and social manners, things in their proper places, physical and moral truth, and "degrading materialism."

The controversial hue and cry set up upon appearance of the *Vestiges* reached a far wider audience than the one which had followed the relatively temperate discussion of uniformitarianism. For several decades all the respectable leaders of scientific opinion, of whatever school, had been actively engaged upon the project of popularizing natural philosophy among mechanics and disseminating science to untutored multitudes.[3] The result, it was thought, could only elevate the moral sentiments of the working class and stabilize its situation by demonstrating the providential and material necessity and the comprehensive beneficence of industrial arrangements. Uniformitarian disputes had not disturbed this hopeful program. But now, it suddenly appeared, it made a great deal of difference what sort of science was popularized. Hitherto scientists themselves, misunderstood to be sure, had been unfairly charged with encouraging infidelity and moral anarchy. And just as they were successfully solidifying the religious cement of industrial society, a real heretic, cleverly and falsely got up in the guise of science, came to undo their labors and to demolish the framework.

The decade separating the *Principles of Geology* and the *Vestiges of Creation* had been one of industry and harmony in the temple of nature. The catastrophist issue tended to become an abstract question of philosophical attitudes rather than a matter of primary importance in explaining geological dynamics, partly because the origins of earth history receded further and further into the distance on a time scale which, if it was not infinite, at least defied common-sense comprehension as firmly as a twentieth-century national debt. Catastrophists actually accomplished more in extending the frontiers of knowledge than uniformitarians did. Sedgwick and Murchison succeeded in identifying the Cambrian and Silurian systems of the Paleozoic and in fixing the position of these formations in the geological succession. Towards the end of the 1830's, Agassiz began to make a name for himself, first with his researches on fossil fish, upon which he became the last word at the time, and later with his convincing demonstration of the existence of a glacial epoch in the temperate zones. The latter discovery, romantic enough to appeal to the popular imagination, gave him great prestige as a source of authoritative pronouncements. Glaciers gave catastrophism a new lease on life, and Agassiz was the most influential individual link between catastrophism and the theological-scientific opposition to Darwinism. Meanwhile, the government was sufficiently impressed with the utility of geology to sponsor the Geological Survey, the earliest official interference in the domain of science. The much criticized British Association was established in 1832. Prominent among the founders were the leaders of the Geological Society, who sought an opportunity for the interchange of ideas and practical applications with other sciences and who were weary of bearing the entire weight of the theological opprobrium which their own studies had called down upon natural philosophy.

At no time during the scientific controversies of these decades, even though these disputes were themselves sufficiently theological, did clerical critics cease their fulminations against science in general and all its works. Buckland and Sedgwick, Agassiz and Hugh Miller, were consigned to perdition as enthusiastically by these writers as were Hutton and Lyell, and later Darwin. Some reasonably reputable theologians, like Edward Bouverie Pusey and Dean Cockburn of York, contented themselves with simple denunciations of science either because in their view it required adoption of strained or at least heterodox opinions about the Bible, or because they thought that it encouraged the human intellect to rely presumptuously on its own powers unaided by divine authority and eventually led to a materialistic, even an atheistic, philosophy. Others, men of the lunatic fringe, like Granville Penn, John Faber, Andrew Ure, and George Fairholme, got out their own fantastic geologies and natural histories, a literature which enjoyed a surprising vogue, but which is too absurd to disinter.[4] None of it marked any advance over Kirwan. Dean Cockburn and his followers made enough of an impression, however, to awaken considerable opposition to Peel's presentment of Buckland to succeed Wilberforce as Dean of Westminster. No one had trod out the Creator's scientific grapes more diligently than Buckland, but Mrs. Buckland remarked gratefully how courageous it was of Sir Robert to appoint a man of science to so prominent a post in the Church.[5] Meanwhile, all during the 1830's, descriptive scientists of all schools continued to publish volumes embodying the results of their researches in the elaboration of a natural theology which was both teleological and mechanistic. Characteristic literary productions in this vein were the eight *Bridgewater Treatises*, of which more will be said later, dealing with "the Power, Wisdom, and Goodness of God, as Manifested in the Creation."

2

In this harmonious chorus insistently singing the beneficence of providential design in nature, the *Vestiges of Creation* struck a stridently discordant note. It may seem odd that it should have done so, because its argument was encased within the framework of natural theology. The *Bridgewater Treatises*, however, emphasized divine design and divine governance; while the *Vestiges* was concerned with naturalistic development, which Chambers, with a certain disregard for logic, sometimes described as a consequence and sometimes as a proof of the proposition that the universe is one of law and the law itself an expression of the Deity's mind:

It being admitted that the system of the Universe is one under the dominion of natural law (natural law being guardedly defined as a mere term for that order which the Deity observes in his operations), it follows that the introduction of species into the world must have been brought about in the manner of law also.[6]

His critics, felt Chambers, had fastened upon the development hypothesis, which he had proposed merely as a plausible explanation of certain unseen phenomena, as if it were the fundamental thesis of his book and had totally ignored that fundamental thesis, which was the dominion of natural law.[7]

Chambers thought that in the concept of "development" he had suggested a physical law of nature which would turn out to be as fundamental and binding as the law of gravitation.

It is most interesting to observe into how small a field the whole of the mysteries of nature thus ultimately resolve themselves. The inorganic has one final comprehensive law, GRAVITATION. The organic, the other great department of mundane things, rests in like manner on one law, and that is, — DEVELOPMENT. Nor may even these be after all twain, but only branches of one still more comprehensive law, the expression of that unity which man's wit can scarcely separate from Deity itself.[8]

In arriving at this, the concluding sentence of his argument, Chambers conducted his readers hastily through the entire domain of natural philosophy. His range of illustration was very wide indeed, his understanding often shallow, and his literary style always pleasing.

The *Vestiges* opens with a description of the outer spaces of the universe, the solar system, and the formation of stars and planets according to the nebular hypothesis. Comte's writings had impressed Chambers very forcibly. Just because our earth has assumed a form which seems final to us, he remarks, we must not suppose that the processes of cooling, condensation, and congelation are not even now forming other systems, unthinkable distances away. Chambers lost no time in suggesting his point of view:

> If we could suppose a number of persons of various ages presented to the inspection of an intelligent being newly introduced into the world, we cannot doubt that he would soon become convinced that men had once been boys, that boys had once been infants, and, finally, that all had been brought into the world in exactly the same circumstances. Precisely thus, seeing in our astral system many thousands of worlds in all stages of formation, from the most rudimental to that immediately preceding the present condition of those we deem perfect, it is unavoidable to conclude that all the perfect have gone through the various stages which we see in the rudimental.[9]

The first half of the book is devoted to a popular description of the geological succession, in which the interpretation is more uniformitarian than catastrophist, and to an exposition of the chronological progression of organic forms, both vegetable and animal. Emphasis was put upon the steadily increasing complication and elaboration of organized beings:

> In pursuing the progress of the development of both plants and animals upon the globe, we have seen an advance in both cases, along the line — or, it may be, lines — leading to the higher forms of organization. . . In short, we see everywhere throughout the geological history, strong traces of a parallel advance of the physical conditions and the organic forms.[10]

This being patently the case, the generally received idea of organic creation required modification, although the source of creation could not, of course, be held in doubt. "That God created animated beings, as well as the terraqueous theatre of their being, is a fact so powerfully evidenced, and so universally received, that I at once take it for granted." [11] But the prevailing notion of the manner in which He had done so, "that the Almighty Author produced the progenitors of all existing species by some sort of personal or immediate exertion," was a very absurd and superstitious formula, a product of miracle mongering and not of science.

How can we suppose an immediate exertion of this creative power at one time to produce zoophytes, another time to add a few marine mollusks, another to bring in one or two crustacea, again to produce crustaceous fishes, again perfect fishes, and so on to the end. This would surely be to take a very mean view of the Creative Power — to . . . reduce it to some such character as that borne by the ordinary proceedings of mankind.[12]

It is more logical, more harmonious, and more befitting the Creator's dignity and craftsmanship to suppose that the organic creation, like the inorganic, was a single event, an exertion of supreme power including in its fiat the simple, fundamental laws which prescribed the course of descent taken by the forms of life from one species to another. "The Eternal One has arranged for everything beforehand, and trusted all to the operation of the laws of his appointment, himself being ever present in all things." [13]

Having derived his theory chiefly from astronomical and geological evidence, Chambers proceeded to illustrate and sustain it by material drawn from natural history, chemistry, embryology, phrenology, philology, and archaeology. His understanding of these subjects was none too sound, but he presented them with attractive ease. Although he criticized Lamarck for the absurdity of his view of the causes and mechanism of transmutation,[14] Chambers was considerably less satisfactory than Lamarck upon this essential point. "Organic life," he remarked, "*presses in* . . . wherever there is room and encouragement for it, the forms being always such as suited the circumstances, and in a certain relation to them." [15] Unfortunately, Chambers placed great emphasis on the life-creating powers of galvanism, chiefly because of the experiments of an obscure Mr. Crosse, who thought he had generated a new species of *acarus* in a wet cell. Mr. Crosse's claims created quite a stir, until it turned out that his creation was a common parasitic mite which had come off his fingers while he mixed his electrolyte.[16]

The presentation of supporting evidence in the *Vestiges* abounded with similar egregious absurdities, misinterpretations, and vagaries. According to Darwin, the later editions were very much improved,[17] and even in the early versions the historical treatment of comparative anatomy presented a serious argument for the basic presumption. But despite Chambers' occasional flashes of insight, no scientist could see any meaning in the only mechanism suggested: *"the fundamental form of organic being is a globule, having a new globule forming within itself*, by which it is in time discharged, and which is again followed by another and another, in endless succession."* [18]

Chambers did the argument no service by relying heavily upon the biological theory of recapitulation. Every individual, he seemed to think, literally goes through embryonic stages of being an invertebrate, a fish, a reptile, and so on.[19] He had very little sense of the limitations of illustrative analogy; the accident that frosted vapor on a windowpane often crystallizes in designs reminiscent of fern leaves, he thought an illustration of the identity of organic and inorganic matter. On another page, a farmer is described as having sowed oats and raised up rye in a practical, if accidental, confirmation of transmutability of forms.[20] Comparative phrenology was not a very satisfactory tool with which to analyze and to explain the relative intellectual capacities, much less the moral characteristics, of man and of the lower orders. And the proposed classification of animated nature had neither descriptive validity nor simplicity to recommend it. Man's place in the system was, of course, the most shocking thing in the book: "Man, then, considered zoologically, and without regard to the distinct character assigned to him by theology, simply takes his place as the type of all types of the animal kingdom." Are there then to be, as conditions change, "species superior to us in organization, purer in feeling, more powerful in device and act, and who shall take a rule over us"? Very likely so, although "the present race, rude and impulsive as it is, is perhaps the best adapted to the present state of things in the world." [21]

"The book," said Chambers in explanation of why he wrote the *Vestiges*, "is an emanation of the higher feelings." [22] His purpose had been simply to show "that the laws of nature appear as the expressions of a Will external to the world, leading us to the conception of a divine originator and ruler of all things." [23] To the accusation that he described inanimate matter as capable of taking on life and mind by its own inherent powers, he replied, "I believe in a personal and intelligent God, and cannot conceive of dead matter receiving life otherwise than from Him, though of course in the manner of order or law." [24] This compulsion to refer all experience to the operation of a unitary system of law was particularly outrageous in the eyes of the critics who deplored the social and religious heresies implicit in the *Vestiges*. For Chambers urged the view that the human intellect was a phenomenon which differed from the mental equipment of lower animals only in point of refinement of operation. Animal instinct, he thought, was clearly a nervous matter, and the training of dogs and horses a process no different from education.[25] Religious philosophy had put itself in a false position by separating mind from biological organization and identifying soul with mind. Human affairs are not to be distinguished from material events. One can, for example, predict the incidence of crime by statistical experience just as one can predict the position of the planets.

This statistical regularity in moral affairs fully establishes their being under the presidency of law. Man is now seen to be an enigma only as an individual; in the mass he is a mathematical problem. It is hardly necessary to say, much less to argue, that mental action, being proved to be under law, passes at once into the category of natural things. Its old metaphysical character vanishes in a moment, and the distinction usually taken between physical and moral is annulled.[26]

This left Chambers face to face with the nemesis of all moralists, a rationalization of evil. The constitution of creation rests upon a beneficent fundamental law of development, the decree of a "Being transcendently kind." [27] But the resultant plan represents the integration of a vast complex of subsidiary laws and goods, and evil is produced in the exceptive case when one of these operates in excess or upon a wrong object. Both wind and sea are useful agencies of transport even though sailors sometimes drown.[28]

Chambers wrote his book in a characteristically Victorian spirit of materialistic reverence. He foresaw, however, that he would be treading upon tender theological toes. He took extraordinary precautions to conceal his identity while arranging for publication, correcting proof, and preparing later editions. A number of objections were anticipated in the text. To the argument that received opinions about creations as opposed to creation were derived from Scripture, Chambers opposed the view — tacitly admitting the unassailability of Holy Writ — that Genesis presents the creative procedure "as flowing *from commands and expressions of will, not from direct acts* . . . 'God *formed* man in his own image' cannot well be understood as implying any more than . . . that man was produced in consequence of an expression of the Divine will to that effect." Similarly with the expressions, "Let there be light — let there be a firmament — let the dry land appear — let the earth bring forth grass, the herb, the tree — let the waters bring forth the moving creature that hath life — let the earth bring forth the living creature after his kind." [29] Indeed, quoted this way, it all sounds rather like development.

To the contention that the development hypothesis was degrading to the dignity of man, Chambers answered with a flat "Nonsense." If it has pleased Providence to arrange our descent from other species, so be it; ours to admire the perfection of the plan, not to criticize it. Anyway, degradation is a relative idea, a product of prejudice.

Were we acquainted for the first time with the circumstances attending the production of an individual of our race, we might equally think them degrading, and be eager to deny them, and exclude them from the admitted truths of nature. Knowing this fact familiarly and beyond contradiction, a healthy and natural mind finds no difficulty in regarding it complacently.[30]

Even more absurd, however, was it to urge that it befitted the Creator's omnipotence, omniscience, and benevolence to suppose Him incapable of arranging His works once for all. To imagine the Divine Craftsman as forever fiddling with His materials, forever so dissatisfied with one creation of rocks or animals that He wiped it out in order to try something else, was to invest Him with mankind's attributes instead of the other way about. Nor could one rationally suppose that He proceeded any differently in the moral, intellectual, and organic aspects of His plan from the way in which He disposed of inanimate materials. The only value of his book, thought Chambers, lay in its religious import, for it took knowledge to admire the divine.

When all is seen to be the result of law, the idea of an Almighty Author becomes irresistible, for the creation of a law for an endless series of phenomena — an act of intelligence above all else that we can conceive — could have no other imaginable source.[31]

3

Chambers had a number of things in common with Hugh Miller, his most damaging critic. They were both Scotsmen. They were both among the last representatives of the self-taught naturalist of universal interests whose cultivation of natural history had turned that genial pursuit into the sciences of geology, biology, paleontology, zoology, and so forth, each of which was becoming so extensive and technical that it was soon impossible for the amateur to keep up with the whole field and increasingly difficult for him to master even one branch of the subject. Like most of their kind, Chambers and Miller were more enthusiastically interested in the meaning of science than in science itself. Both were editors of very influential weekly journals which were pitched to the purse and comprehension of working men. They both wrote well and voluminously and upon a staggering variety of subjects. Although they disagreed explosively about development, their careers offer characteristic examples of the prevailing effort to form popular attitudes by retailing the lessons to be learned from the shape of nature.

Certainly Miller and Chambers satisfied the public's omnivorous appetite for enlightenment with weighty fare. Having turned his hand to very nearly everything else, Chambers could not have been expected to permit the limitations of his knowledge of natural philosophy to prevent him from epitomizing the fundamental lessons to be learned from it. During the course of their publishing partnership, he and his brother provided the grateful booksellers with a series of productions, the titles of which recall the mustily earnest character of the trade. There were *Chambers's Commercial Geography of the World*; *Chambers's Concise Gazetteer of the World, Topographical, Statistical, and Historical*; *Chambers's Biographical Dictionary: The Great of all Times and Nations*; and *Chambers's Encyclopaedia: A Dictionary of Useful Knowledge*. Those who sought rather to cultivate their tastes than to expand their information could turn to *Chambers's Cyclopaedia of English Literature*, which offered "A History critical and biographical of authors in the English tongue from the earliest times until the present day, with specimens of their writings." There were two series to assist the schoolmaster, *Chambers's Graduated Readers* and *Chambers's Educational Course*, which latter included *A Treatise of Practical Mathematics, Mathematical Tables, Rudiments of Vegetable Physiology*, and *Rudiments of Zoology*. Travelers could avail themselves of *Chambers's Handy Guide to London* and *Chambers's Handy Guide to Paris*, and on their way thither could regale themselves with *Chambers's Miscellany of Instructive and Entertaining Tracts*. Stay-at-homes had *Chambers's Home Book; or, Pocket Miscellany*, an improving anthology.[32]

In the periodical field, the house published *Chambers's Edinburgh Journal*, an eight-page weekly begun in February 1832 and continued for some years after its founder's death in 1871.[33] Chambers set the price at three halfpence, and described his objective in the first leading article:

The grand leading principle by which I have been actuated, is to take advantage of the universal appetite for instruction which at present exists; to supply to that appetite food of the best kind, and in such form, and at such a price, as must suit the convenience of *every man in the British dominions.* Every Saturday, when the poorest labourer in the country draws his humble earnings, he shall have it in his power to purchase, with an insignificant portion of even that humble sum, a meal of healthful, useful, and agreeable mental instruction.[34]

Included within the paper's scope would be "Literary and Scientific Subjects; The Formation and Arrangement of Society; The British Constitution; Education; Topography and Statistics, relative to Agriculture, Gardening, Planting, Sheep-farming, The Making of Roads, Bridges, and Canals; the establishment of Ferries, the best means of Conveyance by Land and Water, Increase of Population; the uses of Machinery to simplify Human Labour, Manufactures, etc." The *Journal* never changed its character. Only party politics were excluded, officially so at any rate. There was offered, however, information on emigration for the poor, pieces on political economy of a Benthamite character, bits on history, current events, and foreign affairs, book reviews, agreeable sketches for the naturalist, and for "Artisans . . . instructive little paragraphs from the best writers on the various branches of their industry." Home-bound cottagers, unable to get to church, would find pithy and edifying passages from the Bible and the great British moralists and selections from Bacon, Newton, and the Encyclopedists.[35]

While supervising and preparing this material, Chambers still made time to cultivate his interest in natural philosophy, in the manner of the well-rounded Edinburgh gentleman of the day. He used often to make excursions for the purpose of geologizing, and he would now and again turn his hand to an illuminating dissection. Occasionally he read papers about his observations before the philosophical societies in Edinburgh. About 1841, he retired to the Highlands in order to prepare himself to write the *Vestiges.* His reason for doing so, amateur though he admitted himself to be, was that scientists had become specialized to the extent of being incapable of taking a comprehensive view of their materials. "The consequence is that philosophy, as it exists amongst us at present, does nothing to raise its votaries above the common ideas of their time." [36] Their limited horizons, thought Chambers, explained the all but universal opposition of scientists to his views and justified his flying in the face of prevailing professional opinion. His book, he wrote, "is the first attempt to connect the natural sciences into a history of creation." [37]

He may not, however, have been prepared for the violence of the opposition. Huxley described his reaction to the *Vestiges* as one of savage irritation produced by the "prodigious ignorance and thoroughly unscientific habit of mind manifested by the writer." [38] His review of it, he later declared, was the only piece he had ever written cast in language so extreme as to cause him pangs of remorse. Huxley's attitude owed nothing to religious preconception, but he and Darwin were almost the only naturalists in England of whom this may be said. The modern reader is likely to feel inclined to treat Chambers' works tenderly. One may not, however, captiously dismiss the fact that around 1850 few scientists of any note in Britain had a good word to say for development or a kind one for the author of the *Vestiges*.[39] Catastrophist and uniformitarian, astronomer and biologist, joined in repudiation. Even to quote a sentence or so from each of the leading figures would require pages — they all spoke out: Herschel, Whewell, Forbes, Owen, Prichard, Huxley, Lyell, Sedgwick, Murchison, Buckland, Agassiz, Miller, and others.

So far as they criticized the presentation of the evidence on scientific grounds, there could be very little reason to disagree with their conclusions. With benefit of hindsight, however, it is difficult not to read into the *Vestiges* a certain suprascientific intuitive validity, which its critics almost seem to have felt and feared. One is hard put to it otherwise to account for the tremendous attention it excited. Busy and hard-pressed professional men expended a great quantity of time and ink upon a volume they described as worthless. Other pseudoscientific books, equally unencumbered by original research or understanding, were appearing constantly without receiving any notices at all from scientific men. Even for scientists, then, the trouble with the *Vestiges* was not to be found simply in the violence it did to its subject. The analogous productions of men like George Fairholme, Andrew Ure, and John Pye Smith set forth sillier, less well-informed systems of nature reconciling the Mosaic record with empirically misconceived fact. Their errors cannot have seemed sufficiently damaging to science to merit professional refutation because no one bothered to refute them, but the *Vestiges* struck a note which, besides being erroneous, was "dangerous" — a word which creeps into all the reviews and into all the correspondence and reflects a state of mind transcending scientific disapproval.

Whatever the explanation, the *Vestiges* was enormously read. It went through four editions between October 1844 and April 1845 and eleven editions by 1860.[40] There was, thought Chambers, a great demand for his book among workingmen, and the fifth, sixth, and seventh editions were priced to satisfy it.[41] Very likely, the workingman was not so deeply stirred by this as his betters feared or, indeed, as they were themselves. For months the authorship of the book was a favorite topic for speculation at every *conversazione*, dinner party, and scientific meeting. Nothing like it had occurred since *Waverley*. Among the leading candidates were Thackeray, Lady Lovelace, Sir Richard Vyvyan, Sir Charles Lyell, George Combe, and even Prince Albert.[42]

There was scarcely a single periodical which did not carry a review or an article called forth by the *Vestiges*. Most of the pieces took occasion to discuss the larger question of development and the ultimate meaning of the current understanding of natural history.[43] At this time Sir Henry Holland was writing scientific articles in the *Quarterly*, and in 1849 he summed up the progress achieved in the preceding decade in a forty-page review. The great question had been whether man had evolved or whether he was descended from a single, specially created pair. Let no one object in advance that Scripture already answers this issue; the sacred writings do not teach us science in detail. Reason and research, unaided by the Pentateuch, demonstrate "that all races and diversities of mankind are really derived from a single pair; placed on the earth for the peopling of its surface, both in the times before us, and during the ages which it may please the Creator yet to assign to the present order of existence here." [44] And then, two pages later: "It is, however, this affirmation of the origin and multiplication of mankind from a single pair of created beings which forms the great link between the Scripture narrative and the subject before us." [45] Some similar comment summarized the prevailing argument in the great majority of judgments.

The *Quarterly* reaffirmed the credibility of the Bible, the *Westminster* took advantage of the occasion to emphasize the desirability of informing the workingman about the facts of industrial life, and the *Edinburgh* pointed with alarm to the danger of doing so in a way which would destroy the religious and moral foundations of society. Discussion of the topic of development centered along these three lines, all of which it seemed somehow to bring into question. The *Westminster Review* was almost alone in ignoring the religious and moral implications of the *Vestiges*. It was, they felt, an atrociously bad book, but the fault lay at the door of professional scientists who had abdicated their responsibilities for presenting the results of their work in books comprehensible by the "mass of thinking unscientific men." Indeed, "We feel under obligation to the author, if only for having excited the angry sarcasm of a scientific critic, and tickled the dull repose of collegiate orthodoxy." [46]

This was a shaft aimed at Professor Adam Sedgwick, who, everyone knew, had written the outburst in the *Edinburgh*, quoted at the opening of this chapter. At that time Sedgwick enjoyed a distinguished reputation, not only as a producing scientist but as a progressive educator and as a moralist of considerable importance. A few years previously he had excited a good deal of liberal acclaim in a well-publicized debate with Dean Cockburn of York, who had rather unwisely, if courageously, chosen a British Association meeting as a suitable occasion for imputing unbelief and infidelity to Buckland's irreproachably pious *Bridgewater Treatise*.[47] Now that a real heresy had appeared, Sedgwick stood forth the acknowledged champion of truth and orthodoxy. No one else, thought

McVey Napier, then editor of the *Edinburgh*, could so effectively scotch the "serpent coils" of false philosophy. Sedgwick wrote his review as the spokesman for responsible scientists, and he took into consultation a number of his colleagues — Lyell, Sir Richard Owen, Sir John Herschel, and others.[48] The resulting review was cast in a vein of hysteria, though, even so, it was not so hysterical as Sedgwick's private opinion of the *Vestiges*. He had no trouble, of course, in ridiculing the absurdities in Chambers' book, nor in demolishing its scientific pretensions. But he seems to have been afraid that this was not enough and to have felt that he must set forth an alternative scheme.

I do from my soul abhor the sentiments . . . false, shallow, worthless, and with the garb of philosophy, starting from principles, which are at variance with all sober inductive truth. The sober facts of geology shuffled, so as to play a rogue's game; phrenology (that sink-hole of human folly and prating coxcombry); spontaneous generation; transmutation of species; and I know not what; all to be swallowed, without tasting or trying, like so much horse-physic!! Gross credulity and rank infidelity joined in unlawful marriage, and breeding a deformed progeny of unnatural conclusions! . . . If the book be true, the labours of sober induction are in vain; religion is a lie; human law is a mass of folly, and a base injustice; morality is moonshine; our labours for the black people of Africa were works of madmen; and man and woman are only better beasts! When I read some pages of the foul book, it brought Swift's satire to my mind, and filled me with such inexpressible disgust that I threw [it] down . . . and cried out to myself: "Give me an ounce of civet, good apothecary, to sweeten my imagination." [49]

This frame of mind required Sedgwick to refute the very idea of development. It was not sufficient simply to discredit the *Vestiges*, because, as he wrote Agassiz, there was a danger that the "dark school" which it represented would gain ground in England.[50] His reasoning was a good deal more transparent than his literary style. Even though he admitted the limits of variation within species to be not well known, Sedgwick regarded the failure of naturalists ever to have observed a case of transmutation as a strong indication that it could never have taken place.[51] Neither, of course, had they ever witnessed separate and distinct creations, but this did not occur to him. Geological progression he could not deny, he himself having contributed so much to its comprehension, but he described each epoch in the fashion of a lecturer illustrating his subject with colored slides. The "Hypozoic" flashed upon the student's view full formed and was as suddenly withdrawn to give place to a dark and uneasy void. A mysterious and vaguely inept shuffling in the back of the room, and a panorama of the Paleozoic appeared upon the screen, followed by another interval of blackness before the Triassic leapt into sight. In Sedgwick's kaleidoscope it was empirically impossible to follow events during the intervals when the Creator had his thumb on the button and whirled the bits into a new pattern. In fact, except that Sedgwick's view of dynamics was not uniformitarian, he presented an argument against development very like the one for which he had attacked Lyell some fourteen years earlier.[52]

Sedgwick drew very heavily upon Cuvier and Agassiz in presenting his orthodox cosmogony to the public, emphasizing the unbridgeable gaps between species and organic orders which corresponded with similar gaps between geological periods. The case was summed up in a quotation from Agassiz:

> As for me, I am convinced that species have been created repeatedly and successively . . . and that the changes which they have undergone during any one geological epoch are no more than very secondary and are related only to their greater or lesser fecundity and to the migrations resulting from the influences of the period.

Let those, Sedgwick warned, who would dissolve away the beneficent bonds which give meaning to the universe take heed:

> There is a moral grandeur in this sentence, and it comes to us with the power of demonstration. . . Truth is always delightful to an uncorrupted mind; and it is most delightful when it reaches us in the form of some great abstraction, which links together the material and moral parts of nature — which does not annul the difference between material and moral — but proves that moral

truth is the intellectual and ennobled form of material truth, first apprehended by sense.[53]

This seems a very odd judgment coming from a man whose basic objection to the *Vestiges* purported to be the author's "rank materialism," [54] but odd or not, it represents the prevalent attitude of leading naturalists whose self-imposed duty it was to enlighten the reading public about the meaning of natural history. There was no question but that natural history did have a meaning. For Sedgwick and his school — the prevailing school just then — truth had first to be found in materials apprehended by sense, and then it had to be "ennobled" into morality. One might think that this "annulled the distinction between material and moral" as effectually as Chambers had, but not so.

Does the conclusion at which we have arrived degrade our notion of the Godhead and of his creative power? We think far otherwise. The law of creation is the law of the Divine will, and nothing else besides; and, as the children of nature, how are we to know that will, except by honestly reading the book of nature? . . . In this way we rise to a conception of material inorganic laws, in beautiful harmony and adjustment; and they suggest to us the conception of infinite power and wisdom. In like manner, we rise to a conception of organic laws — of means (often almost purely mechanical, as they seem to us, and their organic functions well comprehended) adapted to an end, — and that end only the well-being of a creature endowed with sense and volition. Thus we rise to a conception both of Divine power and Divine goodness; and we are constrained to believe, not merely that all material law is subordinate to His will, but that He has also (in the way He allows us to see His works) so exhibited the attributes of His will as to show himself to the mind of man as a personal and superintending God, concentrating his will on every atom of the universe.[55]

In order to invest their materialism with moral quality, the scientist-theologians for whom Sedgwick spoke called in what was essentially a series of miraculous dispensations to account for the ultimate dispositions of the materials which were their most certain reality. Biblical fundamentalism was not the issue, and to regard it as such is to misread whatever light the discussion casts upon the Victorian mind — that unsatisfactory and indispensable abstraction. The trouble really lay in the difficulty of relying primarily on the material evidence for the existence and continuing activity of the Deity without accepting materialism — a dilemma which pious and goodhearted men of limited imagination could dodge only by denying self-sufficiency to the cosmic order. They sought to show the necessitarian character of physical phenomena while at the same time the inadequacy of spontaneous natural causation was the proof that the development of the universe took place under divine direction. "Spiritual" was a word very seldom used by this school; and since the demonstration of moral purpose was made to depend chiefly on exhibiting the providential adaptation of structure and behavior to physical circumstances (and the morally good was even implicitly defined as the willing acceptance of the materially necessary), the distinction between material and moral was not a very clear-cut one. Sedgwick and those who thought like him were seeking, in fact, to demonstrate the existence of moral sanctions by techniques which disclose only mechanistic relationships. Unhappy with their unsuitable tools — though it would have distressed them to think this was so — and knowing no others, they turned to miracles and called them supervisory laws.

In any case, development seemed a dangerous idea, and in its place Sedgwick offered Hugh Miller's doctrine of degradation. Within each epoch some forms of life were represented as declining from higher to lower.[56] This was never a very successful answer, since man presented a serious difficulty, and its proponents had to confuse order of size with order of complication. Nevertheless, Sedgwick made much of it in his 442-page preface to the fifth edition of his 94-page *Discourse on the Studies of the University of Cambridge.*[57]

This remarkably arranged dissertation, published expressly for undergraduates, whose moral welfare was always a subject of intense concern to Professor Sedgwick, was designed to lay the development heresy straightway by the heels. The circumstances of publication illustrate the nihilistic implications which development carried in the eyes of "collegiate orthodoxy." The original body of Sedgwick's *Discourse*, a lecture published by academic demand in 1833, had confidently set forth the intellectual, social, and religious benefits which had long been derived from natural philosophy in Cambridge. There was also given a summary of the purpose of the other chief divisions of the curriculum. All this, though unaltered and still ostensibly the subject of the book, was reduced to the character of an appendix by the immense, almost dropsically swollen preface to the fifth edition, an outpouring called forth expressly by the popularity which the *Vestiges* continued to enjoy in 1850.[58]

In order to undo the mischief it had done, Sedgwick set out to justify all the values which, to him, gave meaning to his life as a scientist and a teacher. The central thread lay through an analogical argument in support of Christianity,[59] a faith which he sometimes appears to have derived from the evidence of final cause in nature. While emphasizing the moral insufficiency of unsupported deism, he again urged the view that revealed truth, though indispensable to belief, could be apprehended inductively, by inferring a moral order parallel to natural order. Sedgwick's metaphysical treatment of rationalism and materialism is not very illuminating, and it would scarcely be worth mentioning except for the evidence that he did not feel able to refute the idea of development without bringing in the British constitution, the rise of Christianity and of Anglican doctrine, the consequent amelioration of human relations, the existent social order, the university establishment, the progress of science since Bacon, and the improvement in manufactures, morals, and manners since the Regency. All these good things, he seemed to think, would crumble away at a touch if they could not be referred to the ordinances of a supervisory providence, whose continuous concern was incessantly being demonstrated through the one source of indubitable conviction, the laboratory of nature. Once let the philosophy of the *Vestiges* be

accepted by the multitude as true. What then will follow? The reader can judge for himself: I can see nothing but ruin and confusion in such a creed. . . . If current in society it will undermine the whole moral and social fabric, and inevitably will bring discord and deadly mischief in its train; and on this account also (having a belief in the harmony of nature and in an overruling Providence) I believe it utterly untrue.[60]

4

Professor Sedgwick's rather inchoate opposition to the idea of development probably came closest to epitomizing the instinctive revulsion of contemporary leaders of opinion. Hugh Miller, on the other hand, a more damaging critic even than Sedgwick, knew exactly why he stood where he did.[61] He cast prevailing thought patterns into neat relief, but derived his opposition to development from values older and sounder than any Sedgwick felt, expressed, or understood.[62] Miller was a remarkably interesting person, one of the products of that peculiarly Scottish intellectual democracy which turned up a Carlyle or a Burns from social levels that would have extinguished them in England. It is unfortunate that he is so forgotten, for lyrical geologists are not common phenomena. Miller was entirely self-taught. He had been a stonemason in his youth and spent a poverty-stricken boyhood in Cromarty with a widowed mother who indulged a Gaelic gift of second sight while getting a skimpy living with her needle. This was an improbable background for an accomplished essayist and scientist who was also a crusading editor, political commentator, and religious reformer, influential in all these fields and, in the eyes of many of his countrymen, very nearly an oracle upon whatever issue he saw fit to pronounce.

Miller was probably the last and one of the ablest scientists to develop his professional capacities under the stimulus of an old-fashioned, romantic love of nature. He belongs with Erasmus Darwin and Priestley and the Lunar Society rather than in his own less imaginative generation. Sir Archibald Geikie describes him as a geological poet, and another admirer ecstatically declares that learning geology from the standard texts when Miller's books and public lectures were available would be like thrusting Shakespeare aside to study English literature in the dictionary.[63] And, indeed, many of the passages in his books are very fine. He had a grand, vigorous style, an extraordinary power of evocative description, and an equally impressive manner of delivering political, social, and religious judgments. His original contributions to natural history were sound and important, though not of the first rank. It was as an interpreter and popularizer that his influence was most widely felt.

Miller's American publisher — his books went through a large number of American editions — thought it a particular tragedy that he died in 1856.[64] Had he lived to refute *On the Origin of Species*, that disastrous book would have joined the *Vestiges* in the limbo of forgotten heresies.[65] During his lifetime, it was said, Miller had demonstrated a unique ability for persuading the working classes to take a right view of their circumstances, a view with which their understanding of evolution would clearly become incompatible because Darwinism denied providential order and religion. Hugh Miller had taken his social responsibilities very seriously. His first scientific treatise, *The Old Red Sandstone*, with which he made his reputation, was presented as an object lesson in how to be usefully happy though poor, the maximum of enjoyment consisting, as it does, only in a proper exercise of the intellectual and moral faculties.[66]

Although an edifying homily of this sort was implicit or explicit in nearly everything he wrote, his popularity is not astonishing because somehow, as Robert Chambers remarked, all his work was stamped with interest.[67] Hugh Miller himself had followed exactly the precepts he set the class from which he rose. Though proud of his skill, he had never enjoyed the life of a stonemason. When he lived at home in Cromarty, it had not been too bad because he had been able to write poetry. His verses [68] won him the esteem of his future wife upon whose family estate he was employed for a time, and with whom he conducted an extraordinarily metaphysical and very Scottish courtship. But when jobs gave out in Cromarty and he took work with a gang of laboring masons in Edinburgh, he found the degradation of barrack life more than he could stomach. His fellow masons seemed bestial to him, and their entertainments and improvidence of a Saturday night disgusting.[69] After he had succeeded in writing his way into the intelligentsia, he affected to feel a sympathy for the circumstances of the working classes, and he may have convinced himself that this actually was his attitude. In fact, however, his real feeling for laborers was simple dislike, and like many self-made men, his message to the working class was how to get out of it — not how to live in it. Hugh Miller's scientific essays were a naturalist's chapter in the voluminous self-help literature of the period and, like the other chapters, were particularly appreciated by those who had already helped themselves sufficiently to want to buy books and read them.

Whoever bought and profited from them, his books sold better than any other works which have been mentioned in this study. The first ten editions of the *Vestiges* disposed of about twenty-five thousand copies. Each of Lyell's editions ran to about two thousand. By the end of the century, however, Miller's *Testimony of the Rocks* had sold forty-two thousand copies, his *Footprints of the Creator* had been through seventeen editions, and his *Old Red Sandstone* twenty.[70] Miller's youthful interests and ambitions had been literary before they became scientific. He used occasionally to publish poetry and pieces on Highland antiquities and folklore in *Chambers's Journal*. It was, however, on a religious and nationalist issue that he made his name. In May 1839, the House of Lords sustained the presentment of the minister of Auchterarder whose patron, the Earl of Kinnoul, had refused to accept a parish veto and had carried his refusal to the courts. The case climaxed a growing discontent with what evangelicals felt to be an aristocratic perversion of the revolution settlement, and Miller reports himself as having felt so strongly about it that he could not sleep until he had composed a pamphlet in answer to Lord Brougham's speech which denied Scottish congregations the right to choose their pastors. This *Letter from One of the Scottish People to Lord Brougham and Vaux* [71] had such huge success that the unknown author was offered the editorial chair of *The Witness*, a journal just then being established to express evangelical sentiment upon affairs of the day. Miller accepted the post and held it from 1840 until his death; from it he is commonly reported to have exercised an influence on Scottish opinion second only to that of the Reverend Thomas Chalmers — himself something of a naturalist — with whom he led the Free Church movement which split the Church of Scotland in 1843.

From the impeccable pulpit which his professional situation afforded him, Miller turned his imaginative literary talents to preaching the lessons of natural history. When he had been a stonemason, and later on a bank clerk, he had improved his leisure hours first by teaching himself geology and then by original research in the strata of the old red sandstone. He continued this practice as an editor, and his exhaustive description of that formation was the first to fix its occurrence in Scotland in the general geological succession. The volume was published in 1841, and it immediately won him the attention and acclaim of the English geologists. Both in substance and in its felicitous style, they found it as informative as it was devout.[72] *The Old Red Sandstone* was based in part on information supplied to Miller by another Scottish geologist of equally humble origins, Robert Dick, a baker of Thurso, whose career curiously resembled Miller's except that he communicated his findings in correspondence and never published anything. Samuel Smiles considered Dick's life so edifying that he used it for the final biography in the series exemplifying the virtues of self-help.[73]

Next to his paper, natural history had become Miller's favorite concern, but he did not limit his interests to it. He published political pamphlets, antiquities, travelogues, educational homilies, and theological tracts.[74] He always liked to adorn his literary productions with scientific allusions as well as to enliven his scientific descriptions with literary flavor. The popularization of science seemed to him a religious duty.[75] He prided himself on never using language incomprehensible to the layman, and he devoted a great deal of energy to the lectures he regularly gave before the Edinburgh Philosophical Institute.[76] Perhaps his most successful general book was his autobiography, cast in the form of a story of his education; unlike the student in a more famous education, however, Miller never pretended not to have found one. There were, he knew, millions like himself who needed to learn but had no one to teach them.

They will find that by far the best schools I ever attended are schools open to them all, — that the best teachers I ever had are (though severe in their discipline) always easy of access, — and that the special *form* at which I was, if I may say so, most successful as a pupil, was a form to which I was drawn by a strong inclination, but at which I had less assistance from my brother men, or even from books, than at any of the others. There are few of the natural sciences which do not lie quite as open to the working men of Britain and America as geology did to me.[77]

He admitted himself, however, to have been peculiarly fortunate in having chosen this particular science as a stepping-stone to higher things.

There is no science whose value can be adequately estimated by economists and utilitarians of the lower order. Its true quantities cannot be represented by arithmetical figures or monetary tables; for its effects on mind must be as surely taken into account as its operations on matter, and what it has accomplished for the human intellect, as certainly as what it has done for the comforts of society or the interests of commerce. . . And Geology, in a peculiar manner, supplies to the intellect an exercise of this ennobling character. But it has also its cash value.[78]

Hugh Miller, then, raised an authoritative voice when he spoke out against development. The *Vestiges* did not catch him unawares. He had already devoted an entire chapter of *The Old Red Sandstone* to refuting Lamarck, whose "strange theories" he thought well described by Lyell in the *Principles of Geology*,[79] where they had made their first appearance before the British public. Miller here anticipated his own chief empirical contention against Chambers by arguing that within each of the three great geological epochs the higher forms preceded the lower. And, unlike Sedgwick later, he made no bones about admitting a scientist's necessity for the super-natural.

There is no progression. If fish rose into reptiles, it must have been by sudden transformation. . . There is no getting rid of miracle in the case, — there is no alternative between creation and metamorphosis. The infidel substitutes progression for Deity; Geology robs him of his god.[80]

Whether perpetrated by misguided peers or misguided naturalists, erroneous interpretations awakened a ghost of John Knox in Hugh Miller. He set about immediately the *Vestiges* appeared to compose his answer, in which he performed the unique feat of blending science and religion together instead of bending them together. His book, entitled *Footprints of the Creator*, appeared in 1847 and deservedly enjoyed a huge success. Agassiz arranged for an American edition, for which he provided an appreciative introduction, and which created a steady American market for the rest of Miller's works.[81] The argument, so far as it was geological, rested on a demonstration that within the period with which the author was most familiar, the era of the old red sandstone, fossil forms do not advance in structure according to their chronological position. The method was a case study of the *asterolepis*, the oldest, largest, and — Miller held — most advanced of the ganoid fish. There is no point in following the technical detail or the exposition of corroboratory illustration in other epochs; Agassiz gives a neat summary in his preface. It cannot be said that Miller argued beyond his evidence in rejecting the development hypothesis as inadequate to the facts of the case, or that he suppressed material unfavorable to his own view. The weakest part of the book is the chapter in which he presents evidence of decline of species as an alternative to Chambers' hypothesis, but this is left merely as an intriguing suggestion with the remark that an ingenious theorist might "get up quite as unexceptionable a theory of degradation as of development." [82]

The trouble with development was not, as most of its opponents held, that it vitiated the argument from design, or that it dispensed with a first cause. The purely Christian objection to the hypothesis seemed to Miller much more serious.

There are . . . beliefs, in no degree less important to the moralist or the Christian than even that in the being of a God, which seem wholly incompatible with the development hypothesis. If, during a period so vast as to be scarce expressible by figures, the creatures now human have been rising, by *almost* infinitesimals, from compound microscopic cells . . . until they have at length become the men and women whom we see around us, we must hold either the monstrous belief, that all the vitalities, whether those of monads or of mites, of fishes or of reptiles, of birds or of beasts, are individually and inherently immortal and undying, or that human souls are *not* so. The difference between the dying and the undying, — between the spirit of the brute that goeth downward, and the spirit of the man that goeth upward, — is not a difference infinitesimally, or even atomically *small*. It possesses all the breadth of eternity to come, and is an *infinitely great* distance. . . Nor will it do to attempt to escape from the difficulty by alleging that God at some certain link in the chain *might* have converted a mortal creature into an immortal existence, by breathing into it a "living soul"; seeing that a renunciation of any such direct interference on the part of the Deity in the work of creation forms the prominent and characteristic part of the scheme, — nay, that it constitutes the very nucleus around which the scheme has originated. . . If man be a dying creature, restricted in his existence to the present scene of things, what does it really matter to him, for any one moral purpose, whether there be a God or no? [83]

In all the storm of contentious discussion which followed the *Vestiges*, Hugh Miller's reaction was the only one which impatiently put aside the conventional and arid argument from design as irrelevant. He had nothing to say about Omnipotent Architects. The issue, to him, was not the dispositions of the material universe, but "a belief in the immortality and responsibility of man, and in the scheme of salvation by a Mediator and Redeemer. Dissociated from these beliefs, a belief in the existence of a God is of as little *ethical* value as a belief in the existence of the great sea-serpent." [84]

Christianity, if the development theory be true, is exactly what some of the more extreme Moderate divines of the last age used to make it — an idle and unsightly excrescence on a code of morals that would be perfect were it away.[85]

Hugh Miller's social opinions are not particularly refreshing, but it is refreshing to come upon a religious thinker who required a divinity rather than a landscape gardener for his God, and whose Christianity centered around the redemption, salvation, and immortality of the individual soul. It was the partially educated classes who were, in Miller's opinion, the most liable to corruption.

There is a species of superstition which inclines men to take on trust whatever assumes the name of science. . . And, owing mainly to the wide diffusion of this credulous spirit of the modern type, as little disposed to examine what it receives as its ancient unreasoning predecessor, the development doctrines are doing much harm on both sides of the Atlantic, especially among intelligent mechanics, and a class of young men engaged in the subordinate departments of trade and the law. And the harm, thus considerable in amount, must be necessarily more than merely considerable in degree. For it invariably happens, that when persons in these walks become materialists, they become also turbulent subjects and bad men. That belief in the existence after death, which forms the distinguishing *instinct* of humanity, is too essential a part of man's moral constitution not to be missed when away.[86]

The guise of pseudo science was what made the idea of development particularly sinister in Miller's eyes, because, he thought, the arguments which alone carried conviction in his day were those of "practical philosophy." Speculative theology had been the logical counterpart of metaphysics in a metaphysical age, and natural theology had borne a similar relationship to the mathematical philosophy of Newtonian science. An acquaintance with the great minds of these departments of learning was required of students, both lay and clerical, in the university curriculum of the 1840's, but this was not enough. The clergy, he felt,

do not now seem sufficiently aware — though the low thunder of every railway, and the snort of every steam engine, and the whistle of the wind amid the wires of every electric telegraph, serve to publish the fact — that it is in the departments of physics, not of metaphysics, that the greater minds of the age are engaged. . . Let them not shut their eyes to the danger which is obviously coming. The battle of the Evidences will have to be fought on the field of physical science, as it was contested in the last age on that of the metaphysics.[87]

Hugh Miller could not, like Sedgwick, satisfy himself by inferring the existence of a moral order from an analogy to natural order. He had to try to construct an empirical theology as an integral part of, instead of as a parallel to, his favorite geological science.[88] He was in no sense, however, a literal bibliolater. Why, he asks, should the Bible have been expected to declare the truths of geology when those of astronomy were withheld? The Bible had been intended to tell men what God is and what He expects of them, and upon this it is an infallible and inspired revelation. But except for the one cardinal fact of the divine authorship of the universe, man will look in vain for divine revelations of scientific truth, for it is in accordance with the economy of Providence that everything relating to the actual working of the physical system of things is discovered by the unaided intellectual faculties, after the manner of Sir Isaac Newton or James Watt.[89]

One is to read the Mosaic account of the six creative days — which Miller took to mean periods — not as if it were going to describe the significance of fossil fish or where to dig for coal or how to build a steam engine, but as the vision vouchsafed a seer. Geology, dealing with the manifestations of things and not with their nature, was concerned only with the last three of the six exertions of creative power. These Miller identified with the chief epochs to be discerned in the rocks, the Paleozoic, the Secondary, and the Tertiary, separated from each other by intervals of subsidence in the Creator's activity. This, though not original with Hugh Miller, was presented in a spirit of imaginative devotion which gave it a force entirely lacking in the pedestrian reconciliations with which this literature abounds. The conception was sufficiently allegorical to do justice to contemporary comprehension of the evidence without doing violence to it.[90]

Miller's originality lay chiefly in his interpretation of final cause. At the last

there came a period that differed even more, in the character of its master-existence, from any of these creations, than they, with their many vitalities, had differed from the previous period in which life had no existence. The human period began, — the period of a fellow-worker with God, created in God's own image.[91]

Here was the inadmissibility of development. For after this final, and unprecedented, act of creation, the seventh day began, the day which may still be in existence. The geologist finds no trace of post-Adamic creation. Not even the theologians have sufficiently understood the meaning of the text: *"The work of* REDEMPTION *may be the work of His Sabbath day. . .* During the present dynasty of probation and trial, that special work of both God and man on which the character of the future dynasty depends, is the Sabbath-day work of saving and being saved." [92]

The theory of spontaneous material development had grossly perverted a great scientific and spiritual truth, by misrepresenting the real meaning of progressive evidences:

The existing scene of things is not destined to be the last. High as it is, it is too low and too imperfect to be regarded as God's finished work: it is merely one of the *progressive* dynasties; and Revelation and the implanted instincts of our nature alike teach us to anticipate a glorious *terminal* dynasty. . . Is there to be merely a repetition of the past, — an introduction a second time of "man made in the image of God"? No! the geologist, in the tables of stone which form his records, finds no examples of dynasties once passed away again returning. There has been no repetition of the dynasty of the fish, — of the reptile, — of the mammal. The dynasty of the future is to have glorified man for its inhabitant; but it is to be the dynasty, — the *"kingdom,"* — not of glorified man made in the image of God, but of God Himself in the form of man. In the doctrine of the two natures, and in the further doctrine that the terminal dynasty is to be peculiarly the dynasty of Him, in whom the natures are united, we find that required progression beyond which progress cannot go. Creation and the Creator meet at one point, and in one person. The long ascending line from dead matter to man has been a progress Godwards, —

not an asymptotical progress, but destined from the beginning to furnish a point of union; and occupying that point as true God and true man, as Creator and created, we recognize the adorable Monarch of all the Future. It is, as urged by the Apostle, the especial glory of our race, that it should have furnished that point of contact at which Godhead has united Himself, not to man only, but also, through man, to His own Universe, — to the Universe of Matter and of Mind.[93]

All this may be strange, but to one reader, at least, it is rather impressive. One may or may not be religious, but in either case one may reasonably expect a religious writer to be so, and of all these naturalists who set out to justify God's ways to man, Hugh Miller was the only one whose conception of divinity contained many elements of spirituality. In some ways he is very easy to criticize. Perhaps he never met Chambers' central contention that a unitary plan of creation, set in motion once for all at the beginning, was more befitting divine omnipotence and omniscience than a series of separate creative exertions. As a pundit,[94] too, Hugh Miller is as vulnerable as Samuel Smiles, and in this he differs from his fellow theo-naturalists only in being clearer than they about his alarm lest the workingman be seduced from a state of social grace into a state of social infidelity.

These things being said, however, Hugh Miller's opposition to the idea of development arose from a belief which one can respect: the immortality of the individual human soul. And the impression left by his work is that his philosophy of natural history expressed a spiritual concern which did not require him to shut his eyes to the meaning of his own values as did the materialistic faith of the Sedgwicks, Bucklands, Whewells, and Conybeares. His theory of creation was not in the position of a pot calling the development kettle black. He pictured the creative process as a succession of divine fiats, elevating the level of life through the chief orders of the animal kingdom, until a final decree, differing in kind from its predecessors, introduced the era of God's moral government with man its subject and agent. Hereupon creation was no longer a suitable expression of the divine will, the Lord's work having become the work of redemption preparatory to the terminal dynasty of "everlasting life." [95]

This may not be science, strictly speaking — or even loosely speaking — but it is Christianity. Hugh Miller envisioned a challenge too great for his own understanding: "the battle of the Evidences . . . on the field of physical science." But who is to say he was wrong in seeing "that belief in the existence after death, which forms the distinguishing *instinct* of humanity, is too essential a part of man's moral constitution not to be missed when away"?

5

For all that Hugh Miller was a sympathetic figure, he was also one of the last to write in the tradition he represents, and from the point of view of science it is impossible not to accept the judgment which the Reverend Baden Powell, Savilian professor of geometry at Oxford, put on his books. With these works, thought Powell after Miller's death,

the very last possible resources of Biblical interpretation must be regarded as thoroughly exhausted. They are the very ghost of defunct Biblical geology; and even those who cannot perceive the essential and inherent irrationality of all ideas of mixing up the deductions of science with the language of Scripture, must now admit that all such attempts *have* practically failed; and they must henceforth be content to allow geology uninterruptedly to extend the domain of natural order, through the infinity of past time, while they may learn that the cosmogony of the Mosaic law, with that dispensation of which it is a part, has passed away and been superseded: the one by an inductive philosophy; the other, by a spiritual religion.[96]

It is significant that this is the evaluation, not of a geologist, but of a mathematician and theologian, who later was one of the contributors to the celebrated *Essays and Reviews*,[97] the earliest important British venture into the field of higher criticism. Baden Powell's essay in this volume was not the first of his writings to seem alarming in orthodox circles. Ever since the 1830's he had been insisting in a series of forceful, if somewhat discursive, books that there was simply no relation at all between the words of Scripture and the results of scientific research.[98] A number of geologists also paid lip service to this principle, of course, but, with the possible exception of Lyell, Powell went further than any of them and applied the principle of separation with greater rigor. Geology, he held, and to a less degree the other sciences, directly contradicted many passages in the Old Testament, no matter how tortured an interpretation be put on the texts, and it was no use blinking the fact. But this discredited only those who had misconceived the nature of scientific and scriptural information; it did not impair the validity of either. On the contrary, both would benefit by being freed from a mutually debilitating tradition. Science would be relieved of a host of ridiculous and embarrassing difficulties, while reverence for the real value of the Bible would increase when it was generally recognized that the Lord had manifested Himself to us in the New Testament and that He had imparted His truth to the ancient Jews of the Old Testament through poetic imagery and dramatic allegory, these being the modes of expression best suited to a rude, nomadic society.[99]

Advanced as it was, this position was still a long distance short of Huxley's agnosticism. For in Powell's opinion, the innumerable and futile efforts to square the results of physical research with the Biblical narrative had obscured the real and commanding support which natural philosophy could bring to religious belief. Before Scripture could be accepted as binding in its own sphere, it was first necessary to prove the existence of the sort of deity who could give a revelation. This was preeminently the function of natural theology, which in turn rested wholly on the findings of science. "The investigation of God's works is an essential introduction to the right reception of his word," and Powell went even further and quoted with approval a writer who held that "the study of natural philosophy and natural theology, if rightly pursued, are one; and true science but a perpetual worship of God in the firmament of His power." [100] Powell's discussion of the method by which natural philosophy demonstrated the existence of God was as liberal as his attitude towards Scripture. The very possibility of inductive philosophy (and all *real* science was inductive) depended on recognition of the uniformity, immutability, and sufficiency of natural laws, and this characteristic of nature was also the best assurance that behind it there was an anterior moral purpose.

> Throughout the utmost extent of our investigation of physical causes, we trace the proofs of that moral volition which is *prior* and *superior* to them all; proofs exhibited alike throughout all the vastness and all the minuteness of the universe; increasing and augmenting in overwhelming multiplicity, with no other limit than that imposed on the extent of our observations and inductions.[101]

Design, not interference, argues God. Powell was very scornful of the prevailing tendency to illustrate the divine government of the course of nature by a number of exceptional instances in which God was supposed to have stepped in and controlled events directly. This interpretation began by admitting the very thing which it was the great function of science to prove — the existence of God. There was, moreover, no convincing evidence of occasional interventions, and if there were, it would indicate only that nature was an unpredictable chaos instead of the product of divine omnipotence. Powell, needless to say, supported Lyell against the catastrophists, and he was also one of the few scientists who was sympathetic to the *Vestiges of Creation*.[102]

In his interpretation of the ultimate meaning of science, Powell, though considerably more radical than most scientists in the generation before Darwin's, was far from rejecting the possibility of a natural theology. Quite the contrary, by separating science from Scripture, he hoped to strengthen the connection between science and religion. He had very few supporters, and he did not succeed. Neither, however, did those whose interpretations he opposed.

VII

HOW USEFUL IS THY DWELLING PLACE

The man who has been accustomed to study natural objects philosophically, to be perpetually guarding against the delusions of the fancy, will not readily be induced to multiply words so as to forget things. From observing in the relations of inanimate objects fitness and utility, he will reason with deeper reverence concerning beings possessing life; and perceiving in all the phenomena of the universe the designs of a perfect intelligence, he will be averse to the turbulence and passion of hasty innovations, and will uniformly appear as the friend of tranquillity and order.

— Sir Humphry Davy (1802) [1]

We must, therefore, impregnate the popular mind with the truths of natural science, teaching them in every school, and recommending, if not illustrating them, from every pulpit.

— Sir David Brewster (1854) [2]

I

In early industrial Britain every important department of thought and activity was in some way touched or shaped by the effects of utilitarian social philosophy and evangelical religious belief. The majority of scientists were as practical and as devout as most Englishmen, and in science the influence of the two dominant currents of contemporary opinion is apparent in the importance which scientists attached to speaking and writing for the general public and in the fact that the tone of popular science was both utilitarian and theological. Nor were these characteristics of the literature unrelated. It has often been observed that however different the intellectual background and religious tenets of utilitarianism and evangelicalism, the practical effects of the two movements were frequently parallel if not identical. Both philosophic radicals and evangelicals, for example, enjoined similar types of social behavior. Benthamites urged the individual to take advantage of the dispensations of nature and to appreciate the necessitarian quality of the sanctions which dictated this line of action, while at the same time evangelicals urged the individual to take advantage of the dispensations of Providence and to appreciate the divine quality of the sanctions. The conclusions were already the same, but by means of science even the two arguments could be amalgamated. Since the opening of the century, natural theology, which in Paley's hands had given off an atmosphere of rather arid common sense, had become suffused with the evangelical spirit, and it was the function of natural theology to assimilate nature to Providence and necessity to the divine will.

Geology, then, although it was the most popular science with the British public, was not the only one to be popularized. And although no other science produced disagreements of the sort which afflicted the growth of geology, neither was it the only one to be invested with theological significance. An explanation of the appeal of geology should, therefore, be attempted, after which a consideration of the theology of science and of some of the movements and motives for popularization may cast some light both on the difficulties which cropped up in geological interpretation and on their significance as products of early nineteenth-century opinion in Britain.

2

Throughout England there were, probably, no communities in which physical science was held in such low esteem as it was in Oxford and Cambridge.[3] Even there, however, geology was the most prominent branch of a generally neglected field of study, and in the first half of the century it was the only science to the advancement of which either university made any significant contribution.

At Oxford during the 1820's — and Oxford was always less interested in science than Cambridge — Buckland attracted an average of more than fifty undergraduates annually to his course of lectures on geology and thirty to the series he gave on

mineralogy, so many that his lecture room, one of the famous
sights of the university, had to be enlarged. Over the same
period, Professor Rigaud's course on natural philosophy aver-
aged forty-two students a year, Dr. Kidd's anatomy course
twenty-nine, and Professor Daubeny's chemistry lectures
twenty-eight. Attendance on science lectures fell off radically
after 1830, although the decline did not hit Buckland as badly
as it did his colleagues — in 1835 and again in 1838 Professor
Rigaud would have had no listeners if it had not been for two
or three who turned up from Christ Church in compliance with
that college's requirement that its members attend one course
of science lectures.[4]

The tractarian movement undoubtedly helped to bring about
this discouraging state of scientific affairs in the 1830's, because
even if the antagonism of its leaders to science had had little
effect, the religious issue they raised tended to absorb the attention of the more intellectual members of the university. But
apart from this factor, the declining attendance at public lectures did not necessarily reflect any weakening in the intrinsic
appeal of science. It seems, instead, to have been the effect of
the increasing rigor of the competition for formal honors following upon the introduction in 1830 of separate honors examinations. All candidates for a degree, whether pass or honors, had
to take examinations, not on any of the material presented by
the professors, however, but only on the subjects defined as
mathematics or *litterae humaniores*, for which they were prepared both by the collegiate tutorial body, who also conducted
the examinations, and — increasingly — by private tutors or
crammers.[5] There was, therefore, no curricular incentive for attending lectures — quite the reverse, in fact. In commenting on
the diminishing number of students in his courses and in those
of his colleagues, Buckland thought that it must be attributed
to a basic flaw in the system of education, which discouraged
undergraduates from devoting their time to physical science,
since it had occurred while the study of geology was making
rapid progress elsewhere in England.[6] Buckland's explanation
was confirmed independently by Lyell, who remarked,

It is truly fortunate that, in proportion as Oxford and Cambridge have withdrawn their countenance more and more from studies connected with physical science and natural history, the wants of a high state of civilization, and the spirit of the age, have afforded to them in England an annually increasing patronage.[7]

Contemporary enthusiasm for geology and natural history is reflected in the early Victorian novel in the frequency with which worthy characters are represented as occupying their leisure hours in the accumulation and contemplation of a cabinet of fossils. One of the reasons for the popularity of geology was that the material was easily comprehensible while its interpretation was highly controversial, and one need not be an expert in order to stand a reasonable chance of making important discoveries. In addition, the romantic revival probably attracted numbers of intelligent observers to a study for which the sources lay among sounding cataracts and tempestuous gorges. In books like Mantell's *Wonders of Geology*, the illustrations — not to mention the title — emphasize the weird and the awe-inspiring quality of the ancient countryside.[8] "Geology," thought the astronomer, Sir John Herschel, "in the magnitude and sublimity of the objects of which it treats, undoubtedly ranks, in the scale of sciences, next to astronomy." [9] Very likely, too, traveling conditions before the age of railways were conducive to casual geological observation. An informed contemplation of the landscape was eminently the sort of thing which a gentleman of taste was expected to enjoy. Geology was even thought a suitable accomplishment for ladies. Lady Mary Cole, for example, and her daughters, the Misses Jane and Charlotte Talbot, carried out some of Buckland's preliminary researches in Paviland Cave,[10] and fifteen or twenty years later the attendance of ladies upon the programs of the geological section of the British Association was an annual adornment to the science and the envy of the other divisions. This point particularly impressed the correspondent who reported the meeting of the association at York in 1844 for the readers of *Chambers's Edinburgh Journal*:

The medical, statistical, and mechanical sections were on this occasion thinly attended; the chemical, zoological, and physical moderately; and the geological largely. The last, indeed, seems to be at all times the leading department of the association. The great writers in the science are always present; hence curiosity: then the comparative intelligibleness and popular interest of the subject is attractive. What is strange, there is [*sic*] generally almost as many ladies as gentlemen present.[11]

The geologists had been instrumental in the foundation in 1831 of the British Association for the Advancement of Science, and their enthusiasm was an important element in ensuring its success in the years following.[12] By establishing an annual scientific congress open to the general public, the founders expected to avail themselves of the labors of a host of amateur observers, and by staging their show in the provinces instead of in London, they further hoped to encourage the pursuit of natural philosophy as a hobby.[13] It did, in fact, become something of a pageant. Over the years the titles of the officers grew more and more exalted. The importance of official banquets began to dim the "intellectual sunshine" which, according to Sedgwick, had illuminated the early meetings.[14] It is doubtful whether the association ever became what it intended to be — both a popular forum and a Baconian clearinghouse for the multitude of sciences which were splintering off into their own specialized societies.[15] Still, it was a good show, a serious and solid demonstration of the social utility of science, and well suited to the temper of the times. Rebels against the ethos of industrial capitalism, the Oastlers and Kebles, duly and instinctively attacked the British Association,[16] and possibly the organization did help to precipitate the synthesis of Manchester scholasticism from which it simultaneously sought and won support for science.

The *Edinburgh Review* opened its discussion of the foundation and early years of the British Association with a few reflections on the political and social convulsions which had racked Europe since 1789, and the article implied that enlightened institutions for the propagation of science were to be regarded as a bulwark against anything of the sort in the future. "The education of the people — the diffusion of knowledge —

the encouragement of literature and talent of every kind, are the only ballast for a government like ours, exposed to the double hostility of popular menace and aristocratical inroad." [17] The founders had themselves regarded popularization as a desirable and hopeful by-product of the work of the British Association, but most of the meetings were conducted on an intellectual level which would have been interesting only to a reasonably well-educated audience and on a social level which would have been possible only for a fairly prosperous one. This did not mean, however, that scientists disagreed with the *Edinburgh Review* and with other leaders of opinion on the importance of disseminating an understanding of the principles and meaning of science among the lower classes. Popular lectures by outstanding scientists enjoyed a great vogue. And if the British Association appealed to a primarily middle-class following, science for the masses was the main objective of Mechanics' Institutes and the Society for the Diffusion of Useful Knowledge, both of which were loyally supported by the leaders of the British Association. And the necessity for educating workingmen in the principles of the enterprises which depended on their labors was also one of the arguments most frequently pressed by educational reformers in the thirties and the forties.

These movements are usually said to be examples of a rationalist and humanitarian belief in educational reform as simply a good thing in itself. And, indeed, they were enthusiastically forwarded by the foremost philosophic radicals in the twenties and thirties. The objective of the philosophic radicals was the maximum liberation of individual talents, and towards this end they encouraged the pursuit of the greatest material happiness, it being assumed — if it was not demonstrated — that natural law rendered this felicitous condition the proper yardstick of morality. The bearing of science upon the beneficence of industrial arrangements was eagerly adduced to the same purpose, but that bearing was used less to illustrate natural design than to confirm divine sanction. Perhaps the method of the argument was not so exclusively rational as is often supposed. Outside of Bentham's immediate circle, the assumption of natural law seems to have left lingering doubts even among leaders of progressive opinion. The overwhelmingly theological tone of the social philosophy of science, whether sincere or contrived, suggests either that naturalism was not enough or else that it was not convincing enough.

For example, George Combe, whose reputation as a radical educational reformer has not survived his simultaneous advocacy of phrenology, put "God's secular Providence" at the center of the system of scientific education which was to safeguard British society from vain and destructive revolutions like those of 1848.[18] Despite the impeccable nature of this objective, however, Combe was widely suspected of being dangerous, unsound, and heterodox. He frequently expressed sympathy for the condition of the working classes. Phrenology, although it created quite a stir in the twenties and thirties, was never in good odor among responsible scientists. And Combe accused the churches of having obscured the true character of the divine moral government by picturing God as an Old Testament deity who continually interfered in the affairs of the world to reward or punish directly. Like Chambers (who, in fact, was deeply indebted to Combe's *Constitution of Man* [19]), Combe extended uniformitarianism from natural to moral and political philosophy. The great achievement of physical science, he felt, had been to demonstrate that God governs the material universe through unchangeable laws of behavior and not through supernatural interventions. Moral laws of an equivalent generality govern the political, social, and economic world. It was because the churches had not brought their moral teaching into line with the outlook of science that religion and science sometimes seemed opposed. Properly understood, however, "Science is an exposition of the order of Nature, and the order of Nature is just another form of expression for the course of God's providence in the affairs of this world." [20]

Combe was the leader of a movement for secular education, and since his efforts aroused considerable uneasiness in conservative circles, the limitations of his radicalism cast an interesting light on the ideas of educational reformers. The purpose of Combe's educational system was to demonstrate to all classes that their interest lay in conforming to natural law and not, so far as laborers were concerned, in revolution, nor, so far as manufacturers were concerned, in grinding the last penny of profit out of the poor. It was, however, chiefly to the poor that Combe addressed himself, since only they, he felt, could actually do much to better their own circumstances. "Ignorant minds . . . attribute evils which result from their own gross errors in conduct to the system of things, and fly to dreams of future happiness as the compensation for their miseries instead of proceeding to obey the dictates of nature and remove them." [21]

Combe and his associates in London and Edinburgh employed the term "secular education" in a curious sense, or, as they insisted, in its original sense, for by "secular" they did not mean to exclude religion but only to dispense with its doctrinal, dogmatic, and sectarian elements. These matters, affecting irrelevancies like salvation and immortality, should be left to the churches. Adult-education courses and secondary schools would confine themselves to applying the mandates of "true religion" — i.e., science — to the things of this world. "The divine authority of the Moral Law was especially and most powerfully enforced in Mr. Combe's teaching, and not only moral law and moral duties, but physical law and physical duties were based on the same authority, but only applied to the world." [22] This, according to Combe himself, would "convey to the minds of the young a perception of their actually living under a scheme of Divine Government which favours temperance, frugality, industry, intelligence, morality, and religion in this world." Combe laid the calamities of 1848 to popular ignorance of the "natural laws by which individual and social well-being is determined." [23] Such evils would be averted only when workingmen understood that the truths of physical science, political economy, and moral philosophy were necessitarian because rooted in the decrees of divine Providence. Not only George Combe but the whole chorus of publicists preaching science to the masses referred its message just as insistently, and nearly unanimously, to the ultimate sanction of a providential plan, which shed a more resplendent and commanding light than that of pure naturalism upon the relations of scientist, manufacturer, and mechanic.

Education can be regarded as contributing both to the improvement of social conditions and to making clear the necessity for conforming to the best of possible conditions, and proponents of popular science seldom made any distinction between these objectives. Most of them, indeed, were probably unaware of any distinction. The motives of their opponents were similarly mixed. When the movements for education of the masses are described simply as enlightened humanitarianism, the fact that many Tories and conservative publications like *The Times* and the *Quarterly Review* disliked the idea of popularizing science is usually attributed to benightedness, an opinion often expressed at the time and one which undoubtedly contains considerable truth. It is, also, however, an opinion which can bear some qualification, because not all the advantages which were expected to flow from a wider knowledge of science were of the sort in which a tender social conscience could take unlimited satisfaction, any more than in, say, the Malthusian Poor Law of 1834, which was also attacked by *The Times* and the *Quarterly*.

The editors of these periodicals were suspicious not so much of science as of the groups under whose auspices Mechanics' Institutes and the Society for the Diffusion of Useful Knowledge had grown up. In an article on "Popular Science," the *Quarterly*, for example, dismissed as more than a little absurd the exaggerated hopes of flushing whole coveys of "mute, inglorious Bacons" and "village Newtons" and of reforming human nature through dissemination of science. The reviewer criticized popular science because its message to the populace was Benthamite and its scientific content was superficial. But as to science itself, the *Quarterly* agreed with Bacon, who had assigned "science a two-fold object, the relief of man's estate, and the glory of the Creator. There has never, in this country, been a disposition to underrate its last, and most honoured use. In the same spirit in which they studied the 'book of God's word,' Englishmen have studied the 'book of God's works.' " And the article closed with a disapproving glance at France, where "atheism, without limitation or disguise, has too often been blended with an extensive acquaintance with natural philosophy" — a shallow Gallic tendency of which Comte was the latest and one of the most regrettable instances.[24]

The energy and values of Henry Brougham are a handy and fairly accurate epitome of many characteristics of these decades. His view of the utility of popular science demonstrates that however earnestly radicals pressed for liberation of the individual, they were not unconcerned about securing the group's acquiescence in their brand of liberation. "We ask you," begged Charles Knight, Brougham's amanuensis of Useful Knowledge, "*as a body*, to strive with all your powers to raise the standard of your enjoyment." [25] Workingmen, to whom this plea was addressed, would find the necessary tools, "knowledge, industry, and prudence," [26] in the publications of the Society for the Diffusion of Useful Knowledge, which Brougham founded in 1828. The useful knowledge it diffused was cast in a vein of moralizing condescension. "The peace of the country," thought Brougham, "and the stability of the government, could not be more effectually secured than by the universal diffusion of this kind of knowledge." [27] Both religion and society would benefit, for "the more widely science is diffused, the better will the Author of all things be known, and the less will the people be 'tossed to and fro by the sleight of men, and cunning craftiness, whereby they lie in wait to deceive.' " [28]

Brougham had already been the foremost patron of the London Mechanics' Institute, founded in 1823 upon the suggestion of the *Mechanics' Magazine*.[29] Its supporters anticipated an immediate strengthening of the moral fiber of the British nation so soon as laborers turned their surplus energies to cultivating the intellectual benefits derived from science instead of the dissipations derived from pub, pothouse, and trades combinations.[30] And three years later, the *Edinburgh Review*, in an attack on a pamphlet by an anonymous country gentleman who had expressed the fear that educating the working classes would teach them to aspire above themselves, contrasted the peaceable way in which the laboring classes had suffered the depression and distress of 1826 to their turbulence in similar circumstances in 1817 and 1819; and the reviewer attributed this change largely to the enlightening influence of popular education and popular science.[31] Benthamites were enthusiastic about a good thing when they saw it — besides Brougham and Bentham himself, J. C. Hobhouse, Charles Knight, Francis Place, and William Ellis, one of Combe's associates, were initial subscribers to the institute; and Dr. George Birkbeck, who was prevailed upon to accept the presidency, had for some time been a friend of the two Mills, Grote, Ricardo, and other members of the utilitarian circle.[32] About twenty years before, Birkbeck, at that time professor of natural philosophy at the Andersonian Institution in Glasgow, had been responsible for inaugurating there a highly successful course of popular lectures for workingmen.[33] Earlier in 1823 these lectures at Glasgow, then given by Birkbeck's successor, Andrew Ure, had developed into the Glasgow Mechanics' Institute, which was held up as a model to London artisans. Dr. Ure, incidentally, was also the author of two of the most egregious volumes published in the nineteenth century — one a more than usually forced and insistent reconciliation of geology with Genesis, in which the providential barrier to social chaos is particularly apparent, the other a *Philosophy of Manufacturers*, a really grotesque demonstration of the beneficence of devil-take-the-hindmost natural law in the factories.[34]

Scientists who were requested to give lectures in the new institute responded nobly and generously, but somehow or other trouble began to develop almost immediately in spite of the fact that Mr. Brougham came to nearly every meeting "encouraging, by his own deep attention to the lectures, the attention of others." [35] In less than a year the *Mechanics' Magazine*, edited by Joseph Robertson and Thomas Hodgskin, began to criticize the managers bitterly. Brougham, Birkbeck, and Ellis, felt the editors, were taking control of the institute out of the hands of the laborers for whom it was founded and turning it to their own purposes.[36] The clientele was becoming increasingly middle class; tea was displacing applied philosophy; and the formal lectures, though well attended, were overly moral and insufficiently practical. Provincial institutes seem to have followed the same pattern. Established on a wave of utilitarian enthusiasm for the uplifting educational potentialities of applied science, they soon found themselves ministering to a class of people who already had sufficient leisure and education to appreciate their message.

How far this failure was inevitable and how far it was hastened by over-edification it is difficult to say, but certainly the promoters of the enterprise were motivated by more than the desire to brighten the corners of every humble dwelling with the pure gleam of Newtonian mechanics. There was, of course, sincerity in the reiterated contention that manufacturing would be more efficient if every fireman knew why a steam engine worked, but the underlying objective seems to have been a mass demonstration not only of why the British machine as a whole worked, but of why it should work.

So, at least, thought Henry Brougham. In his view there were two mundane reasons for studying science: its obvious utility to an industrial country, and the satisfaction it afforded the individual, be he a Newton or a humble gleaner of fossils. Besides these,

the highest of all our gratifications in the contemplations of science remains: we are raised by them to an understanding of the infinite wisdom and goodness which the Creator has displayed in all his works. . . It teaches us to look on all earthly objects as insignificant and below our notice, except the pursuit of knowledge and the cultivation of virtue — that is to say, the strict performance of our duty in every relation of society.[37]

Brougham developed this point in vast detail in his edition of Paley's *Natural Theology*, which he found time to bring out while fighting the Reform Bill through the Lords. The preliminary treatise argues that natural theology, and hence science, was necessary to the support of revelation, if revelation was to have any utility. Without these tools, one might indeed prove the existence of a God, but not of a God who took any cognizance of social relations, "as indeed the Epicureans believed in the existence of the gods, but held them to keep wholly aloof from human affairs, leaving the world, physical as well as moral, to itself, without the least interference in its concerns." [38] This would never do, and Lord Brougham seems to say that a miraculous revelation can prove nothing except the exercise of miraculous power, which is in itself no evidence of the trustworthiness of the message it transmits. Without Paley, in other words, one might well be justified in thinking Christ a fraud, however successful He was as a magician.[39]

Nearly everyone who was articulate about his approval of natural science agreed with Brougham upon its twofold *raison d'être*: its utility to the maintenance and extension of British commercial and industrial supremacy, and the evidence it afforded of God's continuing concern for material progress in His creation.[40] The former motivation led the majority of scientists to take an active part in forwarding the application of their researches to industry, agriculture, and mining.[41] The latter put them in the van of the campaign for popularization and dissemination of the "principles" of science.

Sir Humphry Davy, to take one of the most notable examples, devoted some of his best efforts to agricultural chemistry, the miners' safety lamp, and other applications of chemical science. In 1802 he delivered his first series of popular lectures on chemistry at the Royal Institution, and he began with a somewhat stately introductory address which traced the importance of chemistry to science and of science to humanity; his remarks are said to have created a sensation.[42] Thanks to having been "informed through the beneficence of the Deity, by science and the arts," man over the centuries has turned his environment to utilitarian purposes and has transformed himself from a savage, sensual creature into a comfortable, rational being.[43] But material progress, while important, is only the outward and visible sign of the progress of the human spirit. More fundamental is the general improvement of the mind which has resulted from devotion to science, and Davy urged that more people of all classes and stations in life should avail themselves of the opportunity afforded by science to enrich their intellectual enjoyments. What has been accomplished already was only a fraction of what remained to be done. Expanding the cultivation of scientific pursuits was the surest way of ameliorating social relations both because material progress and prosperity would be hastened and because the minds best equipped to understand the essential principles of social well-being were those disciplined and enlarged by the study of nature.

The unequal division of property and of labour, the difference of rank and condition amongst mankind, are the sources of power in civilized life, its moving causes, and even its very soul; and in considering and hoping that the human species is capable of becoming more enlightened and more happy, we can only expect that the great whole of society should be ultimately connected together by means of knowledge and the useful arts; that they should act as the children of one great parent with one determinate end, so that no power may be rendered useless, no exertions thrown away.[44]

Science, therefore, should be actively forwarded as an avocation for members of all classes. It would develop, in the upper ranks, an understanding of the responsibilities attaching to position and, in the lower ranks, an appreciation of the necessity and benefits of just gradations and subordinations.

Davy's political opinions were formed during the period of reaction against the French Revolution. During his lifetime the Tories were in power in the government, and they had not yet developed the social conscience with which, after 1830, some of them responded to the factory conditions, the Poor Law, and the domination of the political scene by liberal political principles, and which made many Tories antipathetic to the increasingly Benthamite character of popular science. Social attitudes, however, did not always neatly follow party lines in these years. Among scientists themselves, as well as among a great many influential laymen, the utility and social significance of science were conceptions comprehensive enough to embrace differences of political outlook. Although Sir John Herschel, to take another prominent illustration, was generally Whiggish in his sympathies, his opinion on the value of science was very like Davy's. Nor, on the other hand, were Herschel's views on its social implications much different from those of the semi-Benthamite Brougham. Unlike Brougham, however, a politician whose only contribution to science was that of a publicist, Herschel was primarily a scientist, and he emphasized a point usually ignored by lay commentators. The ultimate purpose of research, thought Herschel, was the advancement of knowledge for its own sake. It was vulgar, distracting, and harmful to expect immediate applications and useful results to flow from every investigation.[45]

Nevertheless, such results do flow, and both on that account and because of the constructive moral and intellectual influence of science, Herschel made a number of efforts to help keep the public abreast of science. The Lords of the Admiralty had thought it would be well for the officers and even the men of the Royal Navy to occupy their off-duty hours in scientific observations of one sort or another, and Herschel edited a volume of essays outlining the subjects to which sailors might make some avocational contributions and containing instructions on how to observe and record useful information.[46] Assistance and encouragement of this sort should, Herschel felt, be offered to the people generally. A wider comprehension of nature would have a direct influence on political and moral stability in an age when legislation was becoming increasingly scientific, when the theories of political economy had been soundly established, and when, consequently, the conditions of social progress were being isolated and understood.[47] After passage of the Reform Bill of 1832, the importance of a wider dissemination of the principles of social well-being seemed so pressing to Herschel that he accepted the presidency of an institute founded to build a public library and reading room in Windsor and Eton. He insisted that a special section be set aside to provide for the entertainment and the intellectual and moral improvement of the poorer classes. This project he regarded as part of "a process on which it is no exaggeration to say, that the future destinies of this empire will very mainly depend — because on it depends, by a natural and indissoluble link, our capacity as a nation for a high degree of civil liberty." [48]

Most scientists mounted the lecture platform without the slightest reluctance. Seldom did a British Association meeting go by without Buckland or Sedgwick or Murchison addressing a public gathering, usually an outdoor one, on the megatherium or the iguanodon or the origin of British coal deposits, and seldom did a lecture go by without the moral of beneficent Providence being pointed. Sedgwick was particularly anxious to reach the class of artisans, for whom he professed a deep respect.[49] So great was the demand for this sort of thing in lyceums, Mechanics' Institutes, and provincial natural history societies that Lord Arthur Hervey, Bishop of Bath and Wells, urged the universities to establish professorial chairs whose occupants would be relieved of teaching duties in order to devote their energies to popular scientific lectures. "Such men may well think it a mission of no mean importance to light the torch of pure science and hold it out to those who are in danger of being bewildered and seduced." By such a program, thought the bishop, the universities would lay up intellectual treasure with the masses, and the masses would perceive "the advantages which the noble Universities of this land confer upon the wealthier classes" and would "see the knowledge of nature advance hand in hand with the knowledge of the Word of God, till that happy condition of the human mind becomes the portion of the people at large, when Christian truth has the full assent of a cultivated reason, and the truths of science acquire a fresh glow of beauty by being traced to the Wisdom and Power" of the Creator.[50]

Besides the Mechanics' Institutes, London also offered enlightenment to the curious in the lectures at the Royal Institution and at the Society of Arts, revitalized under Prince Albert's presidency after 1843. As professor of natural philosophy at the Jermyn Street School of Mines, Huxley first won public attention by his addresses to workingmen, though he undoubtedly cast his material in a somewhat exceptional framework.[51] Nevertheless, the vast majority of naturalists who undertook to educate the public were perfectly orthodox, none more so than Leonard Horner, first warden of the London University. In 1821 Horner had founded a School of Arts in Edinburgh. "He is a most useful citizen," wrote one Edinburgh gentleman after the opening, "and it is of great importance to have such a person here, not of the law. I have no doubt that with his excellent habits of arrangement and of business, of good manners, science, and whiggism, he will in time greatly raise the character and zeal of our merchants and tradesmen." [52] After 1836 Horner was a leading spirit in the movement to establish after-hours schools for factory children. He even volunteered to act as an inspector under the Factory Acts, and it would be a mistake to regard as simple hypocrisy his picture of the eagerness with which the children sped from loom to primer. Within the limits of the Manchester school philosophy, he sincerely wanted to look out for their welfare.[53]

An astonished German chemist has left an account of one of the fetes of science with which the British public was so frequently regaled. In 1839 the British Association was meeting at Birmingham. Near by lay the famous Dudley Caverns, an artificial cave over a mile in length produced by the quarrying of limestone. Lord Ward, the owner, thought it appropriate to honor the Association by throwing his very profitable cavern open to the public. He spent hundreds of pounds upon candles and torches for illumination and provided boats to carry distinguished guests along the canal which led into the center of the hill to the chief attraction, lectures by Murchison and Buckland on the geology and mineralogy of the iron industry. Several thousand of the more humble visitors, unable to get places in the barges, clambered through paths and passages to the middle of the cave, where they listened to Murchison speak for over an hour about the stratigraphical characteristics of the region and the processes of coal formation. The scene was like Dante's Inferno, according to the somewhat bewildered Herr Schönbein, who, unlike the rest of the audience, had had enough when Murchison stopped speaking.

But that the thirst for knowledge of every one might be satisfied, Buckland went to the gallery, placed himself on a mighty block of stone, and lectured for more than an hour, he and his numerous audience being veiled in the wreathing sulphur smoke, upon the subject already handled by Murchison, but in so original and humorous a manner that he held the attention of his listeners in a way seldom witnessed. . . As is well known, the English have a peculiar love of regarding Nature from a theological point of view, and the celebrated Oxford geologist, as he proved by his last geological work, is no exception to the rule. The immeasurable beds of iron-ore, coal, and limestone, which are to be found in the neighbourhood of Birmingham, lying beside or above one another, and to which man has only to help himself in order to procure for his use the most useful of all metals in a liberal measure, may not, he urged, be considered as mere accident. On the contrary, it in fact expresses the most clear design of Providence to make the inhabitants of the British Isles, by means of this gift, the most powerful and the richest nation on the earth. This theme was treated by Buckland with every permissible variation, to the no small edification of the listening country people, and to my own great pleasure, even though I may not be able to accept his leading idea.[54]

There were very few English scientists who had any doubts about the leading idea, a compound of physical science, Providence, popularization, and patriotism: led by Buckland, the meeting moved back towards the light of day, singing "God Save the Queen."

3

Some few years later Dr. Buckland, then Dean of Westminster Abbey, was reading another side of the message in another limestone cavern. His congregation, he thought, was fortunate in having so little opportunity for error; the lesson of 1848 was clear to all:

Modern professors, in carrying their researches more closely into God's laws, by which He regulates the movements of the material world, have been permitted to gaze more intensely on . . . the infinite wisdom and power and goodness of the Creator. . .

The God of Nature has determined that moral and physical inequalities shall not only be inseparable from our humanity, but co-extensive with His whole creation. He has also given compensations coordinate with these inequalities, working together for the conservation of all orders and degrees in that graduated scale of being which is the great law of God's providence on earth. From the mammoth to the mouse, from the eagle to the humming-bird, from the minnow to the whale, from the monarch to the man, the inhabitants of the earth and air and water form but one vast series of infinite gradations in an endless chain of inequalities of organic structure and of physical perfections. . .

So also there never was, and, while human nature remains the same, there never can be, a period in the history of human society when inequalities of worldly condition will not follow the unequal use of talents and opportunities originally the same: industry and idleness, virtue and vice, lead the same talents, with the same means and opportunities, well used or abused, to most unequal results. . . Equality of mind or body, or of worldly condition, is as inconsistent with the order of Nature as with the moral laws of God. . . There may be equality in poverty: equality of riches is impossible. . . Equality of wealth and property never has and never can exist, except in the imagination of wild transcendental theorists, so long as human nature shall continue to be that imperfect thing which God has placed in this world in a state of moral probation.[55]

This is a view of a necessary order of nature which, together with a demonstration of its beneficence, constituted the central message in the vast literature of natural theology in which early industrial England enshrined its understanding of popular science.

Perhaps the most zealous of the many popular writers on elementary science was Thomas Dick, a Scottish schoolmaster, the success of whose first book, *The Christian Philosopher*, encouraged him to abandon a teaching career in order to devote all his time to spreading the gospel of useful knowledge.[56] Dick sought to stabilize the minds and improve the morals of the slightly educated classes. "As science has it for one of its highest objects to investigate the works of the Creator, an *opportunity should be taken* when imparting scientific instructions, *of adverting to the attributes of the Deity as displayed in his operations.*"[57] Much as Dick appreciated the value of Mechanics' Institutes, he was disturbed by the fact that many of them forbade the discussion of religious topics. This, he feared, might be the first symptom in Britain of a movement to separate science from religion and the diffusion of knowledge from the Christian faith, a tendency which, though not yet far advanced, should be arrested at its earliest appearance. If a separation should actually come about, what would be the inevitable consequence? "The recognition of a Supreme intelligence, to whom we are all accountable, would soon be considered unnecessary in scientific investigations"; and as a result, "there would be no reliance on the superintending care of an unerring Providence, ordaining and directing every event to the most beneficial purposes." [58] The immoralities and horrors of the French Revolution stood as an example of what could come of an atheistic philosophy. In recent years, Dick thought, even British scientists had begun to omit allusions to God and His physical Providence from their publications and lectures, and he warned that if once the bonds of society were loosened, science itself would be swept away in the wreckage.

Dick's alarm was somewhat premature. Before the middle of the century there were, in fact, very few British scientists who did not from time to time refer to the idea that scientific research enlarges our comprehension of the Creator's plans for the world. Disagreements did arise about the way in which those plans had been carried out, but there was no public attack upon the frequently expressed assertion that an understanding of them was the highest, though not the only, benefit derived from the progress of physical knowledge. Whether writers like Lyell fell into the prevailing mode for the sake of conviction or of convention, they never challenged it. Even had they wished to do so, it would, of course, have been very difficult for them. As Lyell complained in a moment of irritation at his clerical detractors, almost all the academic posts for the teaching and advancement of science were restricted to scientists who were also clergymen. This may not have been too serious a deterrent since the universities in any case provided a livelihood for only a very few scientists, but even outside the universities a reputation for doubtful religious views would not have advanced a man's worldly prospects in any line of endeavor in early Victorian England. Although such views were held more often than is sometimes supposed, they were seldom publicized. Nevertheless, there does not seem to have been any general feeling of intellectual cramp among scientists, or any sustained chafing at the theological bonds. Even Roderick Murchison, who privately — very privately — bewailed his inability to believe that God was more than a principle of design, had a clear sense of the utility of natural theology, and he concluded the first volume of his severely descriptive *Silurian System* with the remark: "Geology, therefore, in expounding the former condition of the globe, convinces us, that every variation of its surface has been but a step toward the accomplishment of one great end; whilst all such revolutions are commemorated by monuments, which revealing the course and object of each change, compel us to conclude, that the earth can alone have been fashioned into a fit abode for Man by the ordinances of INFINITE WISDOM." [59]

Other scientists did not often participate in the controversies among geologists, and since the progress and interpretation of research in other fields did not touch upon contentious points within the generally accepted framework of natural theology, most scientists who were not directly concerned with geology were only occasionally and incidentally affected by the theological issues involved in explaining the geological record. The *Vestiges of Creation*, of course, met with general condemnation, but the *Vestiges* was not a product of scientific research. On the other hand, the writings of Sir Richard Owen do reflect a strong theological bent. Like most British scientists, Owen accepted the broad idea that the physical universe is the Deity's handiwork, but in his case, as in that of many geologists, theological influence is also apparent in the cast of his particular theories. Before his reputation had been eclipsed by Darwin's, Owen, an anatomist and paleontologist, was the most prominent biologist in Britain. His approach was that of the *Naturphilosophie* of Oken, Geoffroy Saint-Hilaire, and Goethe. According to the somewhat mystical and now totally rejected doctrines of this school, existing forms of life have resulted from variations on a common archetype produced by the operation of the Platonic idea which was the original model of each particular species and which was conceived of as a specific organizing principle or force.[60] In Owen's view,

The recognition of an ideal Exemplar for the Vertebrated animals proves that the knowledge of such a being as Man must have existed before Man appeared. For the Divine mind which planned the Archetype also foreknew all its modifications. . . To what natural laws or secondary causes the orderly succession and progression of such organic phenomena may have been committed we are yet ignorant. But if, without derogation of the Divine power, we may conceive the existence of such ministers, and personify them by the term "Nature," we learn from the past history of our globe that she has advanced with slow and stately steps, guided by the archetypal light, amidst the wreck of worlds, from the first embodiment of the Vertebrate idea under its old Ichthyic vestment, until it became arrayed in the glorious garb of the Human form.[61]

Owen is particularly interesting because, unlike the continental *Naturphilosophen*, who tended to be uniformitarians and evolutionists in opposition to Cuvier, Owen was not unsympathetic to the catastrophist outlook. His expressions on the descent of species were always peculiarly cloudy, but he remained on the whole a consistent opponent of evolutionism. He is generally supposed to have coached Bishop Wilberforce for his attack on Darwin at the British Association meeting in 1860, and in the 1840's Whewell, Murchison, and Sedgwick had besought him to lend his prestige to the refutation of the *Vestiges*.[62]

In the 1840's and 1850's there was a minor flurry as to whether other planets might be populated, a question which had lain dormant since the early eighteenth century.[63] The argument, however, was conducted largely on geological and religious rather than astronomical grounds. No important astronomers participated in it. Astronomy, it was felt by both sides, might occasion the issue but could not settle it. The discussion produced a large and rather redundant literature, the character of which may be indicated by a brief consideration of the contributions of William Whewell and Sir David Brewster, who led the opposing sides.[64] Whewell, the Master of Trinity College, Cambridge, and something of a scientist as well as a historian of science, was disturbed by the popularity of the supposition that there are a large number of worlds inhabited by human beings. If the notion were true, it would, he felt, prove deeply unsettling — perhaps even fatal — to the Christian belief that the earth is "in a unique and special manner, the field of God's Providence and Government." [65] Whewell had no objection to the existence of lower forms of life elsewhere in the universe, but a religion basing its claim on a unique revelation of truth, and springing from a single set of historical circumstances, could not be reconciled with the admission that other plants also support "intellectual creatures, living, we must suppose, under a moral law, responsible for transgression, the subjects of a Providential Government." [66] The drama of redemption would become meaningless if it had been repeated all over the universe; whereas if it had been different wherever it occurred, then our moral law could not be absolutely true.

Whewell admitted the difficulty of supposing, in the face of the vastness of space and the millions of stars, that our physically insignificant earth had been singled out as the special object of God's attention. This embarrassing dilemma, though it could not be resolved on astronomical grounds, disappears when geology is considered, because geology exhibits actual evidence of the intensity of God's interest in preparing, over ages as inconceivably remote in time as the fixed stars are in space, the surface of our planet to be man's abode and the stage for His moral drama. In Whewell's view, the geological record is a history of events that need never have taken place for any intrinsic reason, and the whole process, therefore, is inexplicable except on the assumption that it was intended and directed toward an end. Since there is no reason to imagine that events have occurred otherwise than naturally on the face of other planets, geology affords good, though in the nature of the case not certain, grounds for regarding our planet as the only physical location for the activities of a moral Providence. The science of the earth comes to the assistance of the moral aspects of religion on a point where astronomy, powerfully though it testifies to design, tends to create, if not infidelity, at least uneasiness.[67]

Whewell's argument, published anonymously, was answered by Sir David Brewster, who had been one of the leading spirits in the foundation of the British Association and who defended the popular belief in a plurality of inhabited worlds. The opposing view, he felt, would lead to loss of faith among the rising generation, since it denied that the universe as a whole had any intelligible purpose.[68] Why would other planets and other suns exist, except to support animal and intellectual life? "To exhibit the Divine attributes, and to display the Divine glory to an intellectual and immortal race," were the only reasons for which a material universe could have been created.[69] "Life was not made for matter, but matter for life; and in whatever spot we see its atoms, whether at our feet or in the planets, we may be sure life is there — life to enjoy the light and heat of God's bounty — to study His works, to recognize His glory, and to bless His name." To suppose otherwise was intolerable. It was to imagine the whole mechanism of the heavens running on aimlessly, "fulfilling no purpose that human reason can conceive, — lamps lighting nothing, — fires heating nothing, — waters quenching nothing, — breezes fanning nothing, — everything around, mountain and valley, hill and dale, earth and ocean, all *meaning nothing*." [70] Brewster, too, referred to the evidence of geology, but his arguments are too strange to follow; he did suggest, reasonably enough, that there is no reason to suppose other planets incapable of having their own geologies. His discussion was, if anything, even more theological than Whewell's. He quoted the Bible at length to show that the inspired writings do not exclude the possibility of other populated planets, and that certain passages even imply that they exist. He entered into a mathematical computation to prove that the earth would not provide room for the myriads of resurrected bodies, and that other planets must, therefore, be livable. And he urged that Whewell had gratuitously put himself in the position of the pre-Christian philosophers, "who had no other guide but reason." [71]

In the geological controversies, the development rather than the design of the order of nature was at the root of the trouble. Owen's theories and the rather ridiculous debate between Whewell and Brewster illustrate that the same difficulty was responsible for the few instances in which theological bias shaped the approach to particular problems in other areas of science. As yet, physicists, chemists, and astronomers were not immediately faced with questions of development in prosecuting and interpreting the results of their researches, which could still be described as evidence of design. Outside of geology there was, therefore, no occasion for an attack on the conceptions of natural theology, while inside that science the disagreements were themselves strongly theological.

On the whole, the opinions of British scientists on the relationship of science to religion may be grouped into three broad patterns, which, if not generalizations of the geological issues, did at any rate parallel them on a wider plane of interpretation. In the first place — although there were no geologists who can be put in this class — there were a few scientists who, like Michael Faraday, thought that there was no connection at all between physical science and religious truth, or who, like Thomas Young and John Dalton, never expressed any views about the subject. Faraday was intensely devout, Dalton moderately so, and Young relatively indifferent.[72] (It may be worth remarking that there is no good reason to suppose that as a social group scientists were either more or less pious than any representative cross section of Englishmen would have been.) Not many belong in this category, and it is perhaps significant that among them are three whose scientific achievements were of the first rank, and that, however different their religious convictions, Faraday, Dalton, and Young were alike in being thoroughly uninterested in political questions.

Secondly, an increasing number of scientists, who subscribed to the idea that science is the witness of a divine plan for the universe, took a uniformitarian position and argued that God's provision for the laws of nature is immutable and that science proves their divine origin by demonstrating the self-sufficiency and invariability of their operation and not by finding evidence of exceptional and miraculous interventions, which, in fact, have never occurred. Playfair, Lyell, Powell, Herschel, Babbage, and — on the popularizing level — Chambers and Combe, were all examples of this interpretation. Scientists whose attitude was of this type usually opposed all efforts to reconcile the results of research with the Biblical narrative, but they did not deny that science had a religious function or that the physical universe exhibits divine purpose.

Finally, there was the tradition, of which Neptunism, catastrophism, and the religious objection to the *Vestiges* were expressions, which held that science discovers a Deity who is not only a first cause but also an active governor of His creation, directly participating in its development, continually adapting means to benevolent ends, and by so doing demonstrating His perpetual watchfulness over its behavior and that of its inhabitants.

Scientists who may be put in the first of these classes, the few for whom science had no bearing on religious truth, did not yet constitute anything in the nature of a conscious school. They were simply occasional individuals who, for one reason or another, were indifferent to the question, and, unlike Huxley and his cohorts later in the century, none of them set out to win converts or to remove a theological incubus from scientific thought. Instead, the disputes that arose were between those for whom the material system of things discloses God's plans and original intentions and those for whom it discloses God's control and perpetual attention. And it was members of the latter group who were most upset about the consequences of disseminating among the people at large the wrong view of God's connection with His physical creation.

An exhaustive discussion of all the titles in the literature of natural theology would be a wearisome affair, and it would serve no useful purpose because the message of the school is epitomized at more than sufficient length in the eight *Bridgewater Treatises*. This strange and, to the modern reader, deadly series was commissioned by the will of the Reverend Francis Henry Egerton, eighth Earl of Bridgewater, a noble clergyman who had always neglected his parish assiduously and who died in 1829. Lord Bridgewater charged his executors, the Archbishop of Canterbury, the Bishop of London, and the president of the Royal Society, with the duty of selecting eight scientific authors capable of demonstrating "the Power, Wisdom, and Goodness of God, as manifested in the Creation; illustrating such work by all reasonable arguments, as for instance, the variety and formation of God's creatures in the animal, vegetable, and mineral kingdoms; the effect of digestion, and thereby of conversion; the construction of the hand of man, and an infinite variety of other arguments; as also by discoveries ancient and modern, in arts, sciences, and the whole extent of literature." [73] All the authors chosen knew something of science at first hand. Four were clergymen, four were physicians, and three of the eight had lectured on geology at one of the universities. [74]

The series was intended to offer a working epitome of each of the main branches of natural science, and its final impact was expected to demonstrate the higher meaning of the order of nature and, in Sedgwick's phrase, to "ennoble" empirical discovery into morality. The argument, repeated incessantly, began with triumphant illustrations of the utility of natural arrangements, organic and inorganic. Next there would be brought out the evidence for unity of design. "The argument of design," remarked one of the authors, "is necessarily cumulative; that is to say, is made up of many similar arguments." [75] Dreadfully cumulative it was, and upon it was erected the contention that so single-minded a universe could not have arisen by chance, that it was statistically impossible for such an infinity of occurrences to work together for good without divine direction. Necessity established, it remained only to demonstrate benevolence — the proximity of Britain's iron ore to her coal and limestone, the Providence which ordained that the vegetable cycle should coincide with the solar year, the transcendent goodness which furnished man with a hand and a codfish which had to live under water with an eye that could see there, and so on and so on — Lord Bridgewater's purpose was not only accomplished but accomplished at incontrovertible length.

The first treatise by Thomas Chalmers dealt with the moral and intellectual nature of man as evidence of necessary and benevolent design, and of this something will have to be said later. The second, by the Reverend John Kidd, was supposed to demonstrate the beneficent adaptation of external nature to the physical condition of man: the utility of animals for food and clothing, the comforts consequent upon divine provision for light and heat, the beneficial effects of sleep upon the constitution. The Reverend Mr. Kidd must have assisted his readers to avail themselves of the latter boon. His book is desperately unreadable, particularly since he would obviously have preferred Chalmers' topic; he is forever spilling over into social morality, and in order to expand his work to appropriate length, he dragged Aristotle in by the heels in order to collate him with Cuvier. Even a pagan classification, thought Kidd, inevitably fell into categories which carry conviction of material design to a Christian mind.[76]

The Reverend William Whewell was the only author who expressed his sense of the moral insufficiency of material proofs and who pointed out that laws of nature are simply descriptive generalizations and are, therefore, very different from manmade laws or moral laws. Nevertheless, he felt that his treatise on astronomy and general physics rendered it "impossible to exclude from our conception of this wonderful system, the idea of a harmonizing, a preserving, a contriving, an intending Mind; of a Wisdom, Power, and Goodness far exceeding the limits of our thoughts." [77] Because Whewell (one of the few Englishmen interested in German philosophy) held that there is "a higher region than that of mathematical proof and physical consequence," Charles Babbage thought that he had unwittingly opened the door to the contention that the facts of science could be opposed to the truths of religion.[78] Babbage wrote his *Ninth Bridgewater Treatise, A Fragment* in order to refute this aspect of Whewell's book.[79] This contribution was not an official part of the series, nor was it a welcome addition. The argument proceeds from the uniformity of natural law, and Babbage's remote and lofty Deity had little in common with the God of the other authors.

Sir Charles Bell, who drew that old favorite, the human hand, was a very prominent physician who had spent his life "maintaining the Principles of the English school of Physiology, and in exposing the futility of the opinions of those French philosophers and physiologists, who represented life as the mere physical result of certain combinations and actions of parts, by them termed Organization." [80] Peter Mark Roget's book on animal and vegetable physiology was intended to be both a religious document and an introduction to natural history, though only to those portions of the subject which illustrated the argument from design and the relation of organic structures to final causes.[81] Like his colleagues, he felt it indelicate to employ the word "God" where he could get around it. "In order to avoid the too frequent, and consequently irreverent, introduction of the Great Name of the SUPREME BEING into familiar discourse on the operations of his power, I have . . . followed the common usage of employing the term *Nature* as a synonym, expressive of the same power." [82]

Buckland was entrusted with the sixth treatise on geology and mineralogy. His volumes, though their appearance was eagerly awaited, contained no surprises. In writing them, he had secured the collaboration of William Broderip, Robert Brown, Louis Agassiz, and Richard Owen. Buckland had abandoned the flood by now, but he was still a catastrophist, and he worked in a number of sections to demonstrate how "a system of perpetual destruction, followed by continual renovation, has at all times tended to increase the aggregate of animal enjoyment, over the entire surface of the terraqueous globe." [83] Being the inventions of benevolence, the carnivorous races, for example, increase the sum total of happiness and decrease the amount of pain in the brute creation by preventing overpopulation and putting the weak and inferior out of their misery.

The Reverend William Kirby, who followed Buckland, was assigned the animal kingdom, a subject which he thought a particularly fortunate manifestation of the power, wisdom, and goodness of God. It offered conclusive demonstration both of the fall of man and of subsequent exertions of creative power. No one could suppose Adam and Eve in their pristine state of glory to have been a prey to such disgusting later creations as the lice, fleas, and intestinal worms which now befall the sinner's lot.[84] Kirby was almost a throwback to Deluc. By dint of Hebraic philology he was able to describe the four cherubim through which God governs the creation as symbols for inertia, gravity, heat, and light.[85] Dr. William Prout closed out the series with a job lot of topics: chemistry, meteorology, and the function of digestion. Prout, a really important chemist, thought chemistry a subject eminently suited to Lord Bridgewater's purpose. Since we know comparatively little about its laws, it is more apt to represent the Deity as a free agent.[86] But like all sciences, and like the function of digestion,[87] it demonstrates that all preceding creations were only anticipatory to the creation and governance of man. For, "what would have been the *use* of all this elaborate design, without an ulterior object?" [88]

Thomas Chalmers was entrusted with the most portentous subject of all, the application to human affairs, nature's "ulterior object," of the general argument from a material Providence which could be proved to be necessary and (fortunately) benevolent. The title he chose is instructive: *On the Power, Wisdom, and Goodness of God as Manifested in the Adaptation of External Nature to the Moral and Intellectual Constitution of Man.*[89] It occurred to Dr. Chalmers that he would find powerful testimony to the wisdom and goodness of God in the moral and intellectual constitution of man himself, because, to any individual mind, the impact and relations of the other minds which, added together, make up human society are the most significant aspects of "external nature." He must, therefore, extend his consideration to the human creation by which men are surrounded as surely as they are by inanimate phenomena.

We thus find access to a much larger territory, which should otherwise be left unexplored — and have the opportunity of tracing the marks of a divine intelligence in the mechanism of human society, and in the frame-work of the social and economical systems to which men are conducted, when they adhere to that light, and follow the impulse of those affections which God has bestowed on them.

But in the progress of our argument, we come at length to be engaged with the adaptation of external nature, even in the most strict and limited sense of the term. In the origin and rights of property, as well as in the various economic interests of society, we behold the purest exemplification of that adjustment which obtains between the material system of things and man's moral nature.[90]

It is in the creation of a moral being who prospers according to his conformity with the material system of things that we have the most conclusive evidence of an exquisite and divinely established harmony.

Did we confine our study to inanimate materials, we should find numerous indications of the "natural perfections of the Godhead," but only the fundamental constitution of the human mind and "the adaptation of that constitution to the external world" can attest to his "moral perfection." [91] The best examples may be found in the way in which men are driven to virtue in pursuit of their own pleasure and self-interest. They are endowed, for instance, with a conscience, the satisfaction of which couples righteousness with pleasure. They are further blessed with a sense of charity, which enables a giver of private alms to revel in a happiness matched only by the exquisite gratification of the recipient.[92] If virtue is not its own reward, contentment is. Even the necessity for obtaining food to sustain life is accompanied by the comfort of dining well.

Such is the mechanism of human society, as it comes direct, from the hand of nature or of nature's God. . .

It is by a summation of particular utilities which each man, under the impulse of his own particular affections, contributes to the general good, that nature provides for the happiness of the world.[93]

Although Chalmers presents almost a caricature of some aspects of political economy,[94] he is nonetheless characteristic of the effort to justify God's social ways to man by bringing the prevailing "higher meaning" of science to the elucidation of a sort of deterministic individualism and to read a divine sanction to total individualism from nature's scripture:

The failure of every philanthropic or political experiment which proceeds on the distrust of nature's strong and urgent and general affections, may be regarded as an impressive while experimental demonstration for the matchless wisdom of nature's God. The abortive enterprises of wild yet benevolent Utopianism; the impotent and hurtful schemes of artificial charity which so teem throughout the cities and parishes of our land; the pernicious legislation, which mars instead of mediates, whenever it intermeddles with the operation of a previous and better mechanism than its own — have all of them misgiven only because, instead of conforming to nature, they have tried to divert her from her courses, or have thwarted and traversed the strongest of her implanted tendencies.[95]

Together with family feeling and hunger, thought Dr. Chalmers, the most important "natural affection," and the one most conducive to the well-being of society, was the desire for property which God had implanted in men. The self-interest which a man has in his person or property alone creates a sense of forbearance in regard to his neighbors.[96] It was for this reason that a poor law, or any public provision at all for paupers, was contrary to the law of nature, since public charity deprived the industrious, the successful, and the virtuous of their property in order to encourage the pauper in his "mean, and crouching, and ignoble sordidness. . . There is no common quality whatever between the clamorous onset of this worthless and dissipated crew, and the generous battle-cry *pro aris et focis*, in which the humblest of our population will join — when paternal acres, or the rights of any actually holden property are invaded." [97]

Besides flattering himself on being a man of science, Chalmers was also a Christian minister and found it necessary to demonstrate that the dictates of nature, in the social as well as the physical world, issued from divine benevolence.

When we look at each striving to better his own condition, we see nothing in this but the selfishness of man. When we look at the effect of this universal principle, in cheapening and multiplying to the uttermost all the articles of human enjoyment . . . we see in this the benevolence and comprehensive wisdom of God. . .[98]

Political economy is but one grand exemplification of the alliance, which a God of righteousness hath established, between prudence and moral principle on the one hand, and physical comfort on the other. However obnoxious the modern doctrine of population, as expounded by Mr. Malthus, may have been, and still is, to weak and limited sentimentalists, it is the truth which of all others sheds the greatest brightness over the earthly prospects of humanity — and this in spite of the hideous and sustained outcry which has risen against it.[99]

For here is a clear adaptation between the external nature of the world and the moral nature of mankind. Let us glorify God that the means of subsistence are insufficient to sustain the population, because only His benevolence could have devised so infallible a system for impressing upon man the necessity, and hence the virtue, of prudence, industry, self-denial, thrift, and forbearance. "And it sheds a revelation, not only on the hopeful destinies of man, but on the character of God — in having instituted this palpable alliance between the moral and the physical; and so assorted the economy of outward nature to the economy of human principles and passions." [100]

4

These quotations from Thomas Chalmers may be an appropriate conclusion to this chapter, even though they are almost too striking an illustration of the relationship between the spirit of the times and a providential attitude toward science. Nevertheless, the inferences which Chalmers wished to draw from the meaning of natural history were very popular among leaders of opinion in early industrial Britain. They serve to bear out the suggestion that the essential obstacles faced by sciences involving time and life arose in part from the instinctive desire of most scientists that their work should support the fabric of society. Chalmers, and all the Bridgewater authors, opposed uniformitarianism when it was still an issue — Chalmers because Lyell's interpretation labored "to demonstrate that by laws, and laws alone, the framework of our existing economy was put together. It is thus that they would exclude the agency of a God from the transition between one system, or one formation, and another, although it be precisely at such transition when this agency seems most palpably and peculiarly called for." [101]

Natural history, geology, political economy, and the factory system might be proved inevitable — particularly to the educated — but God had best be kept handy to declare that the consequences represented His will.

VIII

THE PLACE OF PROVIDENCE IN NATURE

'Tis the crown and glory of organic science that it *does*, through *final cause*, link material to moral. . . You have ignored this link; and, if I do not mistake your meaning, you have done your best in one or two pregnant cases to break it. Were it possible (which, thank God, it is not) to break it, humanity, in my mind, would suffer a damage that might brutalize it, and sink the human race into a lower grade of degradation than any into which it has fallen since its written records tell us of its history.
— Sedgwick to Darwin, on receipt
of *On the Origin of Species* [1]

CHARLES DARWIN had great personal respect for his onetime teacher, but he was not surprised by Sedgwick's hostile reception of his evolutionary theories. In the 1840's Darwin had followed the controversy over the *Vestiges of Creation* with the keenest interest. Although he disapproved of Sedgwick's review of the book, it was, he felt, "a grand piece of argument against mutation of species, and I read it with fear and trembling." [2] As for the *Vestiges* itself, Darwin thought the early ·editions wanting in accurate knowledge and in caution, but he regarded the work as a valuable lightning rod in channeling off the initial thunders of orthodoxy. "In my opinion," he wrote, "it has done excellent service in calling in this country attention to the subject, and in removing prejudices." [3] Darwin may have been a bit sanguine about the dissipation of prejudice. He was, however, prepared to find most scientists and most laymen conditioned against acceptance of his evolutionary ideas, and before publishing his theory, he and his friends foresaw that scientific opposition could not be entirely separated from, nor always distinguished from, theological opposition. [4]

From both the empirical and the interpretative points of view, the progress of geological science in the first half of the

nineteenth century was an essential prelude to the formulation
of a successful theory of biological evolution. There had, of
course, been a number of more or less fanciful evolutionary
schemes suggested ever since the middle of the eighteenth
century. In Huxley's opinion, however, these speculative pro-
posals had little influence on scientific thinking, and it was
rather Lyell's work which was primarily responsible for
smoothing the road for Darwin,[5] so that from this standpoint it
is James Hutton and not Lamarck who ought to be considered
Darwin's intellectual ancestor. Besides being a biologist,
Darwin was himself an experienced geologist. He served as
secretary of the Geological Society from 1838 to 1841. A large
part of *On the Origin of Species* is devoted to describing geological evidence, from which Darwin drew illustrations of what
was by then a generally admitted proposition: that the forms
of organic life which had succeeded each other on the earth
were progressive in character. Even though an evolutionary
mechanism of progression was not accepted before Darwin,
the over-all fact of progression was not disputed. The evidence
had been accumulating ever since William Smith had first
demonstrated that successive strata are distinguished by specific fossil contents and since research in paleontology and
comparative anatomy had elaborated in enormous detail the
knowledge of extinct species. And on the interpretative level,
geologists had begun, though incompletely and with many
trials and tribulations, to draw a naturalistic picture of the development of the earth and the physical system of things. But
uniformitarianism as an attitude toward the course of nature
could not be carried to its logical conclusion in a theory of
organic evolution until a formulation sufficiently scientific to be
compelling could attack the idea of a governing Providence in
its last refuge, the creation of new species, and drive it right
out of the whole field of natural history. This was one, at least,
of Darwin's accomplishments, one which could not have been
achieved by a book like the *Vestiges of Creation* even though
the descriptive sciences had arrived at a level of understanding
that could have been advanced only by a valid construction of
the ideas which Chambers set forth imaginatively.[6]

The conception of providential control over the course of nature was closely tied up with the immutability of species, the more so since in the 1840's and 1850's the creation of new races of living things was the one remaining type of physical phenomenon habitually referred to as concrete evidence for the continuing action of the Deity. "If," wrote Whewell in response to the *Vestiges*, "we allow such a *transmutation of species*, we abandon that belief in the adaptation of the structure of every creature to its destined mode of being, which not only most persons would give up with repugnance, but which, as we have seen, has constantly and irresistibly impressed itself on the minds of the best naturalists, as the true view of the order of the world." [7] Paleyism was deeply ingrained in the thinking of scientists and theologians, and for a long time representatives of both had repeatedly been assuring the reading public that the Paley argument offered a powerful, even a necessary, support to religious belief.

The pervasiveness of this tradition helps to account for the clerical outcry which greeted Darwin's theory and for the initial hostility of most scientists, because in one sense Darwinism is Paleyism inverted. The adaptation of a species to its environment and to the necessities of its existence may be considered either as an explanation of its development or as evidence of a creative purpose. Providence, as Huxley remarked, is the theological equivalent of the scientific conception of order.[8] Darwin himself described how, when an undergraduate at Cambridge, he did not question Paley's premises and, taking these on trust, was "charmed and convinced by the long line of argumentation." [9] But after he hit upon the law of natural selection, the old argument for design seemed to him to fail. "We can no longer argue that, for instance, the beautiful hinge of a bivalve shell must have been made by an intelligent being, like the hinge of a door by man. There seems to be no more design in the variability of organic beings, and in the action of natural selection, than in the course which the wind blows." [10] Actually, although Darwin did not think so, it might still have been possible to interpret the evolutionary process as itself a divine program for the development of the world. The idea of

God as first cause could perhaps have been fitted into an evolutionary view of nature, but only at the price of reducing God to a remote and impersonal postulate because Darwin's theory was necessarily fatal to the idea of God as craftsman and governor.

From the standpoint of the providentialist interpretation of nature, *On the Origin of Species* was a *coup de grâce* rather than an entering wedge. The book represents the final defeat of an argument which had begun to run into difficulties as soon as the geologists brought scientific method to bear upon the development and history of nature. In traditional natural theology, scientific method was held to be the means of proving God's existence. So skillfully constituted a mechanism as science discovers the universe to be could have come about only through the workmanship of an intelligent designer. But at the same time, the empirical proof that God was also an active force as a moral agent in the universe was derived from the supposed necessity of assuming that divine interventions accounted for the physical phenomena which were inexplicable on purely scientific grounds. The proof of the existence of God, therefore, was based on what science had accomplished, and the proof of His continued activity on what it had not. Inevitably this meant that as the sphere of science expanded, that of theology receded; that as more and more events in physical history were explained naturally, there were fewer episodes to be explained supernaturally and fewer empirical illustrations of God's immediate control over the material world.

The role of divine Providence in the course of nature was the central issue, to which the question of the relationship of scriptural history to natural history, while important, was subsidiary. The interpretative problems were not produced by the demands of theology against science. Instead, the fundamental and continuing difficulty lay in the persistence of a quasi-theological frame of mind within science. From the publication of Hutton's *Theory of the Earth* in 1795, every interpretation which marked a definite step forward for the descriptive sciences touched off the same pattern of religious apprehension and disagreement among natural scientists. And after each successive retreat, providential empiricists took up positions on new ground, which their own researches were simultaneously cutting out from under them. The issue of aqueous versus igneous formation of the earth's crust had immediately brought into question the age of the world. Exploitation of the paleontological index had required discussion of the antiquity of species. All these things had soon involved the period of Noah's deluge, then its efficacy as a geological agency, and finally its very existence. Waning of the flood brought on the larger issue of the nature and causation of geological change, whether cataclysmic or constant and gradual. Catastrophists attempted a last-ditch defense by emphasizing the progressive and radical dissimilarity of organic forms. And this, in turn, prepared the ground for Chambers' fanciful answer followed by Darwin's definitive one.

But it was never a black-and-white picture. The providentialists were themselves respectable and productive scientists. And at every stage except the last, progressives admitted that a further step, the possibility of which they disavowed while they unwittingly prepared it, would indeed have had serious implications for orthodox religious fidelity. Playfair, for example, held that Vulcanism did not require a pre-Mosaic antiquity of the human species — only if it had, he thought, would religious truth have been involved. Townsend, Greenough, and Buckland took a similar position on the deluge and the recent appearance of man, while admitting the tremendous age of extinct species. Lyell and the uniformitarians, rejecting the universal flood and attendant catastrophes, contended that they did not touch the only essential matters — man's absolute uniqueness, the immutability of other species, and the separate and distinct character of thousands of special organic creations.[11] Even Chambers wrote ostensibly to demonstrate the immanence and unity of divinely promulgated natural law. His view of Providence, however — and this was always the difference in emphasis between progressive and conservative theorists — envisioned an original fiat; while Sedgwick required a creation resembling an unruly grammar school with a divine director who ordered its affairs as would a hard-pressed headmaster. According to this interpretation, supervision — though immediate — never quite brought order out of chaos; and even when temporary order (the present course of nature) seemed to be achieved, it was never an order sufficient unto itself.

In retrospect it is apparent that, although on the surface the problems raised by Vulcanism, uniformitarianism, the *Vestiges*, and Darwinism were not the same, actually the pattern of reaction was a constant one throughout. Behind the discussion, therefore, was something more than always met the eye: the common tendency of all these theories to remove the hand of God from the course of events in the material world. It would, however, be difficult to offer a simple explanation, first, of why such a large segment of British opinion was reluctant to accept from the developmental sciences those findings which seemed to have this implication, and second, of why the shrinking scope of supernatural causation in physical history should have been accompanied by so much more uneasiness in Britain than in other countries in the same period. Nevertheless, it may be worth attempting a few analytical suggestions to account for the circumstance that the diminishing role of Providence was the ultimate issue underneath the scientific disagreements described in this book, and this may throw some light on their significance as products of the early nineteenth-century environment.

In this connection, the old and somewhat overworked generalization that the English have an innate habit of thinking empirically, though it must sometimes be severely qualified, is nevertheless substantially correct. Another characteristic differentiating English society from continental was the degree and quality of its religiosity. For a long time in England empiricism and piety reinforced each other. Ever since Newton, natural theology, if not quite a distinctively British approach to God, had at least been elaborated in far greater detail and with much more enthusiasm in Britain than in other countries.[12] British theologians and scientists, so many of whom had rested the proof of the existence and activity of God on physical evidence, were, therefore, more distressed than leaders of religious opinion elsewhere when the empirical argument, instead of leading towards God, began to move, if not away from Him, at least in an irrelevant direction. Further, and aside from the internal failure of theological empiricism, the literal-mindedness and philosophical ineptitude of evangelical Protestantism were in part responsible for the idea that naturalistic theories of the growth of the material world were inimical to Christian fidelity. Cardinal Newman's views on the issue, for example, were very different from the prevailing Protestant attitude. In his opinion — and he was as hostile to materialism as to liberalism — the facts of science, when the sense in which they were to be understood was properly appreciated, had no bearing on the spiritual truths or the historical authority of religion. Newman was highly suspicious of what he called physical theology, and though agreeing that the heavens may very well declare the glory of God, he quoted Bacon to the effect that there was no reason for supposing that they also declare His will.[13] In any case, Newman did not rely on astronomy to sustain the faith.

The theological opposition to Darwin's theory and the earlier travails of geology are often attributed to two related sources: a belief, first, in both the inspiration and the literal sense of the Biblical texts; and secondly, a requirement that man be a unique species, specially created as a vessel for the immortal soul which absolutely distinguishes him from all other forms of life, existent or extinct. If it were simply a question of the reaction of clerical opponents of science, who produced a literature of denunciation, reconciliation, and exegesis which has been excluded from this study, this explanation would, on the whole, suffice. But it does not account for the religious difficulties experienced by scientists themselves, by popularizers and theologians of science, and by the more open-minded individuals who made up the greater part of the educated public. And ordained and uninformed critics would probably have attracted less attention if they had not had ready to their vulgarizing hands the contentions of people like Kirwan, Buckland, Sedgwick, and Hugh Miller. Although too neat a generalization would be erroneous, the arguments of one gen-

eration of purely theological disputants more or less reflected
the interpretation of the obstructionist side in the discussions
among scientists of the preceding generation. Granville Penn,
for example, Dean Cockburn of York, and George Fairholme,
to name three of the opponents of geology in Buckland's time,
leveled against the whole of the science — catastrophist as well
as uniformitarian — arguments very similar to those with
which Deluc and Kirwan had attacked the Huttonians twenty-
five years earlier.[14]

Like other pious people, devout geologists and naturalists
felt a real reverence for the Bible, but bibliolatry, though it
may have complicated the difficulties arising from the interpretation of the geological record, was not the root of them.
On the contrary, after Kirwan, no responsible scientist contended for the literal credibility of the Mosaic account of creation.[15] All the people who figure in this book were continually
uttering solemn strictures lest their clerical detractors en-
danger the dignity of religion in the fashion of Galileo's opponents. Even the most obstructive scientists insisted that Scripture, though undoubtedly inspired, was not designed to teach
scientific truth, this being a matter which could be discovered
only inductively upon a basis of observation and experiment.
They were, to be sure, always pleased to remark upon how
their painfully pieced together inductions bore out certain
sweeping generalizations in Genesis. They all agreed that truth
was one and that its two branches — natural and revealed —
must eventually coincide. But in order for this happy conclusion to come about, all serious investigators were willing, as
time went on, to read more and more of the scriptural statements figuratively, though often only after a struggle. The
six days became six indefinite and nearly infinite periods; the
creation of animal life spread out over the geological time
scale; the single, cataclysmic flood became first a series of dynamical catastrophes and then a localized, historical event;
and so on.

Although a Buckland and a Conybeare illogically regarded
the historical universality of a deluge as indispensable, this did
not mean that they were fundamentalists because, at the same

time, they took the six days allegorically and rejected the Mosaic chronology for dumb animals. And, when inescapably put to it, they found themselves able to use the recent appearance of man instead of the flood as the great, confirmatory bridge between the two histories, natural and revealed. When Sedgwick abandoned the Biblical flood as a primary geological agency, he was far from giving up his belief in the necessity for catastrophes produced by divine intervention. Daubeny interpreted deluges resulting from volcanic upheaval as evidence of God's controlling hand, but he did not insist upon identifying them with the Biblical flood. Catastrophists were clinging to the idea of a particular Providence in nature and not simply to the Bible. And before Darwin's time, a succession of obstacles were overcome, which, though they certainly weakened the providential and teleological pattern into which science was fitted, did not yet shatter it.

Nor does it meet the case to turn for an explanation of the continuing difficulties in interpreting science to the necessity that species be immutable lest man be dispossessed of his distinguishing *raison d'être*, his immortal soul. Mutation of species was not seriously under discussion before 1844, and not seriously in prospect until 1859 — nowhere, that is, except in Darwin's immediate and restricted circle. No one rejected mutability more uncompromisingly than Lyell at the time when he himself was the chief object of clerical attack. In general, Lamarck was classified with the visionary speculations of a bygone age, and no more thought to be dangerous than Whiston, or Buffon, or even Lucretius. Until the final episode, then, it was impossible for the common descent of species to have given rise to a spiritual concern for the Christian life after death, and for this to have harassed scientists from within their own ranks. Moreover, as has been pointed out, with the exception of Hugh Miller, the recalcitrant scientists in each stage of the discussion professed a rather unspiritual view of religion.

The interpretative disagreements in the sciences dealing with time and life are not, then, to be explained on the grounds either of a purely religious respect for the Biblical narrative for its own sake, or of an insistence that the spiritual integrity of the human species depends on man's having originated in something like an immaculate conception. These two points, whether taken singly or together, do not account for the persistence of the pattern of controversy even though they were involved in the discussion and were, no doubt, responsible for much of its fervor. Neither, until Darwin, did the issue present itself as an attack on teleology and the idea of final cause in nature. Indeed, it was always the argument of progressive scientists that their hypotheses contributed more powerfully to an exalted understanding of the omnipotence and omniscience of a Creator whose initial design was sufficient for all His purposes than did the Neptunist and catastrophist effort to cast the world into the bosom of an uncertain and ubiquitous Providence. The doctrine of final cause was attacked by no one. The trouble was not that progressives themselves rejected the idea of purposeful design, but that their opponents instinctively felt that eliminating providential direction would lead in that direction. If material phenomena are sufficiently explained by natural causation, the argument for design might be strengthened, but the evidence of control would be weakened. And in the nineteenth century, unlike the eighteenth century, orthodox natural theology was more interested in control than design. It was chiefly on this account that Huttonian and uniformitarian theories were suspect. And, on the popularizing level, Combe and Chambers were attacked, not because they impugned the divine character of the physical universe, which, in fact, they were attempting to illustrate, but because they held that God's Providence, in the social and moral as well as in the organic and inorganic spheres, was a system of unvarying law, and that God never interfered in its working.

The movement for popularization of science and the cult of useful knowledge, which were pushed so enthusiastically in all this period, sprang not only from a desire to disseminate enlightenment for its own sake, but also from a conviction of the necessity that the people at large should appreciate the immanence and understand the dictates of material Providence. Almost to the middle of the century, one of the chief modes of publicizing scientific discovery and theory, at least in the descriptive branches, was in the guise of natural theology. And the principles of behavior and morality preached in this literature were those of the utilitarian social philosophy, backed up by a providential sanction read out of the course of nature. The Bridgewater authors frequently represented the Malthusian population doctrine as a particularly happy illustration of the workings of God's Providence, so that in the eyes of this school the trouble with Darwinism was not simply that it pictured nature as red in tooth and claw. It will have been noticed how largely, in the years before Darwin, the fancied social implications of development, and earlier of a uniformitarian or Huttonian earth history, contributed to the instinctive aversion of the antagonists of these ideas. They feared that if God's role as an immediate, if occasional, adjuster of the material world was whittled away, He would also be displaced as a governor of its inhabitants. There is no reason to suppose that opponents of naturalistic theories of progression were insincere in their anxiety for morality and religion. But it is apparent that, as often happens, they identified these with their concern for the structure of the social complex in which they dwelt, and with which all of them were well satisfied, and that they felt two things: that the stability of society not only depended upon, but was justified by, the direct and immediate attention of a Providence whose arrangements could be empirically demonstrated in the physical universe; and that its stability depended also upon a general conviction that this was the case.

It would, however, do violence to the motives of advocates of catastrophist interpretations to infer from their social ideas that they had conceived their doctrine in the interests of the ruling classes in order to publicize it as a sort of scientific opiate of the people. Plekhanov once claimed Lyell as a geological forerunner of dialectical materialism,[16] but a simple economic explanation of the conflicting attitudes towards God's place in the development of the physical universe would be too neat. Although providentialists seemed to fear that the whole framework both of nature and of the civil order would dissolve unless held together by the hand of the Deity, there was not actually much difference between their social philosophy and that of their critics. Publicists like Combe and Chambers derived practical precepts from a uniformitarian view of nature very like the ones which Buckland and Miller described as the dictates of an immediate Providence. And eventually Darwin would prove as useful to rugged individualism as Providence.

The most that can be said is that the political opinions of providentialists were a continuation of Paley's utilitarian conservatism, whereas the social applications of scientific progressivism reflected Bentham's utilitarian radicalism. Both were utilitarian, however; and it is not, after all, surprising or necessarily Marxist to find that in a pious and bourgeois environment the lessons of science should be interpreted in a pious and bourgeois fashion, and that this should have injected extra-scientific considerations even into the professional discussion of scientific theories. Applied science obviously lay — or could be described as lying — at the basis of England's unique capacity for manufacturing, a capacity which carried with it social stresses also unique to England. This is undoubtedly related to the curious fact that, as Herr Schönbein remarked, "the English have a peculiar love of regarding Nature from a theological point of view."

BIBLIOGRAPHICAL ESSAY

BIBLIOGRAPHICAL ESSAY

What follows makes no claim to being a complete bibliography of the history of geology and the related sciences or of natural theology in Britain. It may, however, be useful as a guide, and it will facilitate critical discussion to arrange the sources topically rather than alphabetically by author. In order to avoid overlapping, I cite each title in full only once, although this involves some arbitrary classification. The bibliography is not so large that anyone will have difficulty in finding any particular author, and since the index covers the bibliography as well as the text, it may be used to locate all the citations to each writer. It will be convenient to take up first the works which are of value bibliographically and other secondary authorities which I have found helpful. Biographical and autobiographical literature comes next, followed by a description of the contemporary materials on which this study is primarily based: works on natural theology, natural science, popular science, education, and other social and political topics; and, finally, periodicals.

1. SECONDARY MATERIALS

There is no bibliography dealing with the history of geology as such. The nearest thing to it is Emmanuel de Margerie, *Catalogue des bibliographies géologiques, redigé avec le concours des membres de la Commission Bibliographique du Congrès [Géologique International]* (Paris, 1896). This work, though intended for the geologist and not the historian and designed as a catalogue of published bibliographical sources rather than as a bibliography of geological literature, is so thorough that it is probably the best starting point both for early nineteenth-century geology and to some extent for the allied sciences. Margerie lists references to 1895. The work was continued by Edward B. Mathews as *Catalogue of Published Bibliographies in Geology, 1896–1920,* no. 36 of the Bulletin of the National Research Council, vol. 6, pt. 5 (Washington, 1923), which, however, is of little use for the period covered by this study.

The rather slim secondary literature dealing with the history of geology is covered in the seventy-three critical bibliographies published in *Isis*, volume I (1913–14) through volume LX, number 120 (May 1949). Though a few earlier items are noticed, these indispensable bibliographies are exhaustive only for materials which were published between the birth of *Isis* in 1913 and November 1948. George Sarton, "La Synthèse Géologique de 1775 à 1918," *Isis*, II (1914–1919), 357–394, though its chief emphasis is on the work of Suess, includes a limited number of bibliographical references for the history of geology.

Several older works should also be mentioned. Robert Watt, *Bibliotheca Britannica; or, A General Index to British and Foreign Literature* (4 vols.; Edinburgh, 1824), is the work of one man and is necessarily incomplete, particularly in its subject index, but it is useful nevertheless. The second volume of Thomas Young, *A Course of Lectures on Natural Philosophy and the Mechanical Arts* (2 vols.; London, 1807), includes a "catalogue of references" which is, in effect, a bibliography of natural philosophy to 1805. The most satisfactory one-volume history of geology is Karl von Zittel, *History of Geology and Paleontology*, translated by Maria M. Ogilvie-Gordon (London, 1901), but it is of only limited bibliographical value. Vicomte Adolphe d'Archiac, *Histoire des progrès de la géologie de 1834 à 1845* (8 vols. in 9; Paris, 1847–1860), a work which changed the final date in its title while it was in progress, extending down to 1859, gives an extensive listing of publications for the period it covers, but with emphasis on French authors; and Charles Sainte-Claire Deville, *Coup d'oeil historique sur la géologie et sur les travaux d'Élie de Beaumont* (Paris, 1878), though it includes a bibliography on pages 583–597, is no more than the title implies and emphasizes Élie de Beaumont rather than geology. Christian Keferstein, *Geschichte und Litteratur der Geognosie* (Halle, 1840), has an enumeration of books and memoirs for the period from 1820 to 1840; and Friedrich Hoffmann, *Geschichte der Geognosie, und Schilderung der vulkanischen Erscheinungen* (Berlin, 1838), refers to some earlier works not mentioned elsewhere.

The English, characteristically, have not been so diligent bibliographically as the French and the Germans. George Wareing Ormerod edited *A Classified Index to the Transactions, Proceedings, and Quarterly Journal of the Geological Society of London* (2d ed.; London, 1870), covering all the memoirs and notices to the end of 1868. The references in Sir Archibald Geikie's charming *The Founders of Geology* (2d ed.; London, 1905), are helpful for the early century. The notes in Frank D. Adams, *The Birth and Development of the Geological Sciences* (Baltimore, 1938), are of too scattered and incomplete a character to be as useful as could be wished. Kirtley F. Mather and Shirley L. Mason (eds.), *A Source Book in Geology* (New York, 1939), contains key excerpts from the work of the great men in the science. Finally, the references in two general works are a rich and indispensable bibliographical mine, and not only for the history of geology: Andrew D. White, *A History of the Warfare of Science with Theology in Christendom* (2d ed.; 2 vols.; New York, 1901), and D. O. Zöckler, *Geschichte der Beziehungen zwischen Theologie und Naturwissenschaft, mit besondrer Rücksicht auf Schöpfungsgeschichte* (2 vols.; Gütersloh, 1877–1879). John F. Fulton has published "A Bibliography of the Honourable Robert Boyle," *Proceedings and Papers, Oxford Bibliographical Society,* vol. III (1931), pt. I.

Recent publications bearing upon the history of geology are Frank D. Adams, "The Scottish School of Geology," *Science*, LXXX (1934), 365–368; H. Hamshaw Thomas, "The Rise of Geology and its Influence on Contemporary Thought," *Annals of Science,* V (1941–1947), 325–341; and F. Sherwood Taylor, "Geology Changes the Outlook," in *Ideas and Beliefs of the Victorians* (London, 1949), pp. 189–196. The general history of science in the period is covered by Sir William C. Dampier, *A History of Science and its Relations with Philosophy and Religion* (3d ed.; Cambridge, England, 1943), a book which does not accomplish all that its title implies. Much more provocative, though not a history, is Alfred North Whitehead, *Science and the Modern World* (New York, 1927). Though superseded as a history, William Whewell, *History of the Inductive Sciences* (3 vols.; London, 1837), gives a useful contemporary account of many of the issues which concern the present study. Robert H. Murray, *Science and Scientists in the Nineteenth Century* (London, 1925), has chapters, none of them entirely satisfactory, entitled "Lyell and Uniformitarianism," "The Precursors of Darwin," and "Darwin and Evolution." Biology, more fortunate than geology, has found excellent historians in Charles Singer, *The Story of Living Things; A Short Account of the Evolution of the Biological Sciences*

(New York and London, 1931); and Erik Nordenskiöld, *The History of Biology, a Survey* (trans. Leonard B. Eyre; New York, 1928). A starting point for the history of scientific organizations is Bernard H. Becker, *Scientific London* (London, 1874), a handy survey, though its historical content rests on current tradition rather than research. Abraham Hume and A. I. Evans, *The Learned Societies and Printing Clubs of the United Kingdom* (London, 1853), is little more than a catalogue. Most of the histories of particular organizations are labors of love rather than of critical scholarship. An exception is Dorothy Stimson, *Scientists and Amateurs: A History of the Royal Society* (New York, 1948), which, however, is a little thin for the nineteenth century, for the early part of which period Charles Babbage, *Reflections on the Decline of Science in England and on Some of its Causes* (London, 1830), is still illuminating. Thomas Sprat, *The History of the Royal Society of London* (London, 1667), is valuable not only for the foundation but for the scientific atmosphere of the period. Horace B. Woodward, *The History of the Geological Society of London* (London, 1907), is somewhat fulsome. Other organizational histories are: Henry F. Berry, *A History of the Royal Society of Dublin* (London, 1915); Sir Henry T. Wood, *A History of the Royal Society of Arts* (London, 1913); O. J. R. Howarth, *The British Association for the Advancement of Science: A Retrospect, 1831–1931* (2d ed.; London, 1931); Robert S. Watson, *The History of the Literary and Philosophical Society of Newcastle-upon-Tyne* (London, 1897). Henry Bence Jones, *The Royal Institution: Its Founder and its First Professors* (London, 1871), goes through the professorship of Davy, whom the author tries to remove from Faraday's shadow. It may be supplemented by Thomas Martin, *The Royal Institution* (rev. ed.; London, 1948), and by *The Prospectus, Charter, Ordinance, and Bye-Laws of the Royal Institution of Great Britain* (London, 1800).

Readers of Élie Halévy will perceive how much my interpretation of the social and intellectual background owes both to his *Growth of Philosophic Radicalism* (trans. Mary Morris; London, 1928), and to his *History of the English People in the Nineteenth Century* (trans. D. A. Barker and E. I. Watkin; 4 vols.; London, 1924–1947). A work of more modest compass, but one which has a number of useful insights into the popular movements of the 1830's and 1840's, is

R. L. Hill, *Toryism and the People* (London, 1929). W. E. H. Lecky, *A History of England in the Eighteenth Century* (8 vols.; New York, 1891), is still the most considerable thing on that period. Lecky's enthusiasm and hopes for rationalism in *History of the Rise and Influence of the Spirit of Rationalism in Europe* (2 vols.; London, 1865) now seem rather dated. The same is true of A. W. Benn, *The History of English Rationalism in the Nineteenth Century* (2 vols.; London, 1906), a somewhat ill-tempered and disappointing book. Leslie Stephen, *The English Utilitarians* (3 vols.; London, 1900), has a discussion of Paleyism and touches on some other topics treated in the present book. Stephen's other major work, *History of English Thought in the Eighteenth Century* (3d ed.; 2 vols.; London, 1902), may be supplemented by Basil Willey, *The Eighteenth Century Background; Studies on the Idea of Nature in the Thought of the Period* (London, 1940), which treats scientific ideas from a literary point of view.

Besides the general intellectual histories, there are several relevant studies of particular topics or ideas. G. V. Plekhanov, *Essays in the History of Materialism* (trans. Ralph Fox; London, 1934), alludes to what the author considers the contribution made by geology to dialectical reasoning. Early opinions on the habitability of the solar system are described by Grant McColley, "The 17th-Century Doctrine of a Plurality of Worlds," *Annals of Science*, I (1936), 385–430; and Katherine B. Collier, *Cosmogonies of our Fathers* (New York, 1934), outlines the major systems of cosmogony proposed in the seventeenth and eighteenth centuries. The most satisfactory account of education is John W. Adamson, *English Education, 1789–1901* (Cambridge, England, 1930). Archibald E. Dobbs, *Education and Social Movements, 1700–1850* (London, 1919), does not live up to its title, and Dorothy M. Turner, *History of Science Teaching in England* (London, 1927), excellent as far as it goes, is very brief and synoptic. My essay, "English Ideas of the University in the Nineteenth Century," appeared in *The Modern University* (ed. Margaret Clapp; Ithaca, N. Y., 1950).

I have not attempted to read the enormous quantity of books, mostly of the late nineteenth century, on the general subjects of natural theology and of science and religion, which are to be found on the shelves of any large library; nor would it serve any purpose to list all those which I have examined. However, a few which are likely to prove useful to anyone interested in the question should be mentioned. On natural theology, a subject somewhat neglected by recent scholars, there are Clement C. J. Webb, *Studies in the History of Natural Theology* (Oxford, 1915), and Charles de Rémusat, *Philosophie religieuse de la théologie naturelle en France et en Angleterre* (Paris, 1864). John W. Draper, *A History of the Conflict between Religion and Science* (New York, 1875), should be read with White and Zöckler — Draper is more extreme than White. Thomas Henry Huxley, "The Lights of the Church and the Light of Science," in *Science and Hebrew Tradition,* volume VI of *Collected Essays* (New York, 1894), gives a highly colored account of the influence of the flood and of theological obscurantism in general after 1830, a subject to which he recurred in many other essays, particularly those in *Darwiniana,* which forms volume II of the same edition.

Two special topics which have received extensive treatment by modern scholars are the encouragement afforded to science by Puritanism and the background of Darwin's theory of evolution. To take, in the first place, the question of Puritanism and the "new philosophy," the two standard monographs, written independently of each other, are Richard F. Jones, *Ancients and Moderns: A Study of the Background of the Battle of the Books,* Washington University Studies, new series, Language and Literature, no. 6 (St. Louis, Mo., 1936), and Robert K. Merton, *Science, Technology, and Society in Seventeenth Century England,* vol. IV, pt. 2 of *Osiris Studies on the History and Philosophy of Science, and on the History of Learning and Culture* (Bruges, 1938). Jones writes from the point of view of intellectual history and is concerned to establish the thesis "that the quarrel out of which Swift's satire sprang had its roots in the conflict between the new science and the old learning, and not in France" (p. vii). He lays great stress upon the influence of Bacon and upon Puritan utilitarianism. Merton, on the other hand, writes as a sociologist and employs the techniques of cultural analysis. In a sense, this results in an application to science of the Weber thesis, for which see Max Weber, *The Protestant Ethic and the Spirit of Capitalism* (trans. Talcott Parsons; London, 1930). Merton's interpretation is psychological rather than intellectual, and he emphasizes the Puritan doctrine of the vocational calling and the idea that experiments were one way of glorifying God through works. Merton regards the Puritans as integrating their theology and their science; Jones interprets the relationship rather as a parallel one. The two books complement each other in an illuminating fashion. For the differences between them, see Jones's review of Merton, *Isis,* XXXI (1939–40), 438–441, and Merton's review of Jones, *Isis,* XXVI (1936), 171–172. Three shorter studies on the same or related topics have been published in *The Bulletin of the History of Medicine:* Dorothy Stimson, "Puritanism and the New Philosophy," III (1935), 321–334; Walter Pagel, "Religious Motives in the Medical Biology of the Seventeenth Century," III (1935), 97–128; and George Rosen, "Left-Wing Puritanism and Science," XV (1944), 375–380. One further article is useful: R. P. Stearns, "The Scientific Spirit in England," *Isis,* XXXIV (1942–43), 293–300.

There is a large literature dealing with evolutionary thought before Darwin. The most general criticism to be applied to most of these studies seems to me to be their failure to reckon with a problem which arises in any attempt to abstract a given idea from its successive environments in order to trace its course over a long period of time. The difficulty is more than a matter of semantics over a word like "development" or a phrase like "natural selection," because the tendency always is to take not only words and phrases but concepts as meaning, if not the same, at least comparable things in the context of different ages. As compared to nineteenth-century thought and science, however, the whole idea of the evolution of animal life would have had such different implications for Greek or patristic or thirteenth-century or even — though to a much smaller degree — for eighteenth-century thought and science, that I question whether any such ideas are fully comparable as between different periods, or whether it has much meaning to trace them abstracted from their cultural surroundings. But however this may be, the following, though not an exhaustive listing, should serve as an introduction to the literature dealing with the theories held by early evolutionists and the value of those theories in the light of modern knowledge.

Darwin himself prefaced the later editions of *On the Origin of Species* with a not very appreciative résumé of the work of some of his predecessors. More valuable for the immediate background is

Huxley's history of his own opinions, published as chapter xiv, entitled "On the Reception of *The Origin of Species,*" in Francis Darwin, *Life and Letters of Charles Darwin.* There is a comparison of the ideas of Erasmus Darwin with those of his grandson in Ernst Krause, *Erasmus Darwin* (trans. W. S. Dallas; New York, 1880), to which Charles Darwin prefixed a biographical memoir which ought to dispose of the charge by Jacques Barzun in *Darwin, Marx, and Wagner* (New York, 1941) that Darwin was jealous of his grandfather.

Isidore Geoffroy Saint-Hilaire, *Histoire naturelle générale des règnes organiques* (3 vols.; Paris, 1854–1862), includes in volume II (pp. 365–429) a history of opinion (chiefly French opinion) on the definition of species and the question of fixity versus variability. Henry F. Osborn, *From the Greeks to Darwin* (3d ed.; New York, 1929), was a pioneer study in its first edition (1894), but is now largely superseded. Many of Osborn's interpretations are corrected by Arthur O. Lovejoy, "Some Eighteenth Century Evolutionists," *The Popular Science Monthly,* LXV (1904), 238–251, 323–340. In the same journal, Lovejoy's "The Argument for Organic Evolution before 'The Origin of Species,' " LXXV (1909), 499–514, 537–549, is an excellent article with which, however, I disagree on a few minor points (see p. 288, n. 39; p. 301, n. 6); and his "Buffon and the Problem of Species," *ibid.,* LXXIX (1911), 464–473, 554–567, does not seem to have carried later writers with him in excluding Buffon from the ranks of thoroughgoing evolutionists. Whether it should have done so, I am not in a position to say. J.-L. de Lanessan, "L'Attitude de Darwin à l'égard de ses prédécesseurs au sujet de l'origine des espèces," *Revue Anthropologique,* XXIV (1914), 33–45, contends — a little patriotically — that most everything in Darwin is to be found in Buffon and Lamarck, hints that Darwin's disdainful attitude toward his predecessors was calculated to conceal this fact, and suggests that Darwin overemphasized the importance of his only real contribution, the struggle for existence. An altogether better discussion is Pierre Brunet, "La Notion d'évolution dans la science moderne avant Lamarck," *Archeion,* XIX (1937), 21–43.

Two authoritative studies by Conway Zirkle trace the history of concepts regarding the mechanism of evolution: "Natural Selection before the 'Origin of Species,' " *Proceedings of the American Philosophical Society,* LXXXIV (1941), 71–123, compiles views held on natural selection from Empedocles to Darwin; and "The Early History of the Ideas of the Inheritance of Acquired Characters and of Pangenesis," *Transactions of the American Philosophical Society*, XXXV (1946), 91–151, shows that the first of these ideas had a long and honorable history and was so widespread that it was practically an assumption when Lamarck applied it to explain his theory of evolution; whereas the idea of pangenesis, adopted by Darwin as the mode by which characteristics are inherited, can also be traced from ancient times, although it never went unchallenged and is, of course, rejected by modern thought.

Nils von Hofsten, "From Cuvier to Darwin," *Isis*, XXIV (1935–36), 361–366, is concerned chiefly with outlining the difference in the approaches to comparative anatomy of Cuvier on the one hand and of Geoffroy Saint-Hilaire and the school of *Naturphilosophie* on the other. This is the summary of a paper in *Nordisk Tidskrift* (1922). On this subject, see also J. Chaine, "La grande époque de l'anatomie comparée," *Scientia*, L (1931), 365–374; Isidore Geoffroy Saint-Hilaire, *Vie, travaux, et doctrine scientifique d'Etienne Geoffroy Saint-Hilaire* (Strasbourg, 1847); and T. H. Huxley, "Owen's Position in the History of Anatomical Science," in Richard Owen, *The Life of Richard Owen*.

As to non-evolutionary views on the origin of species, the most important work by far is Arthur O. Lovejoy's distinguished and stimulating book, *The Great Chain of Being* (Cambridge, Mass.: Harvard University Press, 1936), which is essential reading for anyone interested in the history of theories of organic nature, although it is concerned less with the progress of science than with the influence and persistence of the ancient principles of plenitude and continuity in nature, which began to lose currency at the end of the eighteenth century. Nils von Hofsten, "Ideas of Creation and Spontaneous Generation prior to Darwin," *Isis*, XXV (1936), 80–94, outlines the history of the conception of special creations. He seems to me to be mistaken in describing Lyell as a reluctant rather than a firm adherent of the doctrine of special and successive creations in the 1830's, but this is only the abstract of a longer paper which I have not seen, "Skapelsetro och Uralstringshypoteser före Darwin," *Uppsala Universitets Årsskrift* (1928). Zöckler gives the fullest account I have found of the interpretative vicissitudes undergone by the Biblical creation story.

2. BIOGRAPHICAL SOURCES

The articles on men of science in *The Dictionary of National Biography* are, in general, excellent. Besides this standard work of reference, I have used a fairly large amount of biographical material, which falls naturally into two main categories. On the one hand, the formal biographies, biographical articles, and studies of the work of particular individuals, are essentially secondary sources. On the other hand, there are the older publications — the typical Victorian *Life and Letters* is the most familiar example — which consist chiefly of published correspondence and diaries and which have, therefore, something of the value of primary and contemporary sources.

There do not happen to be any very notable contributions to the art of biography among works which I have classified as secondary. Edward Smith, *The Life of Sir Joseph Banks* (London, 1911), describes Banks's administration of the Royal Society in the late eighteenth and early nineteenth centuries. Sir William Ramsay, *The Life and Letters of Joseph Black, M.D.* (London, 1918), is disappointing. Much more illuminating is E. W. J. Neave, "Joseph Black's Lectures on the Elements of Chemistry," *Isis*, XXV (1936), 372–390. Henry, Lord Brougham, *Lives of the Philosophers of the Time of George III* (London, 1855), volume I of the author's *Works*, is more interesting for Brougham than for the philosophers. F. J. North, "Paviland Cave, the 'Red Lady,' the Deluge, and William Buckland," *Annals of Science*, V (1941–1947), 91–128, based partly on unpublished correspondence, throws a number of sidelights onto the vogue of geology in the 1820's. J. Wilson Harper, *The Social Ideal and Dr. Chalmers' Contribution to Christian Economics* (Edinburgh, 1910), is (so far as I know) the only modern study of a very interesting figure who would probably repay further research.

The best of several biographies of Dalton is Edward M. Brockbank, *John Dalton* (Manchester, 1944). Hesketh Pearson, *Dr. Darwin* (London, 1930), is a mildly entertaining but not a penetrating treatment of the elder Darwin. R. T. Gunther, *The Daubeny Laboratory Register* (3d printing; Oxford, 1924), is a compilation of records with some biographical information on Daubeny. Sir Thomas E.

Thorpe, *Humphry Davy, Poet and Philosopher* (New York, 1896), is slight and uncritical. James G. Crowther, *British Scientists of the Nineteenth Century* (London, 1935), attempts to consider Davy, Faraday, Joule, Thomson, and Clerk Maxwell, not only as scientists but as sociological and psychological specimens. Silvanus P. Thompson, *Michael Faraday, His Life and Work* (London, 1901), relates its subject to his work better than most of these biographies. Sir Edmund W. Gosse, *Father and Son, a Study of Two Temperaments* (9th ed.; New York, 1925), describes the unsuccessful and rather pathetic efforts of a mediocre naturalist to force both his son and his researches into conformity with his religion. A. E. Clark-Kennedy, *Stephen Hales, D.D., F.R.S.* (Cambridge, 1929), gives an excellent account of the eighteenth-century background. Constance A. Lubbock, *The Herschel Chronicle: The Life-Story of William Herschel and his Sister Caroline Herschel* (Cambridge, England, 1933), and C. J. Ducasse, "John Herschel's Philosophy of Nature," *Studies in the History of Culture* (American Council of Learned Societies; Menasha, Wis., 1942), treat the work of this remarkable family.

J. Reilly and N. O'Flynn, "Richard Kirwan, an Irish Chemist of the Eighteenth Century," *Isis*, XIII (1929–30), 298–319, is a useful appraisal of Kirwan as a chemist, but the authors do not emphasize his geological aberrations. William K. Leask, *Hugh Miller* (Edinburgh, 1896), is a patriotic book. William A. Knight, *Lord Monboddo and Some of His Contemporaries* (London, 1900), prints some of the correspondence of less familiar figures of the eighteenth century. Graham Wallas, *The Life of Francis Place* (3d ed.; New York, 1919), includes some information on the Mechanics' Institutes and related movements. Anne Holt, *Joseph Priestley* (London, 1931), treats her subject as a theologian; Sir T. E. Thorpe, *Joseph Priestley* (New York, 1906), views him as a scientist. There is an interesting account of Benjamin Silliman's travels in England and of his acquaintance-ship with the English geologists in John F. Fulton and Elizabeth H. Thomson, *Benjamin Silliman, 1779–1864* (New York, 1947). T. Sheppard, "William Smith, his Maps and Memoirs," *Proceedings of the Yorkshire Geological Society*, XIX (1917), 75–253, is an exhaustive description of Smith's work and publications and includes a sketch of his life and a bibliography. There exists a biography of Werner by Richard Beck, *Abraham Gottlob Werner* (Berlin, 1918), but I have not been able to find a copy of it. Marion R. Stoll, *Whewell's Philosophy of Induction* (Lancaster, Pa., 1929), is less biographical than analytical.

A number of short biographical or critical articles are also useful: Charles F. Mullett, "Charles Babbage: A Scientific Gadfly," *The Scientific Monthly*, LXVII (1948), 361–371; Benjamin Spector, "Sir Charles Bell and the Bridgewater Treatises," *Bulletin of the History of Medicine*, XII (1942), 314–322; D. W. Gundry, "The Bridgewater Treatises and their Authors," *History*, XXXI (1946), 140–152; F. J. North, "Geology's Debt to Henry Thomas de la Beche," *Endeavour*, III (1944), 15–19; E. B. Bailey, "James Hutton: Father of Modern Geology, 1726–1797," *Nature*, CXIX (1927), 582; V. A. Eyles, "James Hutton (1726–1797) and Sir Charles Lyell (1797–1875)," *Nature*, CLX (1947), 694–695; M. MacGregor, "James Hutton, the Founder of Modern Geology," *Endeavour*, VI (1947), 109–111; V. A. Eyles, "John Macculloch, F.R.S., and his Geological Map: An Account of the First Geological Survey of Scotland," *Annals of Science*, II (1937), 114–129; W. T. Gordon, "William Hyde Wollaston," *Nature*, CXXXIV (1934), 86–87.

In nineteenth-century Britain, a man had to be fairly obscure not to leave behind a two or more volume *Life and Letters* or *Memoir*, shepherded through the press by a dutiful son, daughter, or protégé, whose own contribution to the book was seldom more than a thin mortar of narrative holding together thick chunks of correspondence and diary. Very few of these works have any merit beyond the printing of sizable amounts of the subject's private papers, but since they do this at length, they are often more valuable sources of information than the run-of-the-mill biography, in spite of the fact that the index, organization, and standards by which the material was selected are generally very deficient if not wholly lacking. The authors seldom had the will or the skill to stand between their readers and their subject, and the chief difficulty with these books is not what is in them, but that we do not always know what was left out. Some of these works, of course, are intrinsically much better than others. The individual items do not require critical discussion, however, and the scope of the literature will be apparent from a listing of the titles, arranged alphabetically by subject, with occasional comments. In this section, too, are included a number of titles which, though not falling into the pattern just outlined, may be described as primarily autobiographical, as contemporary in their outlook, or as partaking of the character of memoir rather than biography:

Elizabeth C. Agassiz, *Louis Agassiz, His Life and Correspondence* (2 vols.; Boston, 1886); John G. Godard, *George Birkbeck, the Pioneer of Popular Education* (London, 1884); Thomas Birch, *The Life of the Honourable Robert Boyle* (London, 1744); Anna B. Gordon, *The Life and Correspondence of William Buckland, D.D., F.R.S.* (New York, 1894); George Wilson, *The Life of the Honourable Henry Cavendish, Including Abstracts of His more important Scientific Papers* (London, 1851); William Hanna, *Memoirs of the Life and Writings of Thomas Chalmers, D.D., LL.D.* (4 vols.; New York, 1857); Charles Gibbon, *The Life of George Combe* (2 vols.; London, 1878); Frederick C. Conybeare, *Letters and Exercises of the Elizabethan Schoolmaster John Conybeare . . . with Notes and a Fragment of Autobiography by the Very Rev. William Daniel Conybeare, Dean of Llandaff* (London, 1905); William C. Henry, *Memoirs of the Life and Scientific Writings of John Dalton* (London, 1854); Robert A. Smith, "Memoir of John Dalton, and History of the Atomic Theory up to his Time," comprising volume XIII of *Memoirs of the Literary and Philosophical Society of Manchester* (1856), 2d series; George Wilson, "Life and Discoveries of Dalton," in *Religio Chemici* (Cambridge and London, 1862); Francis Darwin, *The Life and Letters of Charles Darwin* (2 vols.; New York, 1888); John Davy, *Memoirs of the Life of Sir Humphry Davy, Bart.*, comprising volume I of *The Collected Works of Sir Humphry Davy* (9 vols.; London, 1839–40); John H. Paris, *The Life of Sir Humphry Davy, Bart.* (London, 1831), a flowery and most unreliable book; Samuel Smiles, *Robert Dick, Baker of Thurso, Geologist and Botanist* (London, 1878), and *Lives of the Engineers* (4 vols.; London, 1862–1865); Richard L. and Maria Edgeworth, *Memoirs of Richard Lovell Edgeworth* (2 vols.; London, 1820); Henry Bence Jones, *The Life and Letters of Faraday* (2 vols.; Philadelphia, 1870); J. C. Shairp, P. G. Tait, and A. Adams-Reilly, *Life and Letters of James David Forbes* (London, 1873); Sir Henry Holland, *Recollections of Past Life* (New York, 1872); Katherine M. Lyell, *Memoir of Leonard Horner* (2 vols.; London, 1890); Leonard Huxley, *Life and Letters of Thomas Henry Huxley* (2 vols.; New York, 1901); Lawrence

Jameson, *Biographical Memoir of the late Professor Jameson* (Edinburgh, 1854); A. F. Tytler of Woodhouselee, *Memoirs of the Life and Writings of the Honourable Henry Home of Kames* (3 vols.; Edinburgh, 1814); Amelia Moillet, *Sketch of the Life of James Keir* (London, 1860); Charles Knight, *Passages of a Working Life* (3 vols.; London, 1864–65), an autobiography; Katherine M. Lyell, *Life, Letters and Journals of Sir Charles Lyell, Bart.* (2 vols.; London, 1881), one of the best of the works of this type; Gideon A. Mantell, *The Journal of Gideon Mantell, Surgeon and Geologist* (ed. E. Cecil Curwen; London and New York, 1940); Hugh Miller, *My Schools and Schoolmasters* (Boston, 1855), an autobiography; Peter Bayne, *The Life and Letters of Hugh Miller* (2 vols.; Boston, 1871); Sir Archibald Geikie, *Life of Sir Roderick I. Murchison* (2 vols.; London, 1875), much the best of these works; Richard Owen, *The Life of Richard Owen* (2 vols.; New York, 1894); Joseph Priestley, *Memoirs of Dr. Joseph Priestley to the Year 1795, Written by Himself, with a Continuation, to the Time of his Decease, by his Son, Joseph Priestley* (2 vols.; Northumberland, Pa., 1806); H .C. Bolton (ed.), *Scientific Correspondence of Joseph Priestley* (New York, 1892); Sir John Pringle, *Six Discourses* (London, 1783), containing an introductory biographical memoir of Pringle by Andrew Kippis; Mary Anne Schimmelpenninck, *Life of Mary Anne Schimmelpenninck* (ed. Christiana C. Hankin; 2 vols.; London, 1858); John W. Clark and Thomas McK. Hughes, *The Life and Letters of the Reverend Adam Sedgwick* (2 vols.; Cambridge, England, 1890); John Phillips, *Memoir of William Smith* (London, 1844); Alfred Russel Wallace, *My Life, a Record of Events and Opinions* (2 vols.; New York, 1905); James P. Muirhead, *The Life of James Watt* (New York, 1859); J. P. Muirhead (ed.), *The Origin and Progress of the Mechanical Inventions of James Watt, Illustrated by his Correspondence* (3 vols.; London, 1854); Eliza Meteyard, *The Life of Josiah Wedgwood, from his Private Correspondence and Family Papers* (2 vols.; London, 1865–66); Janet M. Douglas, *The Life and Selections from the Correspondence of William Whewell, D.D.* (London, 1881), mostly personal and domestic; Isaac Todhunter, *William Whewell, D.D.* (2 vols.; London, 1876), an account of his writings with selections from literary and scientific correspondence; John Randall, *The Wilkinsons* (Madeley, Salop, undated [*c.* 1830]);

George Peacock, *Life of Thomas Young, M.D., F.R.S.* (London, 1855).

3. Contemporary Literature

The contemporary sources, on which this study primarily rests, may be grouped into the three general categories of theology (chiefly natural theology), science, and popular science — a method of arrangement which will leave a few stray titles to be gathered up under a fourth heading as miscellaneous. This scheme of classification should not, however, be looked upon as more than a convenient device by which to organize the material, because to a considerable extent it projects into the past distinctions which were not made in the past, or at least not so sharply made as in modern times. Moreover, the border line between the three types is very blurred. Many of these works include elements which are both theological and scientific, scientific and popular, popular and theological, or all three combined, and the decision on where to place a particular title is often arbitrary. But even when the necessary reservations are made, it still seems worth while, and usually possible, to differentiate between books which would now be regarded as predominantly theological, scientific, or popular in outlook, purpose, and content.

a. *Works of a Theological Character*

My opening remarks in Chapter I on the relationship of Puritanism and science make no claim to originality. They are derived mainly from the work of the authorities cited in the first section of this bibliography. In addition, there are a number of readily available seventeenth- and early eighteenth-century writings which confirm the sympathy then existing between science and theology. What follows is a more or less randomly selected sampling: Robert Boyle, *The Excellency of Theology above Natural Philosophy,* in volume III of *The Theological Works of the Honourable Robert Boyle* (ed. Richard Boulton; 3 vols.; London, 1715), and *Seraphick Love; Some Motives and Incentives to the Love of God, Pathetically Discours'd of in a Letter to a Friend* (4th ed.; London, 1665); Gilbert Burnet, *A Sermon Preached at the Funeral of Robert Boyle* (London, 1692); William Derham, *Astro-Theology; or, A Demonstration of the Being and Attributes of God, from a Survey of the Heavens*

(London, 1715), and *Physico-Theology, or, A Demonstration of the Being and Attributes of God from His Works of Creation* (3d ed.; London, 1714); Joseph Glanville, *Scepsis Scientifica* (London, 1665); John Harris, *The Atheistical Objections, Against the Being of a God, and His Attributes, Fairly Considered and Fully Refuted* (London, 1698); John Ray, *The Wisdom of God Manifested in the Works of the Creation* (London, 1691); John Webster, *Academiarum Examen* (London, 1654); John Wilkins, *Of the Principles and Duties of Natural Religion* (4th ed.; London, 1699).

In the later period, William Paley, *Natural Theology; or, Evidence of the Existence and Attributes of the Deity Collected from the Appearances of Nature* (London, 1802), epitomized, but in no way originated, the empirical approach to God. Among the contributions made to natural theology by scientists of the late eighteenth century were Jean André Deluc, *Lettres sur le christianisme adressées à M. le pasteur Teller* (Berlin, 1801); and Joseph Priestley, *Disquisitions Relating to Matter and Spirit* (2d ed.; 2 vols.; London, 1782), and *Letters to a Philosophic Unbeliever* (2 parts; Bath, 1780, and London, 1787), which were republished with Priestley's other extrascientific works in *Theological and Miscellaneous Works* (ed. J. T. Rutt; 26 vols.; London, 1817–1832).

In the generation after Paley, his argument was often enlarged but seldom improved. The eight *Bridgewater Treatises* are the most characteristic examples of the persistence of Paleyism: Thomas Chalmers, *On the Power, Wisdom, and Goodness of God as Manifested in the Adaptation of External Nature to the Moral and Intellectual Constitution of Man* (2 vols.; London, 1833); John Kidd, *On the Adaptation of External Nature to the Physical Condition of Man* (London, 1833; Philadelphia, 1836); William Whewell, *Astronomy and General Physics, Considered with Reference to Natural Theology* (London, 1833; Philadelphia, 1836); Sir Charles Bell, *The Hand, Its Mechanism and Vital Endowments, as Evincing Design* (London, 1833; Philadelphia, 1836); Peter Mark Roget, *Animal and Vegetable Physiology, Considered with Reference to Natural Theology* (2 vols., London, 1834; 2 vols., Philadelphia, 1836); William E. Buckland, *Geology and Mineralogy, Considered with Reference to Natural Theology* (2 vols., London, 1836; 2d ed., 2 vols., London, 1837); William Kirby, *On the Power, Wisdom, and Good-*

ness of God as Manifested in the Creation of Animals, and in their History, Habits, and Instincts (London, 1835; Philadelphia, 1837); William Prout, *Chemistry, Meteorology, and the Function of Digestion* (London, 1834; 2d ed., London, 1834). In the Philadelphia edition, Kidd, Whewell, and Bell were bound in one volume. Where more than one edition is cited in the list just given, it is to the second that citations in the notes refer. Most of these authors described God as an intervening and superintending deity, and it was on this account that Charles Babbage took issue with them in his independently written *The Ninth Bridgewater Treatise, a Fragment* (2d ed.; London, 1838).

By the 1830's, the question whether God acted through a single set of all-sufficient laws, or whether His control was exerted immediately, had become a major issue in natural theology, and, besides Babbage, other advocates of the uniformitarian interpretation were George Combe, *On The Relation between Religion and Science* (Edinburgh, 1847), and Baden Powell, *The Connexion of Natural and Divine Truth; or, The Study of the Inductive Philosophy Considered as Subservient to Theology* (London, 1838), *The Unity of Worlds and of Nature* (2d ed.; London, 1856), and *The Order of Nature Considered in Reference to the Claims of Revelation* (London, 1859). Powell contributed the essay, "On the Study of the Evidences of Christianity," to *Essays and Reviews* (London, 1860).

The idea of God as a governor was, however, the traditional and the more common assumption, not only among the Bridgewater authors, but among other writers of natural theology, whether scientists or not. This was the attitude underlying Henry, Lord Brougham, *A Discourse of Natural Theology* (4th ed.; London, 1835), the separately published preface to Brougham's edition of Paley; William E. Buckland, *Vindiciae Geologicae* (Oxford, 1820); Thomas Dick, *The Christian Philosopher; or, The Connection of Science and Philosophy with Religion* (London, 1823); John Macculloch, *Proofs and Illustrations of the Attributes of God, from the Facts and Laws of the Physical Universe: Being the Foundation of Natural and Revealed Religion* (3 vols.; London, 1837); Hugh Miller, *The Testimony of the Rocks; or, Geology in Its Bearings on the Two Theologies, Natural and Revealed* (Edinburgh, 1857), and *The Two Records: The*

Mosaic and the Geological (Boston, 1854); and William Whewell, *Indications of the Creator* (Philadelphia, 1845).

The plurality of inhabited worlds was the subject of an exchange between William Whewell, *Of the Plurality of Worlds* (London, 1853), and Sir David Brewster, *More Worlds Than One: The Creed of the Philosopher and the Hope of the Christian* (London, 1854). William Smith's researches were the main subject of Joseph Townsend, *The Character of Moses Established for Veracity as an Historian* (2 vols. in 1; Bath, 1815). Catholic reactions to natural theology may be seen in Nicholas Patrick Cardinal Wiseman, *Twelve Lectures on the Connexion between Science and Revealed Religion* (Andover, N. Y., 1837), and John Henry Cardinal Newman, *The Idea of a University* (London, 1891).

The cosmological literature of the seventeenth and eighteenth centuries, though not always theological in form, nevertheless was generally more theological — or at any rate speculative — than scientific in temper. This is almost as true of George Louis Leclerc de Buffon, *Histoire et théorie de la terre,* in volume I of *Histoire naturelle* (24 vols.; Paris, 1749–1783), in which the theory was only very loosely related to the Biblical account, as of works like Thomas Burnet, *Sacred Theory of the Earth* (6th ed.; 2 vols.; London, 1726), Nehemiah Grew, *Cosmologia Sacra* (London, 1701), and William Whiston, *A New Theory of the Earth, from Its Origin to the Consummation of all Things* (London, 1696), in all three of which considerable importance was attached to squaring the interpretation in some fashion with traditional religious belief.

If the scientific successor of cosmological speculation was serious geological study, its theological descendant was the literature which includes (often in the same book) both clerical attacks upon geology and uninformed attempts to frame theoretical systems reconciling the geological and scriptural records. Characteristic samples are: William Cockburn, *The Bible Defended against the British Association* (London, 1839), and *A Letter to Professor Buckland Concerning the Origin of the World* (London, 1838); George Fairholme, *New and Conclusive Demonstration Both of the Fact and Period of the Mosaic Deluge and of Its Having Been the Only Event of the Kind that Has Ever Occurred upon the Earth* (London, 1837); Philip Gosse, *Omphalos* (London, 1857); Granville Penn, *A Comparative Estimate of the Mineral and Mosaical Cosmologies* (London, 1822), and *Conversations on Geology* (London, 1828); John Pye Smith, *Lectures on the Bearing of Geological Science upon Certain Parts of Scriptural Narrative* (London, 1839); and Andrew Ure, *A New System of Geology, in which the Great Revolutions of the Earth and Animated Nature, are Reconciled at once to Modern Science and Sacred History* (London, 1829).

b. *Scientific Works*

For the purpose of this study, the scientific sources may be divided into those books dealing primarily with geology and the immediately related subjects, and those dealing with other sciences. There is, of course, also much material to be found in the publications of scientific societies, which are listed in the last section of this bibliography. Since the important geological works have already been discussed in the text, further critical comment would be superfluous. Here I have simply listed the writers referred to in the present book in the general chronological order in which their work contributed to the development of geological science:

John Whitehurst, *Inquiry into the Original State and Formation of the Earth* (London, 1778); Richard Kirwan, *Elements of Mineralogy* (London, 1784); James Hutton, *Theory of the Earth, with Proofs and Illustrations* (2 vols.; Edinburgh, 1795); John Playfair, *Illustrations of the Huttonian Theory of the Earth* (Edinburgh, 1802), republished as volume I of *The Works of John Playfair, Esquire* (4 vols.; Edinburgh, 1822); Abraham Gottlob Werner, *New Theory of the Formation of Veins* (trans. Charles Anderson; Edinburgh, 1809); Robert Jameson, *An Outline of the Mineralogy of the Shetland Islands and of the Island of Arran* (Edinburgh, 1798), *Mineralogy of the Scottish Isles* (2 vols.; Edinburgh, 1800), and *System of Mineralogy* (3 vols.; Edinburgh, 1804–1807), including as volume III, *Elements of Geognosy*.

Georges Cuvier and Alexandre Brongniart, *Essai sur la géographie minéralogique des environs de Paris* (Paris, 1811); William Smith, *A Delineation of the Strata of England and Wales* (London, 1815), *Strata Identified by Organized Fossils* (London, 1816), and *Stratigraphical System of Organized Fossils* (London, 1817); Georges

Cuvier, *Essay on the Theory of the Earth* (Edinburgh, 1817), Robert Jameson's translation of *Discours sur les révolutions de la surface du globe*, which was the separately published preface to Cuvier's *Recherches sur les ossemens fossiles, où l'on rétablit les caractères de plusieurs animaux dont les révolutions du globe ont détruit les espèces* (4 vols.; Paris, 1811); George B. Greenough, *A Critical Examination of the First Principles of Geology* (London, 1819), and *Geological Map of England* (London, 1820); William E. Buckland, *Reliquiae Diluvianae; or, Observations on the Organic Remains Contained in Caves, Fissures, and Diluvial Gravel, and on Other Geological Phenomena, Attesting the Action of an Universal Deluge* (2d ed.; London, 1824); George Poulett Scrope, *Considerations on Volcanos, the Probable Causes of their Phenomena, the Laws which Determine their March, the Dispositions of their Products, and their Connexion with the Present State and Past History of the Globe; Leading to the Establishment of a new Theory of the Earth* (London, 1825), and *The Geology and Extinct Volcanos of Central France* (London, 1826); Charles G. B. Daubeny, *A Description of Active and Extinct Volcanos* (London, 1826); Sir Charles Lyell, *Principles of Geology: Being an Attempt to Explain the Former Changes of the Earth's Surface, by Reference to Causes now in Operation* (3 vols.; London, 1830–1833); Gideon A. Mantell, *The Geology of the South-East of England* (London, 1833), an expansion of the same author's *Illustrations of the Geology of Sussex* (London, 1822); Sir Henry T. de la Beche, *Researches in Theoretical Geology* (London, 1834); Sir Roderick I. Murchison, *The Silurian System* (2 vols.; London, 1839); Hugh Miller, *The Old Red Sandstone; or, New Walks in an Old Field* (Edinburgh, 1841).

In addition, there are a number of scientific works which, though not bearing directly on geology, were of importance to the development of that science, or which give useful insights into the character of the general scientific background. Here, too, the chronological method seems the arrangement best suited to the progressive nature of the history of science:

Sir Isaac Newton, *Mathematical Principles of Natural Philosophy* (the Andrew Motte translation of 1729 revised and edited by Florian Cajori; Berkeley, Calif., 1934), which includes Roger Cotes' preface to the second editon of 1713; and *Opticks* (reprinted from the fourth edition of 1730; London, 1931); Stephen Hales, *Statical Essays* (2d ed., 2 vols.; London, 1731); Colin Maclaurin, *A Treatise of Fluxions* (2 vols.; Edinburgh, 1742); Joseph Black, *Experiments upon Magnesia Alba, Quicklime, and Some Other Alcaline Substances* (reprinted from the first edition of 1756; Edinburgh, 1898); Henry Cavendish, *The Scientific Papers of the Honourable Henry Cavendish, F.R.S.* (ed. James Clerk Maxwell, Sir Joseph Larmos, and Sir Edward Thorpe; 2 vols.; Cambridge, 1921), the contents of volume I having been previously published in 1879; Joseph Priestley, *Experiments and Observations upon Different Kinds of Air* (3 vols.; London, 1774–1777), *Experiments and Observations Relating to Various Branches of Natural Philosophy, with a Continuation of the Observations on Air* (3 vols.; London, 1779–1785), often catalogued as volumes IV–VI of the preceding title, and *Doctrine of Phlogiston Established and Composition of Water Refuted* (Philadelphia, 1800); Richard Kirwan, *An Essay on Phlogiston and the Constitution of Acids* (London, 1787), a French translation of which was published by Mme Lavoisier (Paris, 1788); John Hunter, *Essays and Observations on Natural History, Anatomy, Physiology, Psychology, and Geology* (2 vols.; London, 1841), published posthumously; John Dalton, *New System of Chemical Philosophy* (2 vols.; Manchester, 1808–1810); Jean Baptiste de Lamarck, *Recherches sur l'organisation des corps vivants* (Paris, 1802), *Philosophie zoologique* (Paris, 1809), and *Histoire naturelle des animaux sans vertèbres* (7 vols. in 8; Paris, 1815–1822); Georges Cuvier, *Le règne animal distribué d'après son organisation, pour servir de base à l'histoire naturelle des animaux et d'introduction à l'anatomie comparée* (4 vols.; Paris, 1817); James C. Prichard, *Researches into the Physical History of Mankind* (2 vols.; London, 1826); Alexander von Humboldt, *Cosmos; Sketch of a Physical Description of the Universe* (trans. E. C. Otté, B. H. Paul, W. S. Dallas; 4 vols.; London, 1848–1852); Richard Owen, *On the Archetypes and Homologies of the Vertebrate Skeleton* (London, 1848), and *On the Nature of Limbs* (London, 1849); Charles R. Darwin, *On the Origin of Species by Means of Natural Selection; or, The Preservation of Favoured Races in the Struggle for Life* (London, 1859).

c. *Popular Science*

The literature of popular science includes a great variety of works of very unequal merit. Among the better sort were the books which, like the modern textbook or high-level popularization, were written in an objective manner to inform students and the general public about science and its progress. Secondly, there were a number of books of a different type, which were concerned less with dispassionate explanation than with argumentation and the popularization of a controversial theory. And, thirdly, there were the publications of authors who were interested in edifying rather than in informing or in theorizing.

Works of the first type were often written by scientists, and the best of them may be considered to have been scientific in character, differing from the books included in the preceding section of this bibliography in that their purpose was more to explain science than to advance it. Examples are the eighteenth-century descriptions of natural philosophy:

John Keill, *An Introduction to Newtonian Philosophy; or, Philosophical Lectures Read in the University of Oxford, Anno Dom. 1700* (4th ed.; London, 1745); F. Hauksbee, *Physico-Mechanical Experiments on Various Subjects* (2d ed.; London, 1719); Henry Pemberton, *A View of Sir Isaac Newton's Philosophy* (Dublin, 1728); W. J.'s Gravesande, *Mathematical Elements of Natural Philosophy, Confirmed by Experiments; or, An Introduction to Sir Isaac Newton's Philosophy* (trans. J. T. Desaguliers; 3d ed.; 2 vols.; London, 1726), and some of the treatises in *Oeuvres philosophiques et mathématiques de M. G. J. 's Gravesande* (trans. and ed. J. N. S. Allamand; 2 vols. in 1; Amsterdam, 1774); J. T. Desaguliers, *A Course of Experimental Philosophy* (3d ed.; 2 vols.; London, 1763); Pieter van Musschenbroek, *The Elements of Natural Philosophy* (trans. John Colson; 2 vols.; London, 1744); Colin Maclaurin, *An Account of Sir Isaac Newton's Philosophical Discoveries, in Four Books* (London, 1748); John Rutherforth, *A System of Natural Philosophy: Being a Course of Lectures in Mechanics, Optics, Hydrostatics, and Astronomy* (2 vols.; Cambridge, 1748); Benjamin Martin, *Philosophia Britannica; or, A New and Comprehensive System of the Newtonian Philosophy, Astronomy, and Geography* (2 vols.; London, 1747), and *The Young*

Gentleman and Lady's Philosophy, in a Continued Survey of the Works of Nature and Art; by Way of Dialogue (2d ed.; 2 vols.; London, 1772); John Rowning, *A Compendious System of Natural Philosophy: with Notes, Containing the Mathematical Demonstrations, and Some Occasional Remarks* (7th ed.; 2 vols.; London, 1772). An early example of the technical handbook was John Harris, *Lexicon Technicum; or, An Universal English Dictionary of Arts and Sciences, Explaining not only the Terms of Art, but the Arts Themselves* (London, 1704).

In the nineteenth century, there were occasional books published on the whole of natural philosophy, for example, John Playfair, *Outlines of Natural Philosophy* (2 vols.; Edinburgh, 1812), and Sir John F. W. Herschel, *A Preliminary Discourse on the Study of Natural Philosophy* (London, 1831), which, however, was a discussion of method rather than a description of subject matter; but by the latter part of the eighteenth century the exposition of a single science had become the more common type of publication: Joseph Priestley, *The History and Present State of Discoveries Relating to Vision, Light, and Colours* (London, 1772), and *The History and Present State of Electricity* (2d ed.; London, 1769); Samuel Horsley, *Elementary Treatise on the Fundamental Principles of Practical Mathematics* (Oxford, 1801); Joseph Black, *Lectures on the Elements of Chemistry Delivered in the University of Edinburgh by the late Joseph Black, M.D.* (ed. John Robison; 3 vols.; London, 1803); William Smith, *Treatise on the Construction and Management of Waterworks* (London, 1806); John Fleming, *The Philosophy of Zoology; or, A General View of the Structure, Functions, and Classification of Animals* (2 vols.; Edinburgh, 1822); and Sir John F. W. Herschel, *A Treatise on Astronomy* (London, 1841).

A number of manuals and responsible popularizations were published to guide the amateur geologist and to keep the public abreast of the progress of geology in the nineteenth century: Robert Bakewell, *An Introduction to Geology* (London, 1813); William T. Brande, *Outlines of Geology* (London, 1817); William Phillips, *A Selection of Facts from the Best Authorities, Arranged so as to Form an Outline of the Geology of England and Wales* (London, 1818); William D. Conybeare and William Phillips, *Outlines of the Geology of England and Wales* (London, 1822); Sir Henry T. de la Beche,

A Geological Manual (London, 1831), and *How to Observe* (London, 1835); Sir Charles Lyell, *Elements of Geology* (London, 1838); Gideon A. Mantell, *The Wonders of Geology; or, A Familiar Exposition of Geological Phenomena* (2 vols.; London, 1838), and *The Medals of Creation; or, First Lessons in Geology, and in the Study of Organic Remains* (2 vols.; London, 1844); Hugh Miller, *Popular Geology* (Edinburgh, 1858), and *Rambles of a Geologist; or, Ten Thousand Miles over the Fossiliferous Deposits of Scotland* (Edinburgh, 1858), also published in an American edition with *The Cruise of the Betsey; or, A Summer Ramble among the Fossiliferous Deposits of the Hebrides* (Boston, 1859).

The interpretation of science for the layman was the subject of a second type of work, in which the writer's purpose was to persuade as well as to inform his readers. All of the publications listed in the following paragraph are of some interest for the history of scientific thought, either because they were written by people who had a claim to be considered scientists, or because they aroused discussion among scientists. Although many of these books present a good deal of information, in general the authors were more interested in argumentation than in exposition:

John Harris, *Remarks on some Late Papers, Relating to the Universal Deluge: and to the Natural History of the Earth* (London, 1697); Erasmus Darwin, *The Botanic Garden* (2 vols.; London, 1789–1791); *Zoonomia; or, The Laws of Organic Life* (2 vols.; London, 1794–1798), a work which might, perhaps, be classified as scientific rather than popular; and *The Temple of Nature; or, The Origin of Society: a Poem with Philosophical Notes* (London, 1803); Jean André Deluc, *Lettres physiques et morales sur l'histoire de la terre et de l'homme adressées à la reine de la Grande Bretagne* (5 vols. in 6; La Haye, 1779); "Letters to Dr. James Hutton on his Theory of the Earth," *Monthly Review*, II (1790), 206–227, 582–601; III (1790), 573–586; V (1701), 564–585; and *An Elementary Treatise on Geology* (trans. Henry de la Fite; London, 1809); Richard Kirwan, *Geological Essays* (London, 1799); George Combe, *Constitution of Man* (2 vols.; London, 1828); Robert Chambers, *Vestiges of the Natural History of Creation* (London, 1844), with which should be read the preface and notes prepared by Alexander Ireland for the twelfth edition (London, 1884); and *Explanations:*

a Sequel to "Vestiges of the Natural History of Creation" (London, 1845), incorporated into the later editions of the parent work as an appendix; Adam Sedgwick, *A Discourse on the Studies of the University* (4th ed., Cambridge, England, 1835; 5th ed., Cambridge, 1850) — in the latter edition the relevant portion is the enormous prefatory essay refuting the *Vestiges;* Hugh Miller, *The Footprints of the Creator; or, The Asterolepis of Stromness* (Edinburgh, 1847).

Finally, the publications which preached the value of useful knowledge may properly be considered as belonging to the literature of popular science because, although their content was of a moralizing rather than a scientific character, the supposed lessons of science were what pointed the moral, and it was by means of the dissemination of scientific understanding that the authors hoped to enlighten the populace and strengthen the fabric of society:

Thomas Dick, *Celestial Scenery; or, The Wonders of the Heavens Displayed* (London, 1837), and *On the Improvement of Society by the Diffusion of Knowledge* (Glasgow, undated [*c.* 1841]); Henry, Lord Brougham, "Objects, Advantages, and Pleasures of Science," *The Pamphleteer*, XXVII (1826), 497–507, originally written for the Society for the Diffusion of Useful Knowledge as a preliminary treatise to its series, *The Library of Useful Knowledge;* and *Practical Observations upon the Education of the People, Addressed to the Working Classes and their Employers* (London, 1825); George Combe, *Education, Its Principles and Practice* (ed. William Jolly; London, 1879), and *Lectures on Popular Education* (3d ed.; Edinburgh, 1848); John Connolly, *Cottage Evenings* (London, 1829); Sir John F. W. Herschel, *The Admiralty Manual of Scientific Enquiry; Prepared for the Use of Her Majesty's Navy: and Adapted for Travellers in General* (London, 1849), and *Essays from the Edinburgh and Quarterly Reviews* (London, 1857), which includes a number of public addresses not previously published; Lord Arthur Hervey, Bishop of Bath and Wells, *A Suggestion for Supplying the Literary, Scientific, and Mechanics' Institutes of Great Britain and Ireland with Lecturers from the Universities* (Cambridge, 1855); Charles Knight, *The Results of Machinery, Namely, Cheap Production and Increased Employment Exhibited: Being an Address to the Working-men of the United Kingdom* (London, 1831); Andrew Ure, *The Philosophy of Manufactures; or, An Exposition of the*

Scientific, Moral, and Commercial Economy of the Factory System of Great Britain (London, 1835). The latter two titles might, perhaps, be better described as popular technology than as popular science.

d. *Miscellaneous*

There are, to conclude this section, a few works which resist the above classification, but which are, nevertheless, of some importance to the present study: Francis Bacon, *The Works of Francis Bacon* (ed. James Spedding, Robert L. Ellis, and Douglas D. Heath; 15 vols.; Boston, 1860–1864); Thomas Chalmers, *The Christian and Civic Economy of Large Towns* (3 vols.; Glasgow, 1821–1826), and *On Political Economy in Connection with the Moral State and Moral Prospects of Society* (Glasgow, 1832); Jean André Deluc, *Bacon tel qu'il est* (Berlin, 1800), and *Précis de la philosophie de Bacon* (2 vols.; Paris, 1802); J. T. Desaguliers, *The Newtonian System of the World, the best Model of Government: An Allegorical Poem* (London, 1728); William Herschel, *The Universe Around Us* (Ann Arbor, 1932), an exchange of correspondence; Richard Kirwan, *Logick* (2 vols.; London, 1807), and *Metaphysical Essays* (London, 1809); Hugh Miller, *Letter from One of the Scottish People to Lord Brougham and Vaux* (Edinburgh, 1839), and *Poems Written in the Leisure Hours of a Journeyman Mason* (Inverness, 1829); William Paley, *The Principles of Moral and Political Philosophy* (London, 1785).

Samples of contemporary opinion on science and its relation to university education may be found in: Cambridge University Commission, *Report* (London, 1852); Oxford University Commission, *Report* (London, 1852); Charles G. B. Daubeny, *Brief Remarks on the Correlation of the Natural Sciences* (Oxford, 1848); Sir Charles Lyell, *Travels in North America; with Geological Observations on the United States, Canada, and Nova Scotia* (2 vols.; London, 1845), vol. I, chap. xiii; William Whewell, *On the Principles of English University Education* (London, 1837), and *Of a Liberal Education in General; and with Particular Reference to the Leading Studies of the University of Cambridge* (London, 1845).

4. PERIODICALS

Contemporary periodicals are a rich source of information, both for the history of science in the publications of the scientific societies and for the general history of opinion in the reviews which exercised a wide influence in nineteenth-century England. Citations to particular articles will be found in the notes; here only the journals themselves are listed. In each case the period for which I have surveyed them is indicated.

a. *Scientific Societies and their Publications*

The abbreviations which I have employed in citing the journals in the footnotes are given on page 261, below: British Association for the Advancement of Science, *British Association Reports*, I–XIV (1832–1844), volumes I and II bound in one; The Geological Society of London, *Proceedings of the Geological Society of London*, I (1826–1833) and II (1833–1838), which published minutes of meetings, abstracts of papers, presidential addresses, and so forth; and *Transactions of the Geological Society*, series 1, I–V (1807–1821), and series 2, I–VIII (1824–1856), which published memoirs of researches and which was amalgamated with *P.G.S.* in *The Quarterly Journal of the Geological Society*, beginning in 1845; The Literary and Philosophical Society of Manchester, *Memoirs of the Literary and Philosophical Society of Manchester*, I–XIV in two series (1785–1857); The Royal Institution, *The Quarterly Journal of Science, Literature, and the Arts*, I–XXIX (1816–1830); The Royal Irish Academy, *Index to the Serial Publications of the Royal Irish Academy, 1786–1906* (Dublin, 1912), and *Transactions of the Royal Irish Academy*, I–VI (1787–1797); The Royal Society, *Philosophical Transactions*, I–CXL (1665–1850); The Royal Society of Arts, *Transactions of the Society for Encouragement of Arts, Manufactures, and Commerce*, I–LIV (1783–1843), which, however, is of little value for the history of science; The Royal Society of Edinburgh, *Transactions of the Royal Society of Edinburgh*, I–VIII (1788–1818); The Wernerian Society, *Memoirs of the Wernerian Natural History Society*, I–VIII (1811–1839).

b. *General Periodicals and Journals of Opinion*

Articles in most of these periodicals followed (or rather established) the British tradition of journalistic anonymity and were unsigned. In the cases in which I have discovered the identity of an author, either through my own reading in the period or, in the case of the *Edinburgh,* by reference to Walter A. Copinger, *On the Authorship of the First Hundred Numbers of the Edinburgh Review* (Manchester, 1895), I have given his name in the footnotes in brackets before the title of the article.

Several journals were devoted to the popularization of science on what may be described as a middle-class level of comprehension: *Annals of Philosophy,* I–XVI, and new series, I–XII (1813–1826); *Edinburgh Philosophical Journal,* I–XIV (1819–1826), which in 1826 was renamed *Edinburgh New Philosophical Journal,* I–LVII (1826– 1854); and *The Philosophical Magazine,* I–LXVIII (1798–1826), new series (incorporating *Annals of Philosophy*), I–XI (1827–1832), and 3d series, I–XXXVII (1832–1850). *The Mechanics' Magazine,* I–XXVII (1823–1837), and *The Penny Magazine of the Society for the Diffusion of Useful Knowledge,* I–IX (1832–1840), emphasized pieces on popular science and mechanics for a working-class public, a type of article also featured in *Chambers's Edinburgh Journal,* I–XII (1832–1843), new series, I–XX (1844–1853). There are a few useful articles and notices in *The Gentleman's Magazine,* LXX–CIII, and new series, I–XLV (1800–1856). *The Times* gave very little space to the progress of science; it may be surveyed by means of *Palmer's Index.*

Most of the important publications and developments in science served as the occasions for long articles in the three most influential reviews, *The Edinburgh Review,* I–XCII (1802–1850), *The Quarterly Review,* I–LXXXVII (1809–1850), and *The Westminster Review,* I–LIII (1824–1850); and until the 1830's in *The British Critic,* I–XLII (1793–1813), new series, I–XVII (1814–1822). This last periodical suspended publication until 1825, when it resumed as a quarterly, I–III (1825–26). In 1827 it was renamed *The British Critic, Quarterly Theological Review and Ecclesiastical Record,* I–XXIX (1827–1841), but as it came increasingly under high church influences, it ceased publishing reviews of science.

NOTES

NOTES

ABBREVIATIONS

Manchester Memoirs	*Memoirs of the Literary and Philosophical Society of Manchester*
M.W.S.	*Memoirs of the Wernerian Natural History Society*
P.G.S.	*Proceedings of the Geological Society of London*
T.G.S.	*Transactions of the Geological Society of London*
T.R.I.A.	*Transactions of the Royal Irish Academy*
T.R.S.E.	*Transactions of the Royal Society of Edinburgh*

See the Bibliographical Essay for a fuller description of these sources.

PREFACE

1. *History of the Conflict between Religion and Science* (New York, 1875).
2. *A History of the Warfare of Science with Theology in Christendom* (2d ed.; 2 vols.; New York, 1901). Most of the material in this book had already been published piecemeal by the time the first edition appeared (1896), and the general thesis had been stated twenty years earlier in the author's *The Warfare of Science* (New York, 1876), the English edition of which included a preface by John Tyndall (London, 1876).
3. Draper and White should be read with D. O. Zöckler, *Geschichte der Beziehungen zwischen Theologie und Naturwissenschaft, mit besondrer Rücksicht auf Schöpfungsgeschichte* (2 vols.; Gütersloh, 1877–1879). Zöckler treats the subject as *Kulturgeschichte* on the grand scale, and his aim in part is to refute contemporary scientific monism in general and the White-Draper-Tyndall interpretation in particular (I, 1–14, and particularly 12–14, note; see also I, 74–75; II, 717–800).
4. W. E. H. Lecky, *A History of England in the Eighteenth Century* (8 vols.; New York, 1891), II, 571; see also Lecky, *History of the Rise and Influence of the Spirit of Rationalism in Europe* (2 vols.; London, 1865), I, 288–328.
5. A. W. Benn, for example, complains — a little petulantly — that the authority of unthinking science has simply replaced the authority of religious superstition, and he seems not at all sure that this is fortunate (*The History of English Rationalism in the Nineteenth Century* [2 vols.; London, 1906], I, 197–201).
6. Charles Singer, *The Story of Living Things* (London, 1931), pp. 243–244. One need recall only the names of Pallas, Horace Bénédict de Saussure, Guettard, Desmarest, Werner, D'Aubuisson de Voisins, Leopold von Buch, Brongniart, Cuvier, Boué, Prévost, and Élie de Beaumont to

appreciate that this is a somewhat exaggerated view, even though Dr. Singer supports it by remarking, "The very names of the formations suffice to establish this fact."

7. On this point, see Élie Halévy, *A History of the English People in the Nineteenth Century* (4 vols.; London, 1924–1947), I, 487–497.

8. For a confirmatory judgment, see A. O. Lovejoy, "The Argument for Evolution before 'The Origin of Species,'" *Popular Science Monthly*, LXXV (1909), 499–514, 537–549. Professor Lovejoy describes geology as "the ruling science of 1830–60" (p. 506), and remarks, "Geology was, in England, the dominant and the most brilliantly successful science of the first half of the century" (p. 510).

9. See, for example, "The Geology of Russia," *Quarterly Review*, LXXVII (1845–46), 348–380, for a mock-serious lament that about this time geology was just beginning to pass beyond the comprehension of any well-read person (p. 353). See also "Natural History," *Westminster Review*, XLIV (1845), 203–224, pp. 222–223.

10. *British Association Reports*, I (1832), 10.

11. A. O. Lovejoy, *The Great Chain of Being* (Cambridge, Mass.: Harvard University Press, 1936), p. 20.

CHAPTER I. THROUGH NATURE UP TO NATURE'S GOD

1. Robert Boyle, *Seraphick Love; Some Motives and Incentives to the Love of God, Pathetically Discours'd of in a Letter to a Friend* (4th ed.; London, 1665), pp. 53–54.

2. T. H. Huxley, "The Origin of Species" (1860), in *Darwiniana*, vol. II of *Collected Essays* (New York, 1894), p. 52.

3. Francis Bacon, *Novum Organum*, in *Works* (ed. James Spedding, R. L. Ellis, and D. D. Heath; 15 vols.; Boston, 1860–1864), VIII, 114.

4. John Ray, *The Wisdom of God Manifested in the Creation* (London, 1691); John Wilkins, *Of the Principles and Duties of Natural Religion* (4th ed.; London, 1699); Nehemiah Grew, *Cosmologia Sacra* (London, 1701).

5. For a discussion of the point that it was not so much theology as the whole weight of scholastic dogmatism that cramped seventeenth-century scientists, see Zöckler, *Beziehungen zwischen Theologie und Naturwissenschaft*, I, 4–6; II, 36–43, 74–104.

6. John Webster, *Academiarum Examen* (London, 1654), p. 15.

7. *Ibid.*, p. 67.

8. Richard F. Jones, *Ancients and Moderns: A Study of the Background of the Battle of the Books*, Washington University Studies, new series, Language and Literature, no. 6 (St. Louis, Mo., 1936), p. 92. For the preceding remarks, and those in the following paragraph, I am indebted to a number of scholars who have studied the relationship of Puritanism to science. The fullest discussions are the work of R. F. Jones (just cited) and the more analytical treatise by R. K. Merton, *Science, Tech-*

nology, and Society in Seventeenth Century England, vol. IV, pt. 2 of *Osiris Studies* (Bruges, 1938), especially pp. 414–495. For more concise studies leading to similar conclusions, see Dorothy Stimson, "Puritanism and the New Philosophy in Seventeenth Century England," *Bulletin of the History of Medicine,* III (1935), 321–334; and George Rosen, "Left-Wing Puritanism and Science," *ibid.,* XV (1944), 375–380. Walter Pagel has described a similar conjunction in the thought patterns of empiricism and pietism in Germany, "Religious Motives in the Medical Biology of the Seventeenth Century," *ibid.,* III (1935), 97–128.

9. London, 1704.

10. *The Atheistical Objections, Against the Being of a God, and His Attributes, Fairly Considered and Fully Refuted* (London, 1698).

11. Isaac Newton, *Opticks* (reprinted from the fourth edition of 1730; London, 1931), pp. 369–370.

12. Newton, *Mathematical Principles of Natural Philosophy* (trans. Andrew Motte in 1729; rev. and ed. Florian Cajori; Berkeley, Calif., 1934), pp. xxxii–xxxiii.

13. Basil Willey, *The Eighteenth Century Background, Studies on the Idea of Nature in the Thought of the Period* (London, 1940), pp. 136–137. The author contrasts England to France in this respect, and he goes on to say that the alliance "persisted (in spite of Hume) till near the close of the century." It seems to me, as will be apparent, that it actually persisted, though not always smoothly, about fifty years longer than that.

14. For the definitive account of the deist controversy, see Sir Leslie Stephen, *History of English Thought in the Eighteenth Century* (3d ed.; 2 vols.; London, 1902), vol. I and, for an outline, I, 74–90.

15. John Arbuthnot, "An Argument for Divine Providence, taken from the constant Regularity observ'd in the Birth of both Sexes," *Philosophical Transactions,* XXVII (1710–1712), 186–190.

16. William J. 's Gravesande, *Démonstration mathématique de la direction de la providence divine,* in *Oeuvres philosophiques et mathématiques de M. G. J. 's Gravesande* (trans. and ed. J. N. S. Allamand; 2 vols. in 1; Amsterdam, 1774), II, 219–248.

17. Edmund Halley, "Some Considerations about the Cause of the Universal Deluge," read before the Royal Society in 1694 and printed in *Philosophical Transactions,* XXXIII (1724–1725), 118–125.

18. See the books on natural philosophy listed in Robert Watt, *Bibliotheca Britannica* (4 vols.; Edinburgh, 1824); the catalogue of references in Thomas Young, *A Course of Lectures on Natural Philosophy and the Mechanical Arts* (2 vols.; London, 1807), II, 87–520; and the bibliography in Benjamin Martin, *Philosophia Britannica* (2 vols.; London, 1747).

19. The following, dealing either with natural philosophy in general or emphasizing particular aspects such as mechanics, astronomy, or optics, are typical examples: John Keill, *An Introduction to Newtonian Philosophy; or, Philosophical Lectures Read in the University of Oxford, Anno Dom. 1700* (4th ed.; London, 1745); F. Hauksbee, *Physico-Mechanical*

Experiments on Various Subjects (2d ed.; London, 1719); J. T. Desaguliers, *A Course of Experimental Philosophy* (3d ed.; 2 vols.; London, 1763); W. J. 's Gravesande, *Mathematical Elements of Natural Philosophy, Confirmed by Experiments; or, An Introduction to Sir Isaac Newton's Philosophy* (trans. J. T. Desaguliers; 3d. ed.; 2 vols.; London, 1726); Pieter van Musschenbroek, *The Elements of Natural Philosophy* (trans. John Colson; 2 vols.; London, 1744); Henry Pemberton, *A View of Sir Isaac Newton's Philosophy* (Dublin, 1728); Thomas Rutherforth, *A System of Natural Philosophy, Being a Course of Lectures in Mechanics, Optics, Hydrostatics, and Astronomy* (2 vols.; Cambridge, England, 1748); Benjamin Martin, *Philosophia Britannica*; and *The Young Gentleman and Lady's Philosophy, in a Continued Survey of the Works of Nature and Art; by Way of Dialogue* (2d ed.; 2 vols.; London, 1772); John Rowning, *A Compendious System of Natural Philosophy: with Notes, containing the Mathematical Demonstrations, and some Occasional Remarks* (7th ed.; 2 vols.; London, 1772); Colin Maclaurin, *An Account of Sir Isaac Newton's Philosophical Discoveries, in Four Books* (London, 1748).

20. Desaguliers, *Course of Experimental Philosophy*, I, vii.

21. Two vols.; Edinburgh, 1742.

22. Maclaurin, *Account of Newton's Philosophical Discoveries*, pp. vi–vii.

23. *Ibid.*, pp. 377–392.

24. *Ibid.*, p. 382.

25. *Ibid.*, p. 390.

26. *Ibid.*, pp. 391–392.

27. Gravesande, *Mathematical Elements of Natural Philosophy*, I, vii.

28. *Ibid.*, I, ix.

29. Stephen Hales, *Statical Essays* (2d ed.; 2 vols.; London, 1731), II, vii.

30. Gravesande, *Mathematical Elements of Natural Philosophy*, I, 2–3.

31. Musschenbroek, *Elements of Natural Philosophy*, I, 5.

32. *Ibid.*, I, 5–6.

33. Gravesande, *Mathematical Elements of Natural Philosophy*, I, 3.

34. Rowning, *System of Natural Philosophy*, I, xli–xliii.

35. Desaguliers, *Course of Experimental Philosophy*, I, dedication.

36. Quoted from the advertisement in Desaguliers, *The Newtonian System of the World, the best Model of Government: an Allegorical Poem* (London, 1728).

37. Martin, *Philosophia Britannica*, I, preface.

38. John Playfair, *Outlines of Natural Philosophy* (2 vols.; Edinburgh, 1812), I, 2.

39. Desaguliers, *Course of Experimental Philosophy*, I, v.

40. Quoted from Wesley's *Diary* in A. E. Clark-Kennedy, *Stephen Hales, D.D., F.R.S.* (Cambridge, England, 1929), p. 215.

41. For Hales's work, see *Statical Essays*. Volume I is subtitled *Vegetable Staticks* and volume II, *Haemastaticks*. Both are interesting illustrations of the influence of Newtonian mechanics on biology.

42. Lovejoy, *The Great Chain of Being*, p. 183. Most of my remarks in this paragraph are derived from Professor Lovejoy's distinguished study, to which I am much indebted.

43. William Derham, *Astro-Theology; or, A Demonstration of the Being and Attributes of God, From a Survey of the Heavens* (London, 1715).

44. John Hunter, *Essays and Observations on Natural History, Anatomy, Physiology, Psychology, and Geology* (2 vols.; London, 1841). Published posthumously.

45. Two vols.; Edinburgh, 1822; I, xi, 3–4.

46. Derham, *Astro-Theology*, p. 209.

47. Derham, *Physico-Theology; or, A Demonstration of the Being and Attributes of God from His Works of Creation* (3d ed.; London, 1714), p. 433.

48. Willey, *Eighteenth Century Background*, pp. 43–56; Lovejoy, *The Great Chain of Being*, pp. 203–207.

49. Desaguliers, *The Newtonian System of the World*, pp. v–viii.

50. For a brief description of the new societies, see Abraham Hume and A. I. Evans, *The Learned Societies and Printing Clubs of the United Kingdom* (London, 1853); and for a rather general discussion of the more important ones in the capital, see B. H. Becker, *Scientific London* (London, 1874).

51. See the history of the foundation of the society in *T.R.S.E.*, I (1788), 3–14; and also the General Index, *T.R.S.E.* (Edinburgh, 1890), pp. 1–22.

52. *T.R.I.A.*, I (1787), ix–xvii.

53. *Manchester Memoirs*, I (1785), vi–xiii.

54. John Dalton, "Extraordinary Facts relating to the Vision of Colours," *Manchester Memoirs*, V (1798), 28–45.

55. Charles Babbage, *Reflections on the Decline of Science in England* (London, 1830), is the most important discussion of this point. See also Dorothy Stimson, *Scientists and Amateurs: A History of the Royal Society* (New York, 1948), pp. 179–196.

56. Henry Cavendish, *The Scientific Papers of the Honourable Henry Cavendish* (ed. James Clerk Maxwell and Sir Edward Thorpe; 2 vols.; Cambridge, 1921), I, viii, 18–19, 27–28, 349–351; II, 70–73, 249–286.

57. Joseph Priestley, *Theological and Miscellaneous Works* (ed. J. T. Rutt; 26 vols.; London, 1817–1832). For Priestley's view of the relative importance of theology and science, see *Experiments and Observations upon Different Kinds of Air* (2d ed.; London, 1776), II, xix; and *Letters to a Philosophic Unbeliever* (2 pts.; Bath, 1780; Birmingham, 1787), I (dedication), ix.

58. Priestley, *Memoirs* (2 vols.; Northumberland, Pa., 1806), I, 64.

59. The sources of information on the Lunar Society are very scanty. These remarks are based on the following: H. C. Bolton (ed.), *Scientific Correspondence of Joseph Priestley* (New York, 1892); Priestley, *Memoirs*; J. P. Muirhead (ed.), *The Origin and Progress of the Mechanical Inventions of James Watt, Illustrated by his Correspondence* (3 vols.; London, 1854); Hesketh Pearson, *Dr. Darwin* (London, 1930); Mary Anne Schimmelpenninck, *Life of Mary Anne Schimmelpenninck* (2 vols.; London, 1860); Amelia Moillet, *Life of James Keir* (London, 1860); R. L. and M. Edgeworth, *Memoirs of Richard Lovell Edgeworth* (2 vols.; London, 1820).

60. Darwin published *The Botanic Garden* (2 vols.; Dublin, 1790–1793), and *The Temple of Nature; or, The Origin of Society: A Poem with Philosophical Notes* (London, 1803), to instruct as well as to please. The notes to *The Botanic Garden*, besides treating biological and botanical science, contain explanatory comments on meteors, optics, comets, geology, heat, phosphorus, metallurgy and mining technology, and meteorology.

61. Darwin's chief scientific work was *Zoonomia; or, The Laws of Organic Life* (2 vols.; London, 1794–1798). The best discussion of his evolutionism is Ernst Krause, *Erasmus Darwin* (trans. W. S. Dallas; New York, 1880), which includes a prefatory biographical memoir by Charles Darwin.

62. See, for example, Priestley's description of the method of generating silicon tetrafluoride in *Experiments and Observations upon Different Kinds of Air*, II, 191–193; and the passage on the delights of natural philosophy in *History of Electricity* (2d ed.; London, 1769), p. iv.

63. Watt's opinion, quoted in J. P. Muirhead, *Life of James Watt* (New York, 1859), p. 139.

64. A. F. Tytler of Woodhouselee, *Memoirs of . . . Henry Home of Kames* (3 vols.; Edinburgh, 1814), especially III, 82–89, 103–109, 191–259.

65. On Joseph Black, see Sir William Ramsay, *The Life and Letters of Joseph Black, M.D.* (London, 1918).

66. Joseph Black, *Lectures on the Elements of Chemistry* (ed. John Robison; 3 vols.; Philadelphia, 1806–1807), I, 11, 14; II, 415. On these lectures, see E. W. J. Neave, "Joseph Black's Lectures on the Elements of Chemistry," *Isis*, XXV (1936), 372–390.

67. Black, *Lectures*, I, 18.

68. *Ibid.*, dedication.

69. Samuel Smiles, *Lives of the Engineers* (4 vols.; London, 1862–1865), IV, 367–385, 486–487.

70. Eliza Meteyard, *The Life of Josiah Wedgwood* (2 vols.; London, 1865–1866), I, 345–350, 389–391, 419–424, 463–473, 497.

71. Smiles, *Lives of the Engineers*, II, 75–76, 86–87; IV, 423–433.

72. John Randall, *The Wilkinsons* (Madeley, Salop; undated [probably *c.* 1830]), pp. 27–30.

73. *Transactions of the Society for the Encouragement of Arts, Manufactures, and Commerce*, XL (1823), iii. For the history of the Society, see Sir H. T. Wood, *A History of the Royal Society of Arts* (London, 1913). This was not the first organization of the sort. The Royal Dublin Society, whose purposes were entirely similar though its methods were different, had been founded in 1731. See Henry F. Berry, *A History of the Royal Society of Dublin* (London, 1915).

74. *The Prospectus, Charter, Ordinances, and Bye-Laws of the Royal Institution of Great Britain* (London, 1800), p. 7.

75. *Ibid.*, pp. 7–10; see also Thomas Young's plan, printed in Henry Bence Jones, *The Royal Institution: Its Founder and its First Professors* (London, 1871). A more concise account of the foundation will be found in Thomas Martin, *The Royal Institution* (rev. ed.; London, 1948).

76. Bence Jones, *The Royal Institution*, pp. 135–138.

77. *Ibid.*, pp. 222, 258.

78. For a list of the provincial societies, see Hume and Evans, *Learned Societies and Printing Clubs*.

79. Basil Willey discusses this point, *Eighteenth Century Background*, pp. 136–137, 155–157.

80. Quoted in C. C. J. Webb, *Studies in the History of Natural Theology* (Oxford, 1915), p. 2.

81. Samuel Horsley, *Elementary Treatise on . . . Mathematics* (Oxford, 1801), p. xvii; see also W. A. Knight, *Lord Monboddo and Some of His Contemporaries* (London, 1900), pp. 160–170: Horsley to Monboddo, 25 February 1781.

82. Richard Kirwan, *Metaphysical Essays* (London, 1809), pp. 257–277, 447–453.

83. J. A. Deluc, *Lettres sur le christianisme* (Berlin, 1801), *passim*, but especially pp. 4–6. On Kirwan and Deluc, see above, pp. 49–66.

84. John Pringle, *Six Discourses* (ed. Andrew Kippis; London, 1783), pp. lxviii, lxxxii–lxxxiii.

85. C. A. Lubbock, *The Herschel Chronicle* (Cambridge, England, 1933), p. 197.

86. The two letters, dated 9 and 13 October 1809, have been published by the University of Michigan Press under the title *The Universe Around Us* (Ann Arbor, 1932).

87. Quoted by Charles Darwin in his preface to Krause, *Erasmus Darwin*, p. 44. See also *The Temple of Nature*, notes, pp. 54, 142. Darwin's reputation for atheism seems to have originated in the autobiography of Mary Anne Schimmelpenninck (née Galton), which is one of the main sources for the Lunar Society. Her *Life* must be used with caution, however, because when she wrote it she was an old lady whose solace in her declining years was a curiously twisted and ill-tempered piety.

88. George Wilson, *The Life of the Honourable Henry Cavendish* (London, 1851), pp. 180–182.

89. Priestley, *Letters to a Philosophic Unbeliever*, I, 176–177.
90. *Ibid.*, II, iv.
91. See above, pp. 7, 10.
92. Willey, *Eighteenth Century Background*, pp. 171–172.
93. Priestley, *Letters to a Philosophic Unbeliever*, I, xvi.
94. *Ibid.*, pp. iv–viii.
95. Élie Halévy, *The Growth of Philosophic Radicalism* (trans. Mary Morris; London, 1928), pp. 153–154.
96. Priestley, *History of Electricity*, pp. xviii–xix.
97. Priestley, *Experiments and Observations upon Different Kinds of Air* (3d ed.; London, 1781), I, xii–xiii.
98. London, 1785.
99. London, 1802. Citations herein refer to the edition which forms volume I of *The Works of William Paley* (ed. G. W. Meadley; 5 vols.; Boston, 1810).
100. *Moral and Political Philosophy*, p. 423.
101. *Ibid.*, p. i.
102. *Ibid.*, pp. 333–334.
103. G. W. Meadley in the prefatory Memoir to *Natural Theology*, p. 83.
104. Paley, *Natural Theology*, p. 16.
105. *Ibid.*, p. 132.
106. *Ibid.*, p. 311.
107. *Ibid.*, p. 34.
108. *Ibid.*, p. 35.
109. *Ibid.*, pp. 260–279.
110. *Ibid.*, pp. 334–362.
111. *Ibid.*, p. 367.
112. There is, for example, a discussion of this point in a review of one of the most popular of the early treatises, "Reliquiae Diluvianiae," *Quarterly Review*, XXIX (1823), 138–165, pp. 138–139.

Chapter II. Neptune and the Flood

1. Granville Penn, *Conversations on Geology* (London, 1828), pp. 1–3.
2. Karl von Zittel, *History of Geology and Paleontology* (trans. Maria M. Ogilvie-Gordon; London, 1901), p. 46. For a discussion of the importance of this period in the history of geology, see also George Sarton, "La Synthèse géologique de 1775 à 1918," *Isis*, II (1914–1919), 357–394, pp. 358–359.
3. Two vols.; Edinburgh, 1795. For a brief sketch of his life, see M. MacGregor "James Hutton, the Founder of Modern Geology," *Endeavour*, VI (1947), 109–111.
4. For a discussion of this literature in the seventeenth and eighteenth centuries, see K. B. Collier, *Cosmogonies of our Fathers* (New York, 1934).
5. Thomas Burnet, *Sacred Theory of the Earth* (6th ed.; 2 vols.; London, 1726); Georges Louis de Buffon, *Histoire et théorie de la terre*,

in volume I of *Histoire naturelle* (24 vols.; Paris, 1749–1783), I, 65–612. See Collier, *Cosmogonies*, pp. 68–80, 204–218; H. F. Osborn, *From the Greeks to Darwin* (3d ed.; New York, 1929), pp. 159–218; Zöckler, *Beziehungen zwischen Theologie und Naturwissenschaft*, II, 74–92, 122–193.

6. For a pleasant and useful account, see Sir Archibald Geikie, *The Founders of Geology* (2d ed.; London, 1905). Probably the earliest important memoir in English to be entirely free of cosmogony was the Reverend John Michell's "Conjectures Concerning the Cause, and Observations upon the Phaenomena of Earthquakes," *Philosophical Transactions*, LI (1760), 566–634. The Lisbon disaster had stimulated a great deal of interest in earthquakes, but Michell's treatment also includes passages on stratigraphy that are more comprehensive than the title indicates. John Whitehurst, *Inquiry into the Original State and Formation of the Earth* (London, 1778), also offers a good practical description of the arrangement of strata. Unlike Michell, however, Whitehurst freely indulged a taste for cosmogony.

7. F. D. Adams, *The Birth and Development of the Geological Sciences* (Baltimore, 1938), pp. 212–215; see also Geikie, *Founders of Geology*, pp. 233–238.

8. John Playfair, *Illustrations of the Huttonian Theory of the Earth* (Edinburgh, 1802), the chief source for Vulcanist views as they were apprehended by contemporaries. Citations are to the edition which forms volume I of *The Works of John Playfair* (4 vols.; Edinburgh, 1822).

9. This paragraph is condensed from Jameson's summary, which is the most complete statement of the Wernerian theories. Robert Jameson, *Elements of Geognosy*, volume III of his *A System of Mineralogy* (3 vols.; Edinburgh, 1804–1808), III, 78–100.

10. Adams, *Birth of Geological Sciences*, pp. 210–212, 227; Geikie, *Founders of Geology*, pp. 237–239, 333–334; K. von Zittel, *History of Geology*, pp. 47–48.

11. Hutton, *Theory of the Earth*, I, 200.

12. The preceding two paragraphs are condensed from Playfair, *Illustrations*, pp. 19–150.

13. The most serious shortcoming of Vulcanism was its almost total lack of interest in the fossil content of strata — the only characteristic Hutton and Werner shared. Aside from this, Hutton's theory of uplift through the expansive force of heat is not now held in the form he gave it. See Geikie, *Founders of Geology*, pp. 308–315, 334–335; and for a brief estimate of the soundness of Hutton's theories, see E. B. Bailey, "James Hutton: Father of Modern Geology, 1726–1797," *Nature*, CXIX (1927), 582.

14. Priestley, *History of Electricity*, pp. xviii–xix.

15. See the bibliography in J. Reilly and N. O'Flynn, "Richard Kirwan," *Isis*, XIII (1929–30), 298–319; Bibliography, 316–317.

16. Described in *Philosophical Transactions*, LXXI (1781), 7–41; LXXII (1782), 179–236; LXXIII (1783), 15–84.

17. See pp. 8–9 of the *Essay*.

18. *Essai sur le phlogistique* (Paris, 1788).

19. Quoted in Reilly and O'Flynn, "Richard Kirwan," p. 307: Kirwan to Berthollet, 26 January 1791.

20. Reilly and O'Flynn, "Richard Kirwan," p. 300. Kirwan's *Elements of Mineralogy* (London, 1784) was a standard text.

21. Robert Bakewell, *An Introduction to Geology* (London, 1815), p. vii.

22. Kirwan, "Examination of the Supposed Igneous Origin of Stony Substances," *T.R.I.A.*, V (1793), 51–81.

23. Playfair, "Biographical Account of Dr. James Hutton," *Works*, IV, 98–100.

24. The *Essays* were an expansion of an argument first presented in an article, "On the Primitive State of the Globe and its Subsequent Catastrophe," *T.R.I.A.*, VI (1797), 233–308.

25. Kirwan, *Geological Essays*, p. 3.

26. *Ibid.*, pp. 2–3.

27. See his prefatory remarks, *ibid.*, pp. x–xi.

28. *Ibid.*, pp. 1–2.

29. *Ibid.*, pp. 4–6.

30. *Ibid.*, pp. 46–47.

31. *Ibid.*, pp. 47–51.

32. *Ibid.*, pp. 52–53.

33. *Ibid.*, p. 54.

34. *Ibid.*, pp. 60–63.

35. *Ibid.*, pp. 64–65.

36. *Ibid.*, p. 66.

37. *Ibid.*, pp. 84–86.

38. *Ibid.*, p. 105. We do not know the exact age of the earth, but the last violent catastrophe occurred "three thousand six hundred years ago" (p. 97).

39. *Ibid.*, p. 433.

40. *Ibid.*, pp. 481–482.

41. *Ibid.*, pp. iv–viii, xii, 65–67, 433.

42. J. A. Deluc, *An Elementary Treatise on Geology* (trans. Henry de la Fite; London, 1809), p. iii. Though written in French, the book seems to have been published only in translation.

43. Playfair, *Illustrations*, pp. 469, 471. See also Kirwan, *Geological Essays*, p. 61.

44. Hutton, *Theory of the Earth*, I, 377–379, 416, 419; II, 187–195, 213, 231, 367–368.

45. Deluc, *Treatise on Geology*, pp. vi, 414.

46. Five vols. in 6; La Haye, 1779.

47. Deluc, "Letters to Dr. James Hutton on His Theory of the Earth," *Monthly Review*, II (1790), 206–227, 582–601; III (1790), 573–586; V (1791), 564–585.

48. Deluc, "Geological Letters to Professor Blumenbach in Paris," *British Critic*, Ltr. I, 1793 (vol. II, pp. 231–238, 351–358); Ltr. II, 1794 (vol. I, pp. 110–118, 226–237); Ltr. III, 1794 (vol. I, pp. 467–478, 589–598); Ltr. IV, 1794 (vol. II, pp. 212–218, 328–336); Ltr. V, 1794 (vol. II, pp. 447–459, 569–578); Ltr. VI, 1795 (vol. I, pp. 197–207, 316–326).

49. Kirwan, *Geological Essays.*

50. Deluc, *Treatise on Geology* (see above, n. 42); for Playfair, see below, Chapter III, section 1.

51. Deluc, *Treatise on Geology*, p. 45.

52. *Ibid.*, pp. 45, 65, 77–79, 348, 370–371, 376–377.

53. *Ibid.*, p. 65.

54. *Ibid.*, pp. 45–48.

55. *Ibid.*, pp. 26–27, 52–53, 350–351; also *Monthly Review*, II (1790), 216–221.

56. Deluc, *Treatise on Geology*, pp. 78–80, 348, 376–377, 380–381.

57. *Ibid.*, pp. 45, 48, 348, 376–378, 403.

58. *Ibid.*, p. 376.

59. *Ibid.*, p. vi.

60. Deluc, "Letters to Professor Blumenbach."

61. Deluc, *Treatise on Geology*, pp. 389–390.

62. *Ibid.*, pp. 404–405.

63. *Ibid.*, pp. 391–392, 395, 397–398, 401–403, 405–406, 409–415.

64. *Ibid.*, p. 6.

65. *Ibid.*, pp. 2–3.

66. *Ibid.*, pp. 2–4.

67. *Ibid.*, pp. 4–5.

68. *Ibid.*, pp. 17–21, 48–49, 63–64, 71–75, 106–107, 368–371.

69. Deluc, *Lettres sur le christianisme* (Berlin, 1801), p. 4 (my translation).

70. Deluc, *Treatise on Geology*, p. 5.

71. *Ibid.*, pp. 5–6, 377–378.

72. *Ibid.*, pp. 7–8, 11–14, 64, 76–77.

73. *Ibid.*, pp. 12–13.

74. *Ibid.*, pp. 14–15, 22–24.

75. *Ibid.*, pp. 9–10.

76. *Ibid.*, p. 82. See also pp. 31, 47–48, 62–63, 76–80, 348.

77. *Ibid.*, p. 348. Deluc, however, had earlier convinced Dolomieu with this argument: "I shall," wrote Dolomieu, "defend another truth, which appears to me incontestable, and which the works of M. de Luc have rendered evident to me; a truth, of which I see the proof in every page of the *history of man*, and in all those whereon the *phenomena of nature* are recorded. With M. de Luc, therefore, I shall say, that the *actual state of our continents is not ancient*; with him I think that *but a short period of time has elapsed*, since they were given, or restored thus modified, to the dominion of man." Quoted in the *Treatise on Geology*, p. 80, from *Le Journal de physique de Paris* (1792), pt. I, p. 72.

78. Deluc, *Treatise on Geology*, p. 403.

79. *Ibid.*, p. 82.

80. Two vols.; Edinburgh, 1798. For a biographical sketch, see Lawrence Jameson, *Biographical Memoir of the Late Professor Jameson* (Edinburgh, 1854).

81. *The Gentleman's Magazine*, new series, XLI (January 1854), 656–657.

82. The book served as the text for Jameson's lectures in the university (see p. iv), and was so popular that it was sold out a few months after publication (Lawrence Jameson, *Memoir of Jameson*, p. 27).

83. Jameson, *System of Mineralogy*, I, xxii. See also "Mineralogical Queries" and "On Colouring Geognostical Maps," *M.W.S.*, I (1811), 107–108 and 149–161. In the latter, he insisted that only the exact shades recommended by Werner were suitable for representing the work formations.

84. Jameson, "On the Strontian–Lead–Glance Formations" and "On Porphyry," *M.W.S.*, I, 461; II, 217.

85. Jameson, *Elements of Geognosy*, p. 343.

86. See above, pp. 99–100.

87. *Elements of Geognosy*, pp. 348–349.

88. One of Robert Brown's early botanical papers adorns the first volume: "On the Asclepiadeae . . ." *M.W.S.*, I, 12–78.

89. *M.W.S.*, I, xiii-xviii.

90. Volume I (1811), volume II (1818), volume III (1821), volume IV (1822).

91. The appendix to each volume includes a list of the new members in the period covered by its papers.

92. There is no point in citing the title of each, since they all relate the observations of his current researches to Werner's pattern, or pose new questions for others to corroborate. *M.W.S.*, I, 1–7, 107–125, 149–161, 445–452, 461–464, 465–468, 556–565; II, 178–201, 202–216, 217–220, 221–231, 618–634.

93. MacKnight, "On the Mineralogy . . . of Certain Districts in the Highlands," *M.W.S.*, I, 293, 353. For further instances of the society's characteristic approach to research, see the same article, I, 274–276; also MacKnight, "Description of Tinto," II, 125, 134–137; "Lithological Observations on . . . Loch Lomond" (1813), II, 399–403; John Fleming, "Mineralogy of St. Andrew's" (1813), II, 146; R. Bald, "On the Coal-Formation of Clackmanshire" (1808), I, 494–501; Charles Mackenzie, "Outlines of the Mineralogy of the Ochil Hills" (1812), II, 1–2; James Grierson, "Mineralogical Observations in Galloway" (1816), II, 375–378.

94. "On the Geognosy of Germany, with Observations on the Igneous Origin of Trap," *M.W.S.*, IV, 103–104. Jameson's hand may still be seen, however, for though Boué calls the science "geology" in the body of the article, the editor has put "geognosy" in the title.

95. James Grierson, "General Observations on Geology and Geognosy, and the Nature of these Respective Studies," *M.W.S.*, V, 403.

96. *Ibid.*, pp. 405–407.

97. "On the Saphan . . ." (1827), *M.W.S.*, VI, 105–107, 111. Dr. Scot later submitted a paper, "On the question whether Domestic Poultry were Bred Among the Ancient Jews," VI (1830), 391–402, deciding on the whole that they were not, while "expressing my unqualified abhorrence of cock-fighting."

CHAPTER III. FROM VULCANISM TO PALEONTOLOGY

1. William Whewell, *History of the Inductive Sciences* (3 vols.; London, 1837), III, 605.

2. Holland, *Recollections of Past Life* (New York, 1872), p. 81. For a further description of the discussion in Edinburgh, see Benjamin Silliman's account of his visit there in 1805–06, in J. F. Fulton and E. H. Thomson, *Benjamin Silliman* (New York, 1947), pp. 132–133.

3. For example, he went beyond Hutton — and beyond Lyell, as a matter of fact — in recognizing the evidence for glacial transportation (Playfair, *Illustrations*, pp. 384–385). For examples of criticism of errors in Hutton, see Playfair, pp. 341–344.

4. *Ibid.*, pp. 503–514.

5. *Ibid.*, p. 508.

6. *Ibid.*, p. 498.

7. *Ibid.*, pp. 466–467.

8. *Ibid.*, pp. 132, 137, 467–469.

9. *Ibid.*, pp. 130–132.

10. *Ibid.*, p. 136.

11. *Ibid.*, pp. 136–139, 428–432.

12. *Ibid.*, pp. 132–133.

13. *Ibid.*, p. 132.

14. *Ibid.*, pp. 130–132.

15. *Ibid.*, pp. 498–500.

16. *Ibid.*, pp. 502–503.

17. Hutton, "Theory of the Earth" (1785), *T.R.S.E.*, I (1788), 209–304. Volumes V–VIII cover the years of greatest controversy, from 1798 to 1818. Volume V (1805), with fourteen articles, includes only two geological ones: Sir James Hall, "Experiments on Whinstone and Lava" (pp. 43–75), is an experimental verification of some of Hutton's fundamental hypotheses; R. Kennedy, "A Chemical Analysis of . . . Whinstone . . . and Lava" (pp. 76–98), is descriptive mineralogy by a Vulcanist. Succeeding volumes publish a number of papers couched in Neptunist terminology. The proportion of geological papers in each volume was as follows: VI (1812), 7 out of 14 articles; VII (1815), 7 out of 17; VIII (1818), 2 out of 24. The large amount of space devoted to geology in volumes VI and VII probably indicates the interest aroused by the dis-

putes during the height of the controversy, from 1804 or so through 1812 or 1814.

18. Thomas Allen, "Remarks on the Transition Rocks of Werner" (1812), *T.R.S.E.*, VII, 109–110.

19. Allen (1811), *T.R.S.E.*, VI, 408.

20. *Ibid.*, pp. 409–411, 422–428.

21. For descriptions of the experiments, see Hall, "Experiments on Whinstone and Lava" (1798), *T.R.S.E.*, V, 43–75; and "Account of a Series of Experiments, Shewing the Effects of Compression in Modifying the Action of Heat" (1805), *ibid.*, VI, 71–184.

22. Hall, "On the Revolutions of the Earth's Surface" (1812), *T.R.S.E.*, VII, 140.

23. Hall, "Account of a Series of Experiments," pp. 171–172.

24. 1812; *T.R.S.E.*, VII, 139–167, 169–210.

25. *Ibid.*, p. 161.

26. *Ibid.*, p. 210.

27. [W. H. Fitton] "Transactions of the Geological Society," *Edinburgh Review*, XXIX (1817–18), 70–94, p. 70.

28. Geikie, *Founders of Modern Geology*, pp. 332–335.

29. Jean Baptiste de Lamarck, *Histoire naturelle des animaux sans vertèbres* (7 vols. in 8; Paris, 1815–1822); for Cuvier's *Recherches*, citations herein are to the third edition (5 vols. in 7; Paris and Amsterdam, 1825). See above, pp. 99–100.

30. Georges Cuvier and Alexandre Brongniart, *Essai sur la géographie minéralogique des environs de Paris* (Paris, 1811). A portion of this memoir was published in the *Journal des mines*, XXIII (1808), 421–458.

31. John Phillips, *Memoir of William Smith* (London, 1844), pp. 3–25. This is the chief biographical source, but for the best account of the curiously roundabout way Smith's views became known, see [W. H. Fitton] "Geology of England," *Edinburgh Review*, XXIX (1817–18), 311–337, reprinted as "Notes on the History of English Geology," *Philosophical Magazine*, I (1832), 147–160, 268–275, 442–450; II (1833), 37–57. Fitton prints excerpts from Smith's diary not published elsewhere. For an exhaustive description of Smith's work and of his publications, see T. Sheppard, "William Smith, his Maps and Memoirs," *Proceedings of the Yorkshire Geological Society*, XIX (1917), 75–253. This includes a sketch of his life and a bibliography.

32. Smith, *A Delineation of the Strata of England and Wales* (London, 1815). Accompanied by a *Memoir to the Map* explaining the method. An extract is printed in K. F. Mather and S. L. Mason (eds.), *A Source Book in Geology* (New York, 1939), pp. 201–204.

33. "Presidential Address" (1831), *P.G.S.*, I, 274. See also Fitton, "Geology of England." For a discussion of Smith's originality, see John Farey, "Mr. Smith's Geological Claims Stated," *Philosophical Magazine*, LI (1818), 173–180; Thomas Tredgold, "Remarks on the Geological Principles of Werner, and those of Mr. Smith," *ibid.*, pp. 36–38.

34. H. B. Woodward, *The History of the Geological Society of London* (London, 1907), pp. 6–17, 39.

35. See above, p. 67.

36. William Phillips, *A Selection of Facts from the Best Authorities, Arranged so as to Form an Outline of the Geology of England and Wales* (London, 1818).

37. *T.G.S.*, vols. I, II, and III (London, 1811, 1814, 1816).

38. See Nugent, "Account of the Pitch Lake . . . of Trinidad," *T.G.S.*, I, 63–76; Aikin, "Observations . . . on the Great Coal-Field of Shropshire," *ibid.*, pp. 191–212; Phillips, "On the Veins of Cornwall," *ibid.*, II, 110–160; Taylor, "On the Economy of the Mines of Cornwall and Devon," *ibid.*, pp. 309–327.

39. *T.G.S.*, preface to vol. I, p. viii.

40. *Ibid.*, pp. viii–ix.

41. W. A. Copinger, *On the Authorship of the First Hundred Numbers of the Edinburgh Review* (Manchester, 1895), *passim*.

42. See, for example, Playfair's reviews of Archibald Bruce (ed.), *American Mineralogical Journal*, and of Werner, *New Theory of Veins* (trans. Charles Anderson), in the *Edinburgh Review*, XVII (1810), 114–121; XVIII (1811), 80–97.

43. [Fitton] "Transactions of the Geological Society," *Edinburgh Review*, XIX (1811–12), 207–229, pp. 207–209.

44. [Fitton] "Transactions of the Geological Society, Volume II," *Edinburgh Review*, XXVIII (1817), 174–192, pp. 175–177. During this period, the articles in the *Edinburgh* follow so definite a pattern that they appear to be evidence of an organized effort upon the part of geological leaders to win public sympathy. See, for example, Macculloch's letter to Leonard Horner, thanking him for the notice, "calculated to make geology go glibly down among the readers of reviews," which Horner had written on Macculloch's *Islands of Western Scotland* (K. M. Lyell, *Memoir of Leonard Horner* [2 vols.; London, 1890], I, 173–175: Macculloch to Horner, 2 June 1820).

45. "James Kidd, *Outlines of Mineralogy*," *Quarterly Review*, II (1809), 61–74, p. 73.

46. *Ibid.*, p. 66.

47. "Reliquiae Diluvianae," *Quarterly Review*, XXIX (1823), 138–165.

48. *Ibid.*, pp. 139–141.

49. Robert Bakewell, *An Introduction to Geology* (2d ed.; London, 1815); W. T. Brande, *Outlines of Geology* (London, 1817); G. B. Greenough, *A Critical Examination of the First Principles of Geology* (London, 1819); William Phillips, *An Outline of the Geology of England and Wales*.

50. Thomas Martin, *The Royal Institution*, pp. 14–25. Brande's lectures were later published. They follow his book, in general, and one of them contains a good sketch of the general state of geology at this period:

"Outlines of Geology," *The Quarterly Journal of Science, Literature, and the Arts*, XIX (1825), 63–92.

51. Bence Jones, *The Royal Institution*, pp. 276–302.

52. Bakewell, *Introduction to Geology*, p. xx; see also Brande, *Outlines of Geology*, pp. 143–144.

53. Greenough, *Geological Map of England* (London, 1820). Since the map was based on mineralogical rather than paleontological data, it was almost immediately superseded.

54. See, for example, Greenough, *Critical Examination*, pp. 16–17, 73–75, 85–88, 227–229, 233.

55. *Ibid.*, pp. 57, 65, 67–72, 333–336.

56. *Ibid.*, pp. 91–95.

57. *Ibid.*, pp. 184–199.

58. Second ed.; 2 vols. in 1; Bath, 1815. The title above is that of volume I (1st ed.; 1813). Volume II has the same main title and is subtitled *Recording Events Subsequent to the Deluge*. Volume II appeared for the first time in the 1815 edition.

59. Phillips, *Memoir*, pp. 12, 23, 32–35, 49–54, 68–70, 80–89.

60. *Ibid.*, p. 32.

61. Smith, *Memoir of the Map*, p. 201.

62. Phillips, *Memoir*, p. 25.

63. *Ibid.*, pp. 17–18; Smith, *Memoir of the Map*, p. 202.

64. The evidence in the second volume consists of a staggering collation of word stems from English, Greek, Cymric, Gaelic, Erse, Manx, Gothic, and Scandinavian dialects, Sanskrit, Russian, Slavonic, Latin, Hebrew, Laponic, Chaldee, Arabic, Syriac, Ethiopian, and Coptic.

65. Townsend, *The Character of Moses*, I, iv–v.

66. *Ibid.*, p. 437.

67. *Ibid.*, pp. 97–303.

68. The twenty-one original engravings, depicting one hundred and ninety-five characteristic fossil forms, are particularly impressive (*ibid.*, pp. 438ff).

69. *Ibid.*, pp. 415–430.

70. *Ibid.*, p. 430.

71. Townsend's objections to Neptunism, every bit as cogent as Playfair's, had the additional merit of paleontological evidence (*ibid.*, pp. 334–338).

72. *Ibid.*, p. 395.

73. *Ibid.*, pp. 382–397. Particularly in regard to Hutton's explanation of the origin of coal and the fusion of flints.

74. *Ibid.*, pp. 377–378.

75. *Ibid.*, p. 376.

76. *Ibid.*, pp. 335, 398–403.

77. *Ibid.*, p. 436.

78. Erasmus Darwin, whose *Zoonomia* appeared in 1794, made no permanent impression, and although Lamarck proposed his doctrine of evolution in *Recherches sur l'organisation des corps vivants* (Paris, 1802) and published his fully elaborated theory in *Philosophie zoologique* (2 vols.; Paris, 1809), his views seem not to have been widely known in England until after the appearance of Lyell's account of them in 1830 (see above, p. 130). I have not come across any references to Lamarckian ideas in the English publications which have been considered in this chapter, but there are indications that they were occasionally discussed in the 1820's (see p. 118 and pp. 281–282, n. 68; see also Fleming, *Philosophy of Zoology*, I, 311). British ignorance of Lamarck in this period is not surprising when it is recalled that in the eighteenth century evolutionary ideas were developed much further in France than in England (see A. O. Lovejoy, "Some Eighteenth Century Evolutionists," *Popular Science Monthly*, LXV [1904], 238–251, 323–340), and that French thought in general was apt to be regarded with suspicion in England until well into the nineteenth century.

79. There were, of course, many pre-Darwinian evolutionary theories (see below, p. 300, n. 5), but they never won acceptance, and I question whether much was known about them even among naturalists. Certainly the general public, if it thought about the problem at all, simply assumed the permanency of species. For an outline of the history of the idea of special creations, see N. von Hofsten, "Ideas of Creation and Spontaneous Generation prior to Darwin," *Isis*, XXV (1936), 80–94.

CHAPTER IV. CATASTROPHIST GEOLOGY

1. Quoted in Anna B. Gordon, *The Life and Correspondence of William Buckland* (New York, 1894), pp. 41–42.

2. For examples of the contemporary view of the state of the science as the public received it, see W. H. Fitton, "Presidential Address" (1828 and 1829), *P.G.S.*, I, 50–62, 112–134; Adam Sedgwick, "Presidential Address" (1830), *ibid.*, pp. 187–212; [Fitton], "A Description . . . of Volcanoes," *Edinburgh Review*, XLV (1826–27), 295–320, and "Progress of Geological Science," *ibid.*, LII (1830), 43–72; "Transactions of the Geological Society," *Quarterly Review*, XXXIV (1826), 507–540; "Scrope's Geology of Central France," *ibid.*, XXXVI (1827), 437–483; W. D. Conybeare and William Phillips, *Outlines of the Geology of England and Wales* (London, 1822) — the most popular general manual prior to Lyell. This last and the works of Brande, Bakewell, and Greenough (above, p. 275, n. 49) went through new editions every few years.

3. For a sketch of Cuvier's importance and a discussion of his differences with Étienne Geoffroy Saint-Hilaire and the school of *Naturphilosophie*, see J. Chaine, "La Grande Époque de l'anatomie comparée," *Scientia*, L (1931), 365–374.

4. The investigations and memoirs which formed the basis for Lyell's uniformitarian theories were, of course, appearing during these years, but they were very dull and recondite and attracted no popular attention. The public was interested in the theories of scientists, not in their labors, and its fancy could be caught only by neatly generalized formulations, not by dry and dusty technicalities. To the layman, therefore, the disputes of conflicting schools, like the catastrophist and the uniformitarian, seemed much more sudden and dramatic than they did to scientists who had followed the gradual development of the evidence. For a discussion of this point, see [William Whewell], *"Principles of Geology* by Charles Lyell," *British Critic*, IX (1831), 180–206, pp. 180–184.

5. Brongniart and Cuvier, *Essai sur la géographie minéralogique des environs de Paris.*

6. Citations here are to the third edition of 1825.

7. The translation was entitled *Essay on the Theory of the Earth.* Citations are to the third edition (Edinburgh, 1817).

8. Cuvier, *Recherches sur les ossemens fossiles*, I, 8–9 (my translation).

9. For a brief and comprehensive contemporary view of the catastrophist doctrine, see Whewell, *History of Inductive Sciences*, III, 606–609.

10. Cuvier, *Essay on the Theory of the Earth*, pp. 57–60, 88–103.

11. *Ibid.*, pp. 102–127.

12. Because nonpetrified mammalian remains were found in alluvial deposits referred to by Cuvier as resulting from the latest deluge (pp. 127–132, 171–176). Cuvier admitted it to be conceivable, though highly unlikely, that fossilized human bones might exist undiscovered in remote places (pp. 131–132).

13. *Ibid.*, pp. 171–172.

14. For Cuvier's prestige, see, for example, Gordon, *Life of Buckland*, pp. 124–125; K. M. Lyell, *Life, Letters, and Journals of Sir Charles Lyell* (2 vols.; London, 1881), I, 125, 137, 249–250; J. W. Clark and T. McK. Hughes, *Life and Letters of Adam Sedgwick* (2 vols.; Cambridge, England, 1890), I, 271–273, 429; Whewell, *History of Inductive Sciences*, III, 606–609; Sedgwick, "Presidential Address" (1830), *P.G.S.*, I, 197; G. A. Mantell, *The Journal of Gideon Mantell, Surgeon and Geologist* (ed. E. Cecil Curwen; London, 1940), pp. 83–84 (16 August 1830).

15. Whewell, *History of Inductive Sciences*, III, 606–609.

16. Sedgwick, "Presidential Address" (1830), *P.G.S.*, I, 197.

17. Charles Lyell, *Principles of Geology* (3 vols.; London, 1830–1833), I, dedication; Gordon, *Life of Buckland*, pp. 55–56, 84–86, 270; Archibald Geikie, *Life of Sir Roderick Murchison* (2 vols.; London, 1875), I, 115, 123–126; Clark and Hughes, *Life of Sedgwick*, I, 511.

18. Gordon, *Life of Buckland*, p. 23; see also pp. 21–37, excerpts from correspondence of his students.

19. "If the fact I now allude to," wrote Buckland, "were not so generally notorious, that a recent Author [the Reverend Dr. Chalmers] in one of our northern Universities has thought the subject of sufficient importance to devote a chapter of his work on the Evidences of Christianity to what he calls the scepticism of Geologists; it might have been superfluous to introduce the mention of this subject before those who know the strength of the irrefragable moral evidence, on which the general authority of the sacred writings is established, and which cannot be invalidated by occasional differences touching minute details of historical events" (*Vindiciae Geologicae* [Oxford, 1820], pp. 22–23). But judged by the magnitude of his literary efforts to explain them away, Buckland and his fellows could not have thought the difficulties so very minute, after all.

20. *Ibid.*, p. 3, and dedication.

21. *Ibid.*, pp. 4–5.

22. *Ibid.*, p. 11.

23. For a typical illustration, see "Transactions of the Geological Society," *Quarterly Review*, XXXIV (1826), 507–540, pp. 538–540. The word "God" is seldom to be found in this literature and neither, though for different reasons perhaps, is the phrase "supreme being."

24. Buckland, *Vindiciae Geologicae*, p. 13.

25. *Ibid.*, pp. 18–19.

26. *Ibid.*, pp. 23–32.

27. *Ibid.*, pp. 23–24.

28. Buckland, *Reliquiae Diluvianae* (2d ed.; London, 1824), pp. 15–23.

29. Buckland, "An Account of an Assemblage of Fossil Teeth and Bones," *Philosophical Transactions*, CXII (1822), 171–236.

30. See, for example, Henry de la Beche, *A Geological Manual* (Philadelphia, 1832), pp. 171–180.

31. K. M. Lyell, *Life of Charles Lyell*, I, 164: Lyell to Mantell, 3 January 1826. Buckland had intended to kill his first hyena to compare its skull with those from Kirkdale, but he and his friends got fond of it and, instead of dissecting it, kept it as a pet.

32. Gordon, *Life of Buckland*, pp. 55–56: Dawkins to Frank Buckland, undated.

33. Buckland, *Reliquiae Diluvianae*, p. iii.

34. This paragraph is a condensation of the argument. For illustrative examples, see *Reliquiae Diluvianae*, pp. 41–43, 51, 121.

35. *Ibid.*, p. 90. The argument on the antiquity of man is summarized on pp. 164–170. For a discussion of this discovery, and for Buckland's determination to classify the skeleton as postdiluvian, see F. J. North, "Paviland Cave, The 'Red Lady,' The Deluge, and William Buckland," *Annals of Science*, V (1941–1947), 91–128. The lady in question, it may be worth remarking here, is now agreed to have been a tall young man of paleolithic vintage (*ibid.*, p. 92).

36. Buckland, *Reliquiae Diluvianae*, pp. 226–228. For memoirs typical of those which went into the erection of this synthesis, see *T.G.S.*, V (1821), 117–304; I (2d series, 1824), 95–102, 103–123, 124–131, 374–378, 381–389, 390–396; *P.G.S.*, I, 15–16, 48–49, 107–108, 179–180, 189–192.

37. G. P. Scrope, *The Geology and Extinct Volcanos of Central France* (2d ed.; London, 1858), pp. v–xiv, 197–213. I have not seen a copy of the first edition (London, 1826), but, according to the author, the body of the work was unchanged in the second edition (p. xiii).

38. *Ibid.*, p. 208. One reason for the relative neglect accorded Scrope's views may be that during the preceding year he had come out with a somewhat immature volume entitled *Considerations on Volcanos, the Probable Causes of their Phenomena, the Laws which determine their March, the Disposition of their Products, and their Connexion with the Present State and Past History of the Globe; leading to the Establishment of a New Theory of the Earth* (London, 1825). As Scrope admitted in the preface to the *Geology and Extinct Volcanos of Central France*, this, though an anticipation of uniformitarianism, was a somewhat unfortunate effort. The last section (pp. 220–243) is simply imaginative cosmogony and may have had the effect of partially discrediting Scrope's next book.

39. See, for example, his "Presidential Addresses" (1828 and 1829), *P.G.S.*, I, 50–62, 112–134; his articles in the *Edinburgh Review* cited above, p. 277, n. 2; and his later review of Lyell's *Elements of Geology* (London, 1838), in the *Edinburgh Review*, LXIX (1839), 406–466, wherein he takes Lyell to task for (among other things) being over-theoretical. By that time Fitton no longer accepted the diluvial hypothesis, and he had, in fact, always been more uniformitarian than catastrophist in his own attitudes.

40. Geikie, *Life of Murchison*, I, 94–97, 125–126.

41. *Ibid.*, II, 117–118, 156, 316–319. For his earlier papers, see *T.G.S.*, 2d series, II (1829), 97–107, 293–326; 353–368.

42. Clark and Hughes, *Life of Sedgwick*, I, 160–161.

43. Sedgwick, "On Diluvial Formations," *Annals of Philosophy*, new series, X (1825), 18–37, pp. 34–35.

44. Geikie, *Life of Murchison*, II, 306.

45. Conybeare, "On the Hydrographical Basin of the Thames," *Philosophical Magazine*, 2d series, VI (1829), 61–65.

46. Conybeare, "On Mr. Lyell's *Principles of Geology*," *Philosophical Magazine*, VIII (1830), 215–219; "An Examination of those Phaenomena of Geology," *ibid.*, pp. 359–362, 401–406, and IX (1831), 19–23, 111–117, 188–197, 258–270.

47. Charles Lyell, "Presidential Address" (1836), *P.G.S.*, II, 358–359. See also V. A. Eyles, "John Macculloch, F.R.S., and His Geological Map: An Account of the First Geological Survey of Scotland," *Annals of Science*, II (1937), 114–129.

48. John Macculloch, *Proofs and Illustrations of the Attributes of God, from the Facts and Laws of the Physical Universe: Being the Foundation of Natural and Revealed Religion* (3 vols.; London, 1837), III, 571. This work was Macculloch's testament and, though completed before 1830, was published posthumously, having been withheld so as not to compete with the *Bridgewater Treatises* (see above, pp. 209-216).

49. *Proofs and Illustrations*, I, 5.

50. *Ibid.*, III, 425-426.

51. *Ibid.*, p. 573.

52. "Geology of the Deluge," *Edinburgh Review*, XXXIX (1823-24), 196-234, pp. 196-199.

53. Charles Daubeny, *A Description of Active and Extinct Volcanos* (London, 1826).

54. [W. H. Fitton], "Volcanoes," *Edinburgh Review*, XLV (1826-27), 296, 297, 313-315.

55. Daubeny, *Description of Volcanos*, p. 9.

56. "Progress of Geological Science," *Edinburgh Review*, LII (1830), 43-72.

57. *Ibid.*, pp. 66-68.

58. Buckland, *Vindiciae Geologicae*, p. 35.

59. "Reliquiae Diluvianae," *Quarterly Review*, XXIX (1823), 138-165.

60. "Transactions of the Geological Society," *Quarterly Review*, XXXIV (1826), 507-540.

61. *Ibid.*, pp. 508-509.

62. *Ibid.*, pp. 539-540.

63. [Charles Lyell], "Scrope's Geology of Central France," *Quarterly Review*, XXXVI (1827), 437-483.

64. *Ibid.*, pp. 481-482. According to Scrope, this review was Lyell's first essay in the field of geological generalization (Scrope, *Geology of Central France*, p. vii).

65. *British Critic*, I (1825), iii.

66. *Ibid.*, pp. iii-v.

67. Two vols.; London, 1826.

68. "Researches into the Physical History of Mankind," *British Critic*, IV (1828), 33-61, pp. 33-34. Cf. Conway Zirkle, "Natural Selection before the Origin of Species," *Proceedings of the American Philosophical Society*, LXXXIV (1941), 104-105. Professor Zirkle regards Prichard's views on the geographical distribution and environmental variation of races as evolutionary, though he also describes Prichard as having contracted rather than expanded his opinion in his later works. However this may be (and it seems to me that Professor Zirkle reads more into Prichard than is there), Prichard, an early anthropologist, was writing about races, not species. When he refers to species, he supposes each to be descended from a single stock. He accepts, incidentally, the reality and universality of the

flood. See Prichard, *Researches into the Physical History of Mankind*, II, 525–616, and especially pp. 585–591, 602–606.

69. London, 1829.

70. "A New System of Geology," *British Critic*, VI (1829), 387–412, p. 389.

71. *Ibid.*, p. 388.

72. For the typical amateur notice, see James Boaz, "On the Structure of the Earth," *Philosophical Magazine*, LXI (1823), 200–203. The "exercise of Omnipotence" explains the "ghastly fissures and fractures of the shell we inhabit." Mr. Boaz suggests that the divine ordination of centrifugal force may be the agency God uses.

73. *Philosophical Magazine*, new series, IV (1828), 225; V (1829), 387; VI (1829), 92, 136; VII (1830), 54, 321.

74. *Ibid.*, LXV (1825), 412–421. Reprinted from *T.G.S.*, 2d series, I (1824), 381–389.

75. *Philosophical Magazine*, LXVII (1826), 211–219, 249–259. Reprinted from *Cambridge Philosophical Transactions*.

CHAPTER V. THE UNIFORMITY OF NATURE

1. Cuvier, *Theory of the Earth*, p. 12.

2. Lyell, *Principles of Geology*, I, 164–165.

3. Quoted in Geikie, *Founders of Geology*, p. 404.

4. By 1830, the differences over the interpretation of river valleys in particular had almost reached the proportions of a major issue. Two incipient schools, "Fluvialist" and "Diluvialist," had developed and had prepared the positions which uniformitarian and catastrophist would occupy once Lyell made the disagreement explicit and fundamental. For the fluvialist papers and the immediate empirical background of the uniformitarian theory, see, for example, *P.G.S.*, I, 89–91, 170–171; *T.G.S.*, 2d series, II, 195–236, 279–286, 287–292, 337–352. For the anticipatory diluvialist counterattack, see *P.G.S.*, I, 145–149, 189–192; *T.G.S.*, 2d series, I, 95–102; II, 119–130.

5. Fleming, "The Geological Deluge, as Interpreted by Bacon, Cuvier, and Professor Buckland, Inconsistent with the Testimony of Moses and the Phenomena of Nature," *Edinburgh Philosophical Journal*, XIV (1826), 205–239, p. 208.

6. *Ibid.*, pp. 209–215. Like many ex-Wernerians, Fleming had turned to zoology after "geognosy" became discredited. His chief work, *Philosophy of Zoology*, stood very firmly indeed upon the "real existence" of species in nature.

7. Scrope, *Considerations on Volcanos*, pp. iii–ix, 242–243; *Geology of Central France*, pp. vii–viii, 197–213. For evidence of some concessions to the prevailing catastrophist theories, see the former of these titles, pp. iv–v, 215–218.

8. K. M. Lyell, *Life of Charles Lyell*, I, 163: Lyell to his sister, 4 December 1825.

9. *Ibid.*, I, 170: Lyell to his father, 10 April 1827. See also II, 6–7: Lyell to Whewell, 7 March 1837.

10. *Ibid.*, II, 6–7; Lyell, *Principles of Geology*, III, vii–xviii.

11. Lyell, *Principles of Geology*, I, 72.

12. *Ibid.*, III, 1–6.

13. *Ibid.*, I, 144.

14. *Ibid.*, pp. 63–65.

15. [W. H. Fitton], "Mr. Lyell's *Elements of Geology*," *Edinburgh Review*, LXIX (1839), 406–466. The *Elements of Geology* was a condensation and popularization of the *Principles*. On the question of Lyell's debt to Hutton, see V. A. Eyles, "James Hutton (1726–1797) and Sir Charles Lyell (1797–1875)," *Nature*, CLX (1947), 694–695.

16. K. M. Lyell, *Life of Charles Lyell*, I, 269: Lyell to Scrope, 14 June 1830.

17. Lyell, *Principles of Geology*, I, 76–82.

18. *Ibid.*, p. 104.

19. *Ibid.*, III, 52–61.

20. Though he did not think himself guilty of violating it, Lyell would have agreed with Sedgwick's canon, promulgated in criticism of the *Principles*: "The language of theory can never fall from our lips with any grace or fitness, unless it appear as the simple enumeration of those general facts, with which, by observation alone, we have at length become acquainted" ("Presidential Address" [1831], *P.G.S.*, I, 302).

21. Lyell, *Principles of Geology*, III, 272–273.

22. *Ibid.*, III, 270. See also I, 89.

23. *Ibid.*, III, 271–272.

24. *Ibid.*, p. 272.

25. *Ibid.*, II, 179.

26. *Ibid.*, p. 1.

27. *Ibid.*, pp. 2–35.

28. *Ibid.*, p. 65.

29. *Ibid.*, p. 124.

30. *Ibid.*, pp. 179–184.

31. *Ibid.*, p. 270.

32. *Ibid.*, pp. 156–157.

33. *Ibid.*, I, 145.

34. *Ibid.*, quoted from Sir Humphry Davy, *Consolations in Travel*, dialogue iii.

35. Lyell, *Principles of Geology*, I, 145.

36. *Ibid.*, pp. 145–153.

37. *Ibid.*, pp. 155–156.

38. *Ibid.*, p. 156.

39. K. M. Lyell, *Life of Charles Lyell*, I, 271: Lyell to Scrope, 14 June 1830.

40. *Ibid.*, pp. 309–311: Lyell to Scrope, 9 November 1830.

41. Lyell, *Principles of Geology*, I, 65.

42. *Ibid.*, pp. 65–66; on Voltaire and geology, see also White, *Warfare of Science with Theology*, I, 229.

43. K. M. Lyell, *Life of Charles Lyell*, I, 271: Lyell to Scrope, 14 June 1830.

44. *Ibid.*, p. 263: Lyell to his sister, 26 February 1830.

45. *Ibid.*, p. 173: Lyell to Mantell, 29 December 1827. See also Mantell, *Journal*, p. 75 (12 March 1830).

46. K. M. Lyell, *Life of Charles Lyell*, I, 273: Lyell to Scrope, 25 June 1830.

47. [Scrope], "Lyell's Principles of Geology," *Quarterly Review*, XLIII (1830), 411–469. For Lyell's satisfaction, see K. M. Lyell, *Life of Charles Lyell*, I, 309–311: Lyell to Scrope, 9 November 1830.

48. For a somewhat highly colored account of the theological opposition, both in the 1830's and later, see T. H. Huxley, "The Lights of the Church and the Light of Science," in *Science and Hebrew Tradition*, volume VI of *Collected Essays* (New York, 1894), pp. 201–238.

49. See, for example, Sedgwick, "Presidential Address" (1831), *P.G.S.*, I, 304; Whewell, *History of Inductive Sciences*, III, 616–617; and see also Whewell's remarks in his review in the *British Critic*, IX (1831), 180–206, especially pp. 184–186, 202–204.

50. Two vols.; London, 1839. Nor did Murchison's reviewer in the *Edinburgh Review* make any application of the work to interpretative controversies (LXXIII [1841], 1–41).

51. Lyell, *Principles of Geology*, I, 76.

52. For the first three months, volume I of the *Principles*, of which 1500 copies were printed, sold fifty copies a week. After this, sales, instead of declining, picked up enough to necessitate a second edition, of which Murray expected to sell one thousand copies in a year, but which in fact was bought up before that. In 1835, a third edition of the whole sold 1750 copies in ten months, and a fourth edition of 2000 was sold out in 1836 (K. M. Lyell, *Life of Charles Lyell*, I, 311–312, 383, 449, 464).

53. For example, W. D. Conybeare, who headed the catastrophist counterattack: "The great interest of this treatise seems to me to arise from its necessary tendency to force the current of scientific attention . . . to certain points of theoretical inquiry, for the investigation of which the science has been for some time growing more and more mature" (*Philosophical Magazine*, VIII [1830], 215). See also Whewell in the *British Critic*, IX (1831), 180.

54. Sedgwick, "Presidential Address" (1831), *P.G.S.*, I, 302.

55. K. M. Lyell, *Life of Charles Lyell*, I, 316–317: Lyell to Mantell, March, 1831.

56. Mantell, *Journal*, pp. 122, 129 (1 May and 13 November 1835).

57. *The Geology of the South-East of England* (London, 1833); *The Wonders of Geology; or, A Familiar Exposition of Geological Phenomena* (4th ed.; 2 vols.; London, 1840); and *The Medals of Creation; or, First Lessons in Geology, and in the Study of Organic Remains* (2 vols.; London, 1844).

58. *Illustrations of the Geology of Sussex* (London, 1822).

59. Mantell, *Geology of the South-East of England*, p. 15. In the terminology of diluvialist geology in the 1820's, materials more recent than tertiary formations were classified as alluvial and diluvial. The former means loose, superficial accumulations deposited by the mechanical action of surface water since the time of the retreat of the sea. The latter refers to materials deposited during a major inundation.

60. Mantell, *Wonders of Geology*, I, 115–116.

61. *Ibid.*, pp. 69–77, 114.

62. *Ibid.*, pp. 5–7.

63. The reference is to Buckland's *Bridgewater Treatise* (see above, p. 212).

64. Mantell, *Wonders of Geology*, II, 115–116.

65. *A Geological Manual* (Philadelphia, 1832 [1st ed.; London, 1831]); and *How to Observe* (London, 1835). For De la Beche's work in establishing the Geological Survey, see F. J. North, "Geology's Debt to Henry Thomas de la Beche," *Endeavour*, III (1944), 15–19.

66. De la Beche, *Geological Manual*, p. 32.

67. De la Beche, *Researches in Theoretical Geology* (London, 1834), pp. 240–241.

68. *Geological Manual*, pp. 131, 158–165, and *passim*; see also his "Notes on the Excavation of Valleys," *Philosophical Magazine*, VI (1829), 241–248; "Notes on the Formation of Extensive Conglomerate and Gravel Deposits," *ibid.*, VII (1830), 161–171; and an anonymous criticism of several of his papers, *ibid.*, pp. 189–194.

69. K. M. Lyell, *Life of Charles Lyell*, I, 317–318, 330, 444; Geikie, *Life of Murchison*, I, 203, 266–267.

70. K. M. Lyell, *Life of Charles Lyell*, I, 317–318: Lyell to his sister, 7 April 1831.

71. Charles Daubeny, "On the Diluvial Theory, and on the Origin of the Valleys of Auvergne," *The Edinburgh New Philosophical Journal*, X (1830–31), 201–229, pp. 204–205.

72. K. M. Lyell, *Life of Charles Lyell*, I, 312: Lyell to his sister, 14 November 1830.

73. Whewell, *History of Inductive Sciences*, III, 601–602.

74. Conybeare, "On Mr. Lyell's *Principles of Geology*," *Philosophical Magazine*, VIII (1830), 215–219; "An Examination of those Phaenomena of Geology which Seem to Bear Most Directly on Theoretical Speculation," *ibid.*, pp. 359–362, 401–406; IX (1831), 19–23, 111–117, 188–197, 258–270.

75. *Ibid.*, IX, 190.
76. Sedgwick, "Presidential Address" (1831), *P.G.S.*, I, 313.
77. K. M. Lyell, *Life of Charles Lyell*, I, 276: Lyell to his sister, 9 July 1830.
78. *Ibid.*, pp. 445–456: Lyell to Fleming, 7 January 1835.
79. Sedgwick, "Presidential Address" (1831), *P.G.S.*, I, 311–313; Lyell, *Principles of Geology*, III, 272–273.
80. K. M. Lyell, *Life of Charles Lyell*, I, 328: Lyell to Fleming, 29 August 1831. See also II, 3–5: Lyell to Whewell, 7 March 1837.
81. *Ibid.*, I, 318: Lyell to his sister, 7 April 1831.
82. Sedgwick "Presidential Address" (1831), *P.G.S.*, I, 300–301.
83. Conybeare, "Report on Geology," *British Association Reports* (1831–32), I and II (bound in one), 406.
84. Sedgwick, "Presidential Address" (1831), *P.G.S.*, I, 305.
85. *Ibid.*, pp. 305–306.
86. "Lyell — *Principles of Geology*," *British Critic*, IX (1831), 194.
87. Sedgwick, *A Discourse on the Studies of the University* (4th ed.; Cambridge, England, 1835), pp. 26–27.

CHAPTER VI: THE VESTIGES OF CREATION

1. Robert Chambers, *Vestiges of the Natural History of Creation* (2d ed.; London, 1844), p. 223. Authorship was not certainly known until the twelfth edition in 1884, when Alexander Ireland, who acted as go-between in arranging for the initial publication, disclosed the author's identity with a view of doing justice to his memory and out of a commendable interest in "saving the time of curious and diligent inquirers who might fruitlessly investigate the matter in future times" (*Vestiges* [12th ed.], p. ix).
2. [Sedgwick], "Natural History of Creation," *Edinburgh Review*, LXXXII (1845), 1–85, p. 3.
3. See above, Chapter VII, pp. 184–201.
4. Andrew D. White, *Warfare of Science with Theology*, deals definitively with this aspect of the story. For bibliographical suggestions and a brief description of this literature from a point of view opposite to White's, see Zöckler, *Beziehungen zwischen Theologie und Naturwissenschaft*, II, 474–475, 572 (note 115), 576 (notes 136, 137).
5. Gordon, *Life of Buckland*, p. 220: Mrs. Buckland to Sir Philip Egerton, November 1845. Her letter is an interesting indication of the peculiarly English quality of the questions discussed in this book.
6. Chambers, *Vestiges* (12th ed.), appendix, pp. lxix–lxx.
7. *Ibid.*, p. lxx.
8. *Ibid.* (2d ed.), p. 362.
9. *Ibid.*, p. 20.
10. *Ibid.*, pp. 149–151.
11. *Ibid.*, p. 153.

12. *Ibid.*, p. 154.
13. *Ibid.*, p. 184.
14. *Ibid.*, pp. 232–233.
15. *Ibid.*, p. 161.
16. *Ibid.*, pp. 185–186, 205.
17. Charles Darwin, *On the Origin of Species* (New York, 1864), p. vii. Opponents were equally sensible of the improvements in the later editions. "The author of the *Vestiges*," wrote James Forbes upon the appearance of the fourth edition and the *Sequel* (see note 41 below), ". . . has shown himself a very apt scholar, and has improved his knowledge and his arguments so much since his first edition that his deformities no longer appear so disgusting. It was well that he began to write in the fullness of his ignorance and presumption, for had he begun now he would have been more dangerous" (J. C. Shairp, P. G. Tait, and A. Adams-Reilly, *Life and Letters of James David Forbes* [London, 1873], p. 178: Forbes to Whewell, 8 January 1846).
18. Chambers, *Vestiges* (2d ed.), p. 173.
19. *Ibid.*, pp. 198–203. Chambers attached more importance to this than to the real evidence of comparative anatomy, which he presented more sketchily (pp. 191–198).
20. *Ibid.*, pp. 166–167, 222.
21. *Ibid.*, pp. 274–278.
22. Quoted from Chambers' anonymously conducted correspondence, "Appendix to the Introduction," *Vestiges* (12th ed.), p. xxviii.
23. *Ibid.*, appendix, p. lxiv.
24. *Ibid.*, appendix, p. lxvii.
25. *Ibid.* (2d ed.), pp. 327–330, 337–350.
26. *Ibid.*, pp. 333–334.
27. *Ibid.*, pp. 365–369.
28. *Ibid.*, pp. 366–367.
29. *Ibid.*, pp. 156–157.
30. *Ibid.*, p. 236.
31. *Ibid.*, p. 158.
32. These items are not listed in my bibliography. I have glanced at them, with respect both for their readers and for the publishers, who participated far more intimately in the compilation than such people do today. Either Robert Chambers or his brother, William, actually wrote a large part of the material.
33. From 1854 to its demise in 1897 it was known as *Chambers's Journal of Popular Literature, Science, and Arts.*
34. *Chambers's Edinburgh Journal*, vol. I, no. 1 (4 February 1832).
35. *Ibid.*
36. Chambers, *Vestiges* (12th ed.), p. xxii.
37. *Ibid.* (2d ed.), p. 392.
38. T. H. Huxley, "On the Reception of *The Origin of Species*," chap-

ter xiv of Francis Darwin, *Life and Letters of Charles Darwin* (2 vols.; New York, 1888), I, 541–542. See also Leonard Huxley, *Life and Letters of T. H. Huxley* (2 vols.; New York, 1901), I, 179–183.

39. It is interesting that Alfred Russel Wallace thought it "an ingenious hypothesis strongly supported by some striking facts and analogies, but which remains to be proved by more facts and the additional light which more research may throw upon the problem" (A. R. Wallace, *My Life* [2 vols.; New York, 1905], I, 254: Wallace to H. W. Bates, 28 December 1847). When the *Vestiges* was published, however, Wallace was only twenty-one and had scarcely begun to educate himself as a scientist, so that his opinion was not of much moment at the time. For Darwin's privately expressed view of the *Vestiges*, see above, p. 217. Compare my remarks, however, with A. O. Lovejoy's discussion in "The Argument for Organic Evolution before 'The Origin of Species,' " *Popular Science Monthly*, LXXV (1909), 499–514, 537–549, especially pp. 501–507. Professor Lovejoy sets aside the testimony of Huxley (and other contemporaries) as an emotional rather than a scientific reaction and describes the *Vestiges* as an example of "scientific method" (p. 504) and Chambers as the British writer by whom "a logically cogent argument for the theory [was] first brought together" (p. 499), one which ought to have convinced scientists in the then state of knowledge. I cannot agree with this interpretation. Even if an argument of the type of the *Vestiges* could properly be described as logically cogent, then Erasmus Darwin ought to have this credit rather than Chambers — though, to be sure, the general state of knowledge was far less advanced in Darwin's time.

40. Ireland's Introduction to the twelfth edition.

41. See Chambers' correspondence, extracts printed in the "Appendix to the Introduction," *Vestiges* (12th ed.), p. xxviii. Each edition was revised and improved, a fact which made many critics somewhat uncomfortable. After the appearance of the fourth edition, Chambers published a separate volume dealing with the criticism he had evoked: *Explanations: A Sequel to "Vestiges of . . . Creation"* (London, 1845). Later the sequel was incorporated into the parent work as an appendix. It argued that his critics, by refusing to accept his interpretation as a scientific premise, were driven to rely upon successive visitations of a causation essentially miraculous.

42. Ireland's Introduction, *Vestiges* (12th ed.), pp. xvii–xix. See also references throughout the correspondence cited in this chapter.

43. Some editors, like those of the *Quarterly Review*, ignored the *Vestiges*; they commissioned reviews of some of the more orthodox works then appearing and thus dealt with the issue without admitting its existence.

44. [Holland], "Natural History of Man," *Quarterly Review*, LXXXVI (1849–50), 1–40, pp. 6–7.

45. *Ibid.*, p. 9. Holland dismissed the *Vestiges* in a footnote (p. 14).

46. "The Vestiges, Etc.," *Westminster Review*, XLIV (1845), 152-203, p. 153. The latter part of the review dealt with Humboldt's *Kosmos* and seemed not unsympathetic to ideas of development, though the reviewer felt he "need scarcely say" that he rejected the idea of development "through the medium of the ordinary process of generation" (p. 199).

47. Clark and Hughes, *Life of Sedgwick*, II, 76-80; see also *Chambers's Edinburgh Journal*, new series, II (1844), 322-323.

48. For a sample of the correspondence, see Richard Owen, *The Life of Richard Owen* (2 vols.; New York, 1894), I, 252-256.

49. Clark and Hughes, *Life of Sedgwick*, II, 83-84: Sedgwick to Lyell, 9 April 1845.

50. *Ibid.*, p. 86: Sedgwick to Agassiz, 10 April 1845.

51. For a statement of this argument, see Sedgwick, *A Discourse on the Studies of the University of Cambridge* (5th ed.; Cambridge, England, 1850), pp. xxv-xxvi.

52. Above, pp. 145-146.

53. Quoted from Louis Agassiz, *Recherches sur les poissons fossiles* (5 vols.; Neuchâtel, 1833-1843), in [Sedgwick], "Natural History of Creation," *Edinburgh Review*, LXXXII, 56.

54. Sedgwick, "Natural History of Creation," p. 3.

55. *Ibid.*, pp. 62-63.

56. *Ibid.*, pp. 28-51.

57. Sedgwick, *Discourse*, pp. lx-lxix.

58. *Ibid.*, pp. xx, cccxxiii.

59. See Clark and Hughes, *Life of Sedgwick*, II, 161: Sedgwick to Hugh Miller, 3 September 1849.

60. Sedgwick, *Discourse*, pp. clxx-clxxi.

61. According to Chambers, these two were his most difficult critics, but he respected Miller. See *Vestiges* (12th ed.), pp. xxix, xl.

62. Miller entered into extensive correspondence about the issue with Sedgwick, Murchison, Agassiz, *et al.*, but Sedgwick was flattering himself in thinking their religious opinions very nearly parallel (Clark and Hughes, *Life of Sedgwick*, II, 159-161: Sedgwick to Miller, 3 September 1849).

63. See Geikie's memoir in W. K. Leask, *Hugh Miller* (Edinburgh, 1896), pp. 147-151. Also, Miller, *Popular Geology* (Boston, 1859), editor's preface, pp. 12-13.

64. Miller had always been a man of turbulent intensity, given to occasional hallucinations. He always went armed, possessed of a pathological fear of burglars, and in his latter years the symptoms of incipient insanity became increasingly apparent. He grew morbidly afraid of walking in his sleep, and of what he might do in such a situation. At last, he shot himself in a sudden rush of madness one night, having seen what must have been some unbearable vision. His appearance must have been striking, to judge from the likeness printed in *My Schools and Schoolmasters*. He was tall, but the picture is of a squat figure, strong to the point of

being misshapen; a huge head covered with masses of hair, out of proportion to the body in a startling way; a delicate though large face, prominent nose, forehead broader than it ought to be, and wary eyes.

65. Peter Bayne, *The Life and Letters of Hugh Miller* (2 vols.; Boston, 1871, I, viii; II, 449.

66. Miller, *The Old Red Sandstone* (Edinburgh, 1841), pp. 25–41.

67. Quoted in Bayne, *Life of Miller*, II, 494. Miller never found out who wrote the *Vestiges*, and he and Chambers were friends all this time.

68. *Poems Written in the Leisure Hours of a Journeyman Mason* (Inverness, 1829). His poetry was very bad.

69. Miller, *My Schools and Schoolmasters* (Boston, 1855), pp. 303–315, 321–327.

70. Above, Chapter V, p. 284, n. 52; Chambers, *Vestiges* (12th ed.), p. vi; Leask, *Hugh Miller*, p. 124. By 1876, *On the Origin of Species* had sold 16,000, and Darwin thought this very good indeed (Francis Darwin, *Life of Charles Darwin*, I, 70).

71. Edinburgh, 1839.

72. Even Huxley, who never had any use for what he thought the obscurities of natural theology, found *The Old Red Sandstone* illuminating (Leask, *Hugh Miller*, p. 143).

73. Smiles, *Robert Dick, Baker of Thurso, Geologist and Botanist* (London, 1878).

74. Many of these were collected only posthumously. A full bibliography will be found in Leask, *Hugh Miller*, pp. 155–157.

75. See, for example, his *Rambles of a Geologist* (Boston, 1859), pp. 260–262 (published with *The Cruise of the Betsey*). This is a characteristic book, including antiquities, scenery, folkways, geography, nautical lore, geology, religion, morals, and society.

76. Miller, *Popular Geology*, pp. 12–13.

77. Miller, *My Schools and Schoolmasters*, p. iv. This book was written while his mind was cracking up, but no one would guess that from its context.

78. Miller, *The Old Red Sandstone*, pp. 217–218.

79. *Ibid.*, p. 62.

80. *Ibid.*, pp. 68–69.

81. Miller, *The Footprints of the Creator; or, The Asterolepis of Stromness* (Boston, 1850). See the preface by Louis Agassiz, p. xi. Agassiz was in close touch with English geologists in the 1830's and 1840's and was the chief authority on fossil fish and, in the early forties, on glacial geology. He was, as is well known, very devout and adamant in his opposition to theories of transmutation of species. It is interesting that, before he came to America, much of his research was financed in England. His great work on fossil fish had over twice as many English as French subscribers (Elizabeth C. Agassiz, *Louis Agassiz, His Life and Correspondence* [2 vols.; Boston, 1886], I, 248–297).

82. Miller, *Footprints of the Creator*, p. 189.
83. *Ibid.*, pp. 38–39.
84. *Ibid.*, p. 42.
85. *Ibid.*, p. 41.
86. *Ibid.*, pp. vi–vii.
87. *Ibid.*, pp. 44–45.
88. Although his views are scattered through all his writings, he pulled them together in a series of lectures, which were published posthumously under the title, *The Testimony of the Rocks; or, Geology in its Bearings on the Two Theologies, Natural and Revealed* (Boston, 1857).
89. Miller, *Testimony of the Rocks*, pp. 373–391.
90. *Ibid.*, pp. 148–178. See also the splendid passage, pp. 206–210.
91. Miller, *My Schools and Schoolmasters*, p. 365.
92. Miller, *Footprints of the Creator*, pp. 331–332.
93. Miller, *My Schools and Schoolmasters*, pp. 366–367.
94. "A Brahman versed in Hindu science, laws, and religion" — *Webster's Dictionary*.
95. Miller, *Footprints of the Creator*, pp. 330–331.
96. Baden Powell, *Christianity Without Judaism* (London, 1857), pp. 257–258.
97. London, 1860. Powell contributed the essay, "On the Study of the Evidences of Christianity."
98. Powell, *The Connexion of Natural and Divine Truth* (London, 1838); *The Unity of Worlds and of Nature* (2d ed.; London, 1856); *The Order of Nature Considered in Reference to the Claims of Revelation* (London, 1859).
99. Powell, *The Connexion of Natural and Divine Truth*, pp. 204–269.
100. *Ibid.*, pp. 273, 4.
101. *Ibid.*, p. 187.
102. Chambers, *Vestiges* (12th ed.), p. xxxi; Powell, *The Unity of Worlds and of Nature*, pp. 329–430.

CHAPTER VII: How Useful Is Thy Dwelling Place

1. Sir Humphry Davy, "A Discourse Introductory to a Course of Lectures on Chemistry," in *The Collected Works of Sir Humphry Davy, Bart.* (ed. John Davy; 9 vols.; London, 1839–40), II, 325–326.
2. Sir David Brewster, *More Worlds than One, the Creed of the Philosopher and the Hope of the Christian* (New York, 1854), p. 264.
3. See D. M. Turner, *History of Science Teaching in England* (London, 1927), pp. 69–74; J. W. Adamson, *English Education, 1789–1902* (Cambridge, England, 1930), pp. 70–89; and the account of the Oxford educational system in Charles Lyell, *Travels in North America* (2 vols.; London, 1845), I, 261–316. A comparison of Harvard with Oxford and Cambridge led Lyell into a full discussion of English university education, and, though very critical, his description does not warrant quite so

minimal a view of the place of science (particularly before 1830) as is presented by Miss Turner.

4. These figures are taken from a pamphlet by Charles G. B. Daubeny, *Brief Remarks on the Correlation of the Natural Sciences* (Oxford, 1848), where they are reproduced from a report by the professors concerned which had been attached to a proposal to reform the system of studies. The proposal had been submitted to, and rejected by, Convocation in 1839. The occasion for this pamphlet was the renewed agitation and criticism which in 1850 led to the issuing of the Royal Commissions on the universities. It is worth remarking that Daubeny, though a reformer and proponent of science in the curriculum, had very modest ideas regarding the scientific attainments to be desired in a candidate for the degree (see pp. 8–18). For a brief account of the work of the commissions, see Adamson, *English Education*, pp. 171–195. A list of the students who attended the chemistry lectures will be found in R. T. Gunther, *The Daubeny Laboratory Register* (Oxford, 1924), pp. 65–135. For description and discussion of the place of science in the universities, see Oxford University Commission, *Report* (London, 1852), pp. 60–83, and Cambridge University Commission, *Report*, pp. 89–114, and "Evidence," pp. 76–137.

5. Examinations themselves had been instituted by a statute of 1800, but competition for honors appears not to have been severe until after the separate examination was established. The universities were subjected to an increasing barrage of criticism up to the middle of the century, partly from people who were science-minded and resented what they thought the arid scholasticism of classical studies, and partly from people who were liberal-minded and resented the restrictiveness of the universities and their clerical character. These lines of attack often converged. Anyone interested in these issues — and in the uniformity over the centuries of such questions as overemphasis on grades, the lecture versus the discussion method, science versus the humanities, and professional education versus liberal education — may consult, besides the authorities already cited, William Whewell, *On the Principles of English University Education* (London, 1837), and *Of a Liberal Education in General; and with Particular Reference to the Leading Studies of the University of Cambridge* (London, 1845). For examples of the attacks on the universities, see the following articles by Sir William Hamilton in the *Edinburgh Review*: "English Universities — Oxford," LIV (1831), 478–504; "Patronage of Universities," XLIX (1834), 196–227; "Study of Mathematics — University of Cambridge," LXII (1835–36), 409–455.

6. This is the gist of a letter of 1839 published in Daubeny, *Correlation of the Natural Sciences*, pp. 22–23.

7. Lyell, *Travels*, I, 310.

8. Mantell's *Journal* substantiates this point (see especially pp. viii, 10–56, 172–173), and it offers additional documentation for the popularity of geological lectures with the general public and for the frequency with

which geology furnished the subject of the *conversazione* given by the intelligentsia.

9. Sir John Herschel, *A Preliminary Discourse on the Study of Natural Philosophy* (The Cabinet Cyclopaedia; London, 1831), p. 287.

10. See above, pp. 109–110. F. J. North, "Paviland Cave and William Buckland," quotes extensively from their correspondence (*Annals of Science*, V, 91–128).

11. *Chambers's Edinburgh Journal*, new series, II (23 November, 1844), 322. See also "Natural History," *Westminster Review*, XLIV (1845), 203–224, p. 219; and "The Vestiges, Etc.," *ibid.*, 152–302, p. 152. Justus Liebig, who attended the 1844 meeting, was also impressed, though not favorably, by the predominant interest in geology: "The meeting at York, which was very interesting to me from the acquaintance of so many celebrated men, did not satisfy me in a scientific view. It was properly a feast given to the geologists, the other sciences serving only to decorate the table" (H. Bence Jones, *The Life and Letters of Faraday* [2 vols.; London, 1870], II, 189: Liebig to Faraday, 19 December 1844). Despite their many successes, the geologists were, in Liebig's opinion, like most British scientists in that they were too exclusively empirical in their approach and displayed too little knowledge of the allied sciences.

12. In 1832 Buckland acted as host to the Association at Oxford, and the year following Sedgwick extended the patronage of Cambridge. Sedgwick succeeded Buckland as president, and in the first few years about half the other officers were geologists. See *British Association Reports*, I (1832), 17–41, 42, 46–47, and II, 111; Gordon, *Life of Buckland*, pp. 120–128; Geikie, *Life of Murchison*, I, 184–189, 237–238; Mantell, *Journal*, pp. 102–105. For accounts of the foundation and the early years, see "The British Scientific Association," *Edinburgh Review*, LX (1834–35), 363–394; and O. J. R. Howarth, *The British Association for the Advancement of Science* (2d ed.; London, 1931), especially pp. 1–107.

13. Geikie, *Life of Murchison*, I, 187–188.

14. Gordon, *Life of Buckland*, p. 134: Sedgwick to Buckland, undated. For reports of a typical meeting (that at Bristol in 1836), see *The Times* for 1836: 17 August, p. 3; 22 August, p. 3; 24 August, p. 3; 25 August, p. 3; 26 August, p. 4; 27 August, p. 5; 29 August, p. 1; 30 August, p. 4; 1 September, p. 3; 7 September, p. 2. It should be noted, however, that *The Times* was hostile to the Association and tended to ridicule the meetings.

15. The concern aroused by Charles Babbage's criticism of dilettantism in the Royal Society and of specialization in the learned societies of each science undoubtedly contributed to the foundation of the Association. Babbage also compared unfavorably the neglect of science in the universities and by the government to the careful fostering it received on the Continent. See Babbage, *Reflections on the Decline of Science in England*. He thought the Geological Society one of the few which were really

contributing to the advancement of science (p. 45). For an evaluation of Babbage's critique, see C. F. Mullett, "Charles Babbage: A Scientific Gadfly," *Scientific Monthly*, LXVII (1948), 361–371.

16. Gordon, *Life of Buckland*, p. 136; Lyell, *Travels*, I, 295–297; Richard Oastler, *Fleet Papers* (29 October 1842), quoted in R. L. Hill, *Toryism and the People* (London, 1929), p. 159; White, *Warfare of Science with Theology*, I, 406. The *Quarterly Review* was very hostile, and so too was *The Times*, which was then flirting with the anti-Poor Law agitation (Geikie, *Life of Murchison*, I, 187; II, 64–65). For the scornful attitude of *The Times*, see, for example, the issues of 4 September 1835, p. 3; 24 August 1838, p. 4; and 29 August 1839, p. 4.

17. "The British Scientific Association," *Edinburgh Review*, LX, 365.

18. For a brief summary of Combe's educational theory, see his *Lectures on Popular Education* (3d ed.; Edinburgh, 1848), p. vi. The first edition of these lectures was published in 1833, following their delivery before the Edinburgh Philosophical Institute. They were reprinted in *Chambers's Journal*, and Combe was constantly in demand by lyceums and literary and philosophical societies all over the United Kingdom.

19. London, 1828.

20. Combe, *On the Relation between Religion and Science* (3d ed.; Edinburgh, 1847), p. 35.

21. Charles Gibbon, *The Life of George Combe* (2 vols.; London, 1878), II, 182.

22. George Combe, *Education, Its Principles and Practice* (ed. William Jolly; London, 1879), p. 718: Mathieu Williams to Jolly, 17 December 1877. This volume is a compilation of all Combe's writings on education. Williams was headmaster of the school Combe established in Edinburgh in 1848 especially — according to the prospectus (p. 201) — to avert a reenactment of the February revolution in Britain.

23. *Ibid.*, pp. 202–203.

24. "Popular Science," *Quarterly Review*, LXXXIV (1848–49), 307–344, pp. 341, 344.

25. Knight, *The Results of Machinery, Namely, Cheap Production and Increased Employment Exhibited* (London, 1831), p. 205.

26. *Ibid.*, p. 206. Stopping at an inn, convivial fellow-commercials would inquire of Mr. Knight, "Pray, Sir, what do you travel in?" "In Useful Knowledge, Sir!" Knight would answer. Apparently he and his associates encountered considerable sales resistance before their customers could be made to "discover that political economists were not striving to enforce laws of their own or of anybody's making, but simply seeking to interpret the laws of God" (Knight, *Passages of a Working Life* [3 vols.; London, 1864–65], II, 76; III, 220–221). In these last remarks Knight is quoting a Mr. Solly "whose labours in the establishment of Working Men's Clubs appear to be as successful as they have been arduous."

27. Brougham, *Practical Observations upon the Education of the People* (London, 1825), p. 5. This tract went through ten editions in one year, Brougham devoting the proceeds to the London Mechanics' Institute.

28. *Ibid.*, p. 32.

29. *Mechanics' Magazine*, I (15 November 1823), 177–192, describes the opening meeting of the Institute. This magazine had itself been founded earlier in the same year with the object of diffusing among mechanics a better acquaintance with the history and the principles of the arts they practiced (*ibid.*, I, iii). It enjoyed a huge success the first few years, possibly because of the opposition of the editors (J. C. Robertson and Thomas Hodgskin) to the domination of the Mechanics' Institute by its patrons.

30. *Ibid.*, I, 119, 182–183, and *passim*. "Mechanics' Institutions," *Westminster Review*, XLI (1844), 416–445.

31. "Diffusion of Knowledge," *Edinburgh Review*, XLV (1826–27), 189–199.

32. J. G. Godard, *George Birkbeck, The Pioneer of Popular Education* (London, 1884), pp. 32, 66–67.

33. *Mechanics' Magazine*, I, 100–101, 115, 190; II, 306–309. See also "Mechanics' Institutions," *Westminster Review*, XLI, 416–445.

34. Andrew Ure, *A New System of Geology* (London, 1829), and *Philosophy of Manufactures* (London, 1835). See particularly the latter, pp. 3–8, 23, 279–290, 408–428. The calumnies uttered by factory reformers against mill and mine owners over child labor seemed to Ure comparable in injustice only to those uttered by pagans against primitive Christians, accused "of enticing children into their meetings in order to murder and devour them" (p. 290). Factory children, Ure pointed out, had never before been so well off.

35. *Mechanics' Magazine*, II (1 May 1824), 125.

36. *Ibid.*, pp. 306–309, 323, 378, 409–412, 428, 436–442, and appendix. See also Godard, *George Birkbeck*, pp. 51–61, 71–75; and Graham Wallas, *The Life of Francis Place* (3d ed.; New York, 1919), pp. 112–113.

37. Brougham, "Objects, Advantages, and Pleasures of Science," extract from the preliminary treatise of the *Library of Useful Knowledge* printed in *The Pamphleteer*, XXVII (1826), 506–507.

38. Brougham, *A Discourse of Natural Theology* (4th ed.; London, 1835), p. 204.

39. *Ibid.*, pp. 205–209. See also pp. 81–97, 126–137.

40. Footnotes to this point could be multiplied almost indefinitely. See, for example, Conybeare, "Report on Geology," *British Association Reports*, II (1832), 365; Gordon, *Life of Buckland*, pp. 24–26; Townsend, *The Character of Moses*, pp. 415–430; Phillips, *Memoir of William Smith*, pp. 18–20; Bakewell, *Introduction to Geology*, p. 454; "Principles of Geology," *Quarterly Review*, XLIII (1830), 411–414; Sedgwick, "Natural History of Creation," *Edinburgh Review*, LXXXII, 62–64.

41. Buckland's interest in applied science is a good example. Peel often

consulted him over agricultural improvements and drainage projects; he was instrumental in founding the Jermyn Street School of Mines; and, as Dean of Westminster, he struggled with the problems of public health in London (Gordon, *Life of Buckland*, pp. 150–166, 182–184, 247–254).

42. T. E. Thorpe, *Humphry Davy, Poet and Philosopher* (New York, 1896), pp. 76–77.

43. Davy, "A Discourse Introductory to a Course of Lectures on Chemistry," *Works*, II, 318–319.

44. *Ibid.*, p. 325.

45. Herschel, *Preliminary Discourse on Natural Philosophy*, pp. 10–17. On this treatise, see C. J. Ducasse, "John Herschel's Philosophy of Science," *Studies in the History of Culture* (The American Council of Learned Societies; Menasha, Wis., 1942), pp. 279–309.

46. *The Admiralty Manual of Scientific Enquiry; Prepared for the Use of Her Majesty's Navy: and Adapted for Travellers in General* (London, 1849). Herschel also published several popular manuals on his own field; for example, *A Treatise on Astronomy* (The Cabinet Cyclopaedia; London, 1841).

47. Herschel, *Preliminary Discourse on Natural Philosophy*, pp. 73–74.

48. Herschel, "An Address to the Subscribers" (1833), *Essays from the Quarterly and Edinburgh Reviews* (London, 1857).

49. Clark and Hughes, *Life of Sedgwick*, II, 46. See also I, 440, 515–516; II, 80, 242–244; K. M. Lyell, *Life of Charles Lyell*, II, 41–43: Lyell to Horner, 6 September 1838; and Mantell, *Journal*, pp. 102–104, 17–24 June 1832.

50. Lord Arthur Hervey, *A Suggestion for Supplying the Literary, Scientific, and Mechanics' Institutes of Great Britain and Ireland with Lecturers from the Universities* (Cambridge, 1855), pp. 16–17, 20. See also "Natural History," *Westminster Review*, XLIV (1845), 203–224.

51. Huxley undertook the post in 1854. For his popular lectures, see Leonard Huxley, *Life of T. H. Huxley*, I, 149–150. See also Adamson, *English Education*, pp. 387–400.

52. K. M. Lyell, *Memoir of Leonard Horner*, I, 196: Henry Cockburn to Thomas Kennedy, 25 October 1821.

53. *Ibid.*, pp. 194–200, 226, 329–330, 351–356, 367.

54. Quoted in Gordon, *Life of Buckland*, pp. 79–83, from C. F. Schönbein, *Mittheilungen aus dem Reisetagebuche eines deutschen Naturforschers* (Basel, 1842). See also Bayne, *Life of Miller*, II, 409: Murchison to Miller, undated.

55. Sermon in the Abbey on 23 April 1848 (Gordon, *Life of Buckland*, pp. 242–243). Readers of A. O. Lovejoy's *The Great Chain of Being* will recognize what is, probably, one of the last echoes of that idea in the nineteenth century. It had been many years since the chain of being had been regarded as a satisfactory schematization of organic nature, and it is probable that Buckland was unconsciously led to adopt this manner of expres-

sion because of its suitability to the social application he wished to make of science — an application, incidentally, which was very like the one which in the eighteenth century was often referred to the chain of being. See *The Great Chain of Being*, pp. 203–207.

56. After *The Christian Philosopher* (Edinburgh, 1823), Dick published a number of books which sold well enough to secure him a livelihood. There is no point in citing all the titles — a typical example is *Celestial Scenery; or, The Wonders of the Heavens Displayed* (London, 1837). Most of his works were pirated in American editions, for which his only tangible return was an honorary LL.D. from Union College. Dick was the first editor of the *Educational Magazine and Journal of Christian Philanthropy*, and he wrote several small treatises, published by the Religious Tract Society, on the solar system, the atmosphere, and optical instruments.

57. Dick, *On the Improvement of Society by the Diffusion of Knowledge* (Glasgow, undated [apparently *c.* 1840]), pp. 319–320.

58. *Ibid.*, pp. 312–313.

59. *Silurian System*, I, 576. See also Geikie, *Life of Murchison*, I, 261–262: Murchison to Sedgwick, 19 January 1838.

60. Richard Owen, *On the Archetypes and Homologies of the Vertebrate Skeleton* (London, 1848), p. 172.

61. From *On the Nature of Limbs* (London, 1849), quoted by T. H. Huxley, "Owen's Position in the History of Anatomical Science," in Owen, *Life of Richard Owen*, II, 316–317.

62. Owen, *Life of Richard Owen*, I, 252–256. The generally accepted opinion is that it was at least partly personal jealousy which induced Owen to attack Darwin.

63. For the early history of this question, see Grant McColley, "The Seventeenth-Century Doctrine of a Plurality of Worlds," *Annals of Science*, I (1936), 385–430.

64. For accounts of the controversy, see Zöckler, *Beziehungen zwischen Theologie und Naturwissenschaft*, II, 432–434, 567–568; and Isaac Todhunter, *William Whewell* (2 vols.; London, 1876), I, 184–210.

65. William Whewell, *Of the Plurality of Worlds* (London, 1853), p. 248.

66. *Ibid.*, p. 30.

67. *Ibid.*, pp. 52–112.

68. Brewster, *More Worlds than One*, pp. 253–255.

69. *Ibid.*, p. 142.

70. *Ibid.*, pp. 186–187.

71. *Ibid.*, p. 15.

72. It is noteworthy that in the first third of the century three of the four individuals (Davy being the fourth) who would appear in any list of great English scientists came from Nonconformist backgrounds. Faraday was a Sandemanian, a rigidly individualistic Calvinist sect of a confessional

and fundamentalist type. Dalton was a Quaker. Young had been brought up as a Quaker, though in later life he abandoned the doctrines of the Friends and joined the Church of England. See Bence Jones, *Life of Faraday*, II, 195–196; S. P. Thompson, *Michael Faraday, His Life and Work* (London, 1901), pp. 286–299; W. C. Henry, *Memoirs of the Life and Scientific Writings of John Dalton* (London, 1854), pp. 209–216; George Wilson, "Life and Discoveries of Dalton," in *Religio Chemici* (London and Cambridge, 1862), pp. 304–364; George Peacock, *Life of Thomas Young, M.D., F.R.S.* (London, 1855), pp. 58–59, 481.

73. Quoted in the first treatise, Thomas Chalmers, *On The Power, Wisdom, and Goodness of God as Manifested in the Adaptation of External Nature to the Moral and Intellectual Constitution of Man* (2 vols.; London, 1833), I, ix. The other treatises (for full citations see the bibliography, above, pp. 246–247) were: John Kidd, *Adaptation of External Nature to the Physical Condition of Man*; William Whewell, *Astronomy and General Physics*; Sir Charles Bell, *The Hand, Its Mechanism and Vital Endowments*; Peter Mark Roget, *Animal and Vegetable Physiology*; William E. Buckland, *Geology and Mineralogy*; William Kirby, *The Power, Wisdom, and Goodness of God as Manifested in the Creation of Animals*; William Prout, *Chemistry, Meteorology, and the Function of Digestion*. The books sold well. Dates of the first editions and the number of subsequent English editions were as follows:

Author	First Edition	Subsequent Editions
Chalmers	1833	8 by 1884
Kidd	1833	7 by 1887
Whewell	1833	9 by 1864
Bell	1833	7 by 1865
Roget	1834	5 by 1870
Buckland	1836	9 by 1860
Kirby	1835	6 by 1853
Prout	1834	4 by 1855

Whether Pickering, the London publisher, originally printed the same number of copies of all the treatises, I do not know, but the first two editions of Chalmers consisted of 1500 copies each, which were sold out immediately on publication. See William Hanna, *Memoirs of the Life and Writings of Thomas Chalmers, D.D., LL.D.* (4 vols.; New York, 1857), III, 312.

74. For biographical sketches of the authors and a somewhat more generous judgment than mine regarding the quality of their product, see D. W. Gundry, "The Bridgewater Treatises and their Authors," *History*, XXXI (1946), 140–152. See also Leslie Stephen, *The English Utilitarians* (3 vols.; London, 1900), II, 349–351; and White, *Warfare of Science with Theology*, I, 43–44.

75. Prout, *Chemistry, Meteorology, and Digestion*, p. xii.

76. Kidd, *Adaptation of External Nature to Physical Condition of Man*, pp. 176–196.

77. Whewell, *Astronomy and General Physics*, p. 19.

78. On Whewell, see Marion R. Stoll, *Whewell's Philosophy of Induction* (Lancaster, Pa., 1929).

79. Second ed.; London, 1838, pp. iv–vii (advertisement) and x (preface).

80. Bell, *The Hand*, p. ix. Bell had collaborated with Brougham in getting out the latter's edition of Paley. For a discussion of Bell's eminence as a physician and for an opinion that his teleological philosophy was more profound and successful than it seems to me to have been, see Benjamin Spector, "Sir Charles Bell and the Bridgewater Treatises," *Bulletin of the History of Medicine*, XII (1942), 314–322.

81. Roget, *Animal and Vegetable Physiology*, I, viii-x.

82. *Ibid.*, p. 25, n. 1.

83. Buckland, *Geology and Mineralogy*, I, 129.

84. Kirby, *Creation of Animals*, pp. 7–9.

85. *Ibid.*, pp. lii–lxxi. I think this is what is meant, though it is hard to be sure.

86. Prout, *Chemistry, Meteorology, and Digestion*, pp. 10–23; see also pp. 95–104, 163–187.

87. The last section is a devout description of the alimentary canal.

88. *Ibid.*, p. 404.

89. Chalmers was professor of divinity at the University of Edinburgh. He had a great reputation as a preacher and moralist, both in England and Scotland. He was leader of the evangelical party in the schism which gave rise to the Scottish Free Church in 1843, a close associate of Hugh Miller, and a serious student of natural history, astronomy, mathematics, and political economy.

90. Chalmers, *Adaptation of External Nature to the Moral and Intellectual Constitution of Man*, I, 5–6.

91. *Ibid.*, p. 38.

92. *Ibid.*, pp. 57–98, 169–178.

93. *Ibid.*, pp. 255–257.

94. Among Chalmers' many publications was a treatise, *On Political Economy in Connection with the Moral State and Moral Prospects of Society* (Glasgow, 1832). In some important respects, notably as to the danger of gluts, he differed with the orthodox school (for a discussion, see Stephen, *English Utilitarians*, II, 242–250), and though the book was not very well received, it was "the favourite child of his intellect" (Hanna, *Life of Chalmers*, III, 301). For an enthusiastic, though not very critical, appraisal of Chalmers as an economist, see J. Wilson Harper, *The Social Ideal and Dr. Chalmers' Contribution to Christian Economics* (Edinburgh, 1910).

95. Chalmers, *Adaptation of External Nature to the Moral and Intellectual Constitution of Man*, I, 228–229.

96. *Ibid.*, pp. 238–274.

97. *Ibid.*, II, 9. In fairness to Chalmers, it should be pointed out that, like Malthus, he genuinely wanted to improve the condition of the poor by inculcating in them the virtues of self-reliance. As a parish minister in Glasgow, he had organized a system of parish self-help tempered by church relief which was successful so long as he managed it himself. See Hanna, *Life of Chalmers*, II, 302–322; Stephen, *English Utilitarians*, II, 247–249; and for Chalmers' own writings, *The Christian and Civic Economy of Large Towns* (3 vols.; Glasgow, 1821–1826). But if anything, his real hatred of pauperism makes his attitude more rather than less interesting.

98. Chalmers, *Adaptation of External Nature to the Moral and Intellectual Constitution of Man*, II, 36.

99. *Ibid.*, p. 49.

100. *Ibid.*, p. 50.

101. *Ibid.*, I, 28.

CHAPTER VIII: THE PLACE OF PROVIDENCE IN NATURE

1. Clark and Hughes, *Life of Sedgwick*, II, 357–358: 24 December 1859.

2. Francis Darwin, *Life of Charles Darwin*, I, 312: Darwin to Lyell, 8 October 1845.

3. Darwin, *On the Origin of Species*, pp. vii–viii.

4. The immediate reaction of scientists to *On the Origin of Species* was, as Darwin had anticipated, unfavorable, and it was several years before the tide of professional opinion began to swing the other way. "On the whole, then," wrote Huxley, "the supporters of Mr. Darwin's views in 1860 were numerically extremely insignificant. There is not the slightest doubt that, if a general council of the Church scientific had been held at that time, we should have been condemned by an overwhelming majority" (Huxley, "On the Reception of the 'Origin of Species,'" Francis Darwin, *Life of Charles Darwin*, I, 540).

5. *Ibid.*, I, 543–544. Besides Robert Chambers; Buffon, Maupertuis, Benoît de Maillet, Erasmus Darwin, Treviranus, and Lorenz Oken were among the originators of different theories of evolution. Even the more solid doctrines of Lamarck and Geoffroy Saint-Hilaire seem to have been outside the contemporary stream of scientific development. The pre-Darwinian theory of evolution has been discussed by a number of scholars, most of whom have been chiefly concerned either with the question of species or with the degree to which particular writers anticipated Darwin rather than with the more general problem of the elimination of providentialism from natural history, which is the angle from which this chapter will approach the subject. Although there is considerable disagreement

about just how the ideas of early evolutionary philosophers are to be interpreted, it is at least clear that Darwin did not invent the concept of biological evolution, but that before Darwin neither was biological evolution generally accepted as a fact. See H. F. Osborn, *From the Greeks to Darwin*, with which should be read three articles in the *Popular Science Monthly* by A. O. Lovejoy: "Some Eighteenth Century Evolutionists," LXV (1904), 238–251, 323–340; "The Argument for Organic Evolution before 'The Origin of Species,'" LXXV (1909), 499–514, 537–549; and "Buffon and the Problem of Species," LXXIX (1911), 464–473, 554–567 (which unlike most interpretations regards Buffon as having been an evolutionist in only a very limited sense); see also J.-L. de Lanessan, "L'Attitude de Darwin à l'égard de ses prédécesseurs au sujet de l'origine des espèces," *Revue anthropologique*, XXIV (1914), 33–45; Pierre Brunet, "La Notion d'évolution dans la science moderne avant Lamarck," *Archeion*, XIX (1937), 21–43; and for the history of three major subsidiary concepts in the modern theory of evolution, see three articles by Conway Zirkle: "Natural Selection before the 'Origin of Species,'" *Proceedings of the American Philosophical Society*, LXXXIV (1941), 71–123, and "The Early History of the Ideas of the Inheritance of Acquired Characters and of Pangenesis," *Transactions of the American Philosophical Society*, XXXV (1946), 91–151.

6. Despite the fact that transmutation of species was being widely discussed in the 1840's, I cannot entirely agree with A. O. Lovejoy in his excellent article, "The Argument for Organic Evolution before 'The Origin of Species,'" in thinking that the circumstance that most of the facts and definite arguments used by Darwin were then current means that the theory of evolution was, therefore, substantially complete. I doubt whether the facts and arguments themselves should be regarded as independent of the whole scientific situation, which included a factor that Professor Lovejoy appreciated, but which he does not seem to me to allow for sufficiently. I mean the persistence into the 1840's of the idea of a superintending Providence in natural history. Referring to special creations, Professor Lovejoy says, "And while all these miraculous interpositions were taking place in order to keep the organic kingdom in a going condition, the Creator was not for a moment allowed by the orthodox geologists to interfere in a similar manner in their own particular domain of the inorganic processes" (p. 506). Now this was just what Sedgwick, Buckland, and Whewell, for example, did object to in uniformitarianism (about which the quotation would be correct) and in the nonorganic parts of the *Vestiges*.

7. Whewell, *Indications of the Creator* (Philadelphia, 1845), p. 36. As Master of Trinity College, Cambridge, Whewell excluded *On the Origin of Species* from the college library (Stoll, *Whewell's Philosophy of Induction*, p. 4).

8. Huxley, "On the Reception of 'The Origin of Species,'" pp. 556–557.

9. Francis Darwin, *Life of Charles Darwin*, I, 41.

10. *Ibid.*, pp. 278–279.

11. Compare, however, my remarks on Lyell's attitude toward special creations, both here and in Chapter V, to N. von Hofsten, "Ideas of Creation and Spontaneous Generation prior to Darwin," *Isis*, XXV (1936), 80–94.

12. For a discussion of this point, see Charles de Rémusat, "La Théologie naturelle en Angleterre," *Revue des deux mondes*, XXV (1860), 537–573. This article was later incorporated into the author's *Philosophie religieuse de la théologie naturelle en France et en Angleterre* (Paris, 1864).

13. J. H. Newman, *The Idea of a University* (New York, 1891), pp. 33–39, 60–66, 219–227, 428–455.

14. See Granville Penn, *Conversations on Geology*, especially pp. 291–320; William Cockburn, *The Bible Defended Against the British Association* (London, 1844), and *A Letter to Professor Buckland Concerning the Origin of the World* (2d ed.; London, 1838); George Fairholme, *New and Conclusive Physical Demonstration Both of the Fact and Period of the Mosaic Deluge* (London, 1837).

15. Perhaps an exception ought to be made here for Philip Gosse, but *Omphalos* (London, 1857) did not question the facts of science in attempting to reconcile them with the Bible. It was by no means an original book.

16. G. V. Plekhanov, *Essays in the History of Materialism* (trans. Ralph Fox; London, 1934), p. 172.

INDEX

HARVARD HISTORICAL STUDIES